HIS GARDEN

CONVERSATIONS WITH A SERIAL KILLER

ANNE K. HOWARD

WILDBLUE
PRESS

WildBluePress.com

HIS
GARDEN

Table of Contents

Preface

In just nine months, from February to October 2003, seven individuals in and around New Britain, Conn., went missing. All of their bodies were subsequently found in close proximity to one another in a wooded lot behind a suburban strip mall. The mall could not have appeared more ordinary in location or style—and yet, for many years, as patrons ate at Subway, paid to have their car mufflers fixed or their hair cut, purchased their beer, or poked around Daddy's Junky Music Store, the bodies of the killer's victims lay rotting on the swampy earth located just a few hundred yards away.

I first heard about the then-unsolved murders in early 2015, while researching some other open murder cases not far from my home along Route 8 in Northwest Connecticut. Every time I searched the Internet for information about the Route 8 murders that occurred between 1988 and 2004, articles about the unsolved New Britain strip mall murders would appear in the results. Reading that someone was on the loose and had left the remains of seven individuals— all of them prostitutes, most with drug addictions—in the wooded land beside a busy commercial roadway in a nearby suburb literally sent shivers up my spine. The first skull was discovered by a hunter in August 2007; within two weeks, 50 bones of three women were found. In April 2015, the remains of four more victims were unearthed. Who was this monster and how had he managed to escape getting caught?

I live near Winsted, Conn., a town devastated by the flood of 1955, when the overflow of the Mad River wiped out one side of Main Street. Like most New England towns, Winsted contains many ghostly legends, including the myth of The Winsted Wildman. As the story goes, in the summer of 1895, a local town official was out picking berries and saw a "large man, stark naked and covered in hair all over his body" emerge from the bush. News quickly got out that there was a Bigfoot in the area. A more plausible explanation was that an insane artist, Arthur Beckwith, had reportedly escaped from a New York asylum the year before. Wandering around naked in the bushes would not be unusual for Beckwith, as he had previously escaped from a Litchfield asylum and was discovered six months later living *sans vêtements* in the tropics of Cuba.[1]

When I read about the killer who had left the bodies of six women and one man behind the strip mall in New Britain, my mind conjured up The Winsted Wildman: a giant beast of a man; half human, half wild boar; driven to kill and dismember his victims because he was both hungry and insane. Little did I know that I would soon meet and get to know the subject of my darkest fears.

My relationship with William Devin Howell started in July 2015, shortly after he was named as a person of interest in the New Britain serial murders, but not yet officially charged with the crimes. It began with written correspondence and evolved into monthly face-to-face meetings at a high maximum prison in Suffield, Conn., where Howell was serving a 15-year sentence for the murder of Nilsa Arizmendi. At all times, he knew that the sole purpose of our communications was my plan to write a book about him and he also knew that what I would end up writing would not always be to his liking.

His two attorneys, William Paetzold and Jeffrey Kestenband, had done a good job of warning their client of the dangers of getting involved with a journalist pending trial. They later remarked on the "psychological dynamic" that I had with Howell whereby Howell often stood up to them and went against their legal advice in order to stay connected with me. Predictably, our author/subject relationship was complicated, confusing, surprisingly intense and, quite frankly, a head-trip of the highest order. Many times I wondered what I had gotten myself into by deciding to write a book about a man alleged to have committed such heinous crimes. Howell suggested that I title the book, "Dancing With the Devil." Though I did not choose that title, it aptly describes the last three years of my life.

A thread that runs throughout this story involves the drug epidemic that afflicts our nation, and seemingly upscale states including Connecticut are certainly not immune from the epidemic's ruinous effects. Once addicted to poisons such as heroin or crack cocaine, otherwise ordinary people engage in extremely high risk, illegal activities including prostitution in order to fund their costly habits. One thing is irrefutable: there is no such thing as a "typical" prostitute. "Wild Bill's" victims came from all walks of life. Based on my interviews conducted with some of their family members and investigative reports contained within the legal discovery that was given to me by the killer himself, it is clear that the victims wanted to be free of their nightmarish addictions. Many engaged in drug rehabilitation programs and remained clean for long periods of time before succumbing to the addiction's clutches and returning to life on the streets.

Tragically, the drugs, coupled with the prostitution, exposed these individuals to a murderous monster. I truly believe that if it were not for the drugs, most of Howell's victims would be alive today, as they would have never placed themselves in the dangerous position of setting foot into his van, the infamous "Murder Mobile," where they met their demise. On the issue of whether all of Howell's victims were engaged in prostitution at the time of their deaths, the transcripts of police interviews that took place during the investigation indicate that they were, although at least one family member of a victim contests that fact. It also appears that the only victim that was not addicted to drugs was Danny Whistnant.

In theory, local and state police should dedicate equal time and zeal to every missing person's case. In reality, it is often assumed that the prostitute overdosed and died or skipped town with her john, so less energy is put into the investigation. To their credit, the many law enforcement officers referenced in the story that you are about to read did not fall into that pattern of apathy. Det. Robert DeRoehn of the Wethersfield Police Department, New Britain Police Chief James Wardell and many others aggressively pursued justice as though the victims in question were members of their own family. Each one has my deepest respect and the gratitude and respect of the people of Connecticut. I see these men and women as protectors of the vulnerable.

This story also tackles the issue of sexual assault head on. As with the drug epidemic, sexual assault is rampant in our society. For almost two decades, my law practice has focused on representing individuals seeking Social Security disability benefits because they cannot sustain employment due to severe mental and physical impairments. I have encountered literally hundreds of women and men who were sexually molested in childhood or suffered sexual assault in adulthood. The residuals of their traumas last a lifetime: acute anxiety involving flashbacks, nightmares and the fear of being around others, along with periods of deep depression that stem from feelings of hopelessness and low self-worth. For readers who have experienced sexual abuse, I offer a word of warning. The contents of this book, especially the disturbing information contained in Part Two, may be too upsetting for you to read. Please proceed with caution and put the book down if it results in emotional distress.

Finally, I would like to address the issue of journalistic accuracy. The great challenge for any true-crime writer involves drafting a page-turning story that reads like well-crafted literature (with stylistic and thematic traits that transcend traditional journalism) and simultaneously survives the most detailed of fact checks. It is an impossible endeavor because it carries the assumption that truth is discernible at all levels and 100 percent of the facts can always be known. Like all forms of art, true-crime literature seeks to capture what is non-decipherable; paradoxically, without fabricated layers of myth and conjecture, truth laid bare is not really truth at all. At some point in the creative process, the questioning and ruminations of the author— and the reader—combine to create a unique perception of reality that flies in the face of the reporter, the lawyer and the skeptic.

That said, the body of the work strives for accuracy. It is derived from thousands of pages of trial transcripts, affidavits, police interviews, newspaper articles, discussions with victims' family members and hundreds of pages of letters from the serial killer to the author. Details regarding our face-to-face visits come from my oral transcriptions into a digital recorder in the minutes after I left the prison. Most of the killer's confessions were recorded on a phone line at my law office or conveyed in letters that he wrote following his guilty plea hearing on Sept. 8, 2017. "But how do you know if Howell is telling you the truth?" people have asked me. I don't know. That is for the reader to decide. I also provided Howell with the manuscript before submitting it to the publisher and many endnotes contain his objections to the way in which I portray events.

Certain details in the book have been imagined by the author: small things, such as the rock the killer sat on in the forest after depositing the body of Nilsa Arizmendi, or the dialogue with the jailhouse snitch, Tommy Rodriquez, concerning the horrible prison food. I visualized a rock in the woods behind the strip mall; there are, after all, thousands of such rocks in Connecticut. I placed Howell's observations made about the chicken chow mein and oatmeal in his dialogue with Tommy Rodriguez, just to give it color. Those comments actually came from a letter Howell wrote to me in which he described the terrible prison food and the content of that chapter came from Det. DeRoehn's investigative report. On the rare occasions when this technique is applied, the information given does not materially alter the probative findings derived from legal documentation and other reliable sources.

Other miscellaneous details are on point. The visual descriptions of the killer's hometown of Hampton, Va., are based on an exploratory trip that I took in the fall of 2017. And what about Nilsa Arizmendi singing Christian hymns as she walked along the Berlin Turnpike after a long night of turning tricks? Though it may seem like a schmaltzy fabrication, it is a fact. According to a close family member, Nilsa reassured her mother, a devout Christian, that she still trusted in God, despite her reckless lifestyle. "I sing hymns, Mami," she said. "I sing them out loud as I walk along the Berlin Turnpike at night."

To this day, I cannot say for certain what prompted me to get to know a serial killer, other than to say that I needed to figure out what made the man tick. How did an innocent infant transform into a wild beast wreaking havoc on the lives of so many and, perhaps more importantly, why do we live in a world where such evil exists?

Disclaimer: Some names have been altered to protect the privacy of individuals.

Excerpts from letters written by William Devin Howell are in unedited, original form, and include typos.

In Memoriam

Christo Lassiter
1957–2017

A brilliant law professor and loyal friend, Christo taught me that criminal procedure is an intricate chess game whereby the greatest mind wins.

*"Words have no power to impress the mind
without the exquisite horror of their reality."*

Edgar Allan Poe

1.

July 25, 2003

The monster stirred inside him. Most times, he could tame it. Keep it hidden. Silence its screams. But tonight, the beast demanded release.

She lifted her head up. "You're taking too long. I'm done."

He pressed her head back down. "You're done when I say you're done ..."

She wriggled beneath the firmness of his grip. "No!" she protested, forcing herself up from his lap. She stared him straight in the eyes—defiant and unafraid. "That's all I'm doing for you, Devin."

His calloused fingertips nervously tapped the upholstered backbench and his spine tingled with an odd mixture of excitement and fear. The beast was rising. There was no going back. Not now. Not ever. "Rape her," the monster instructed. "Rape the whore!"

*

It had been a long night of hustling for Nilsa Arizmendi and Angel "Ace" Sanchez. Maybe it was the hot weather, but the regular johns were being especially cheap and irritable, and Nilsa was forced to negotiate smaller fees. Ordinarily, she charged $30 for a half hour, but tonight's tricks were turning a maximum of only $20 and some demanded blowjobs for a measly 10 bucks. Like shrewd customers at a turn-of-the-century street market, the johns knew that the vendor in question was desperate for cash.

Ace loitered around the corners of New Britain Avenue, where his girlfriend worked. He stared glumly at the filthy surroundings, trying not to think about Nilsa's activities. He did not like their lifestyle. In fact, he despised it. But how else could he and Nilsa score drugs? The couple's shared habit was not cheap. In July 2003, they were each smoking about 20 to 30 pieces of crack per day and shooting up a bundle-and-a-half of heroin, which translated to about 10 to 15 bags on the streets. Sometimes, Nilsa used up to three bundles of heroin a day, depending on the amount of crack she smoked. It was a nasty cycle. The crack got Nilsa and Ace ramped up and wired and the heroin brought them down. They needed both to survive.

Without the drugs, sickness set in. Being drug sick was terrible—worse than having the flu. In the darkness of their motel room, the childhood sweethearts huddled together in sweat-soaked sheets, shivering with nausea and chills. Every joint and bone ached as invisible bugs furiously crawled beneath the surface of their skin. In between fits of vomiting, their bowels loosened and the bed became soiled. Nilsa kept the curtains drawn and placed the Do Not Disturb sign on the outside door handle for days at a time. The room was a mess. Their lives were a mess. Besides the incessant and all-consuming craving for heroin, she felt shame.

"This shit has to stop," Ace thought as he watched Nilsa emerge from the back seat of an old man's car. She walked toward him, tucked her tie-dyed T-shirt into her dungaree shorts and offered a faint smile. Normally 140 pounds, the 5'2", dark-haired woman was now only skin and bones. "I'm tired," she said. "Let's go home."

On the walk back, Nilsa briefly disappeared and scored a blast of crack at Goodwin Park in Hartford. She returned to Ace and attempted to take his hand. He pulled away. "I'm done with this shit. You gotta go to rehab, Nilsa. We both gotta go."

She acted like she did not hear him. It was usually the best way to avoid a fight.

But tonight, Ace would not let up. "I'm done with the fucking drugs," he mumbled, running his hand through his greasy dark hair. Normally, he kept it long, but a few days before, he had cut it short. "Done with the hustling. Fuck. Fuck this shit."

Their shadowy figures forged into the night, softly illuminated by the neon lights of outdated motels. Rolling hills of forest stood far in the distance, strangely comforting and yet somehow sinister. When Nilsa's high wore down, they started to quarrel. This time, Ace would not take no for an answer. They both had to go to rehab in the morning.

Nilsa was reluctant. She had been in and out of rehab for years and it never did her any good. Still, she loved her four children and desperately wanted to be done with the drugs and get clean forever and for good. Overhead, the night sky opened and a warm drizzle began to fall. The blue rock watch on Nilsa's frail wrist ticked into the early morning hours. They walked southbound along the pike, past Cedar Hill Cemetery containing the corpses of Connecticut's affluent class, including legendary actress Katharine Hepburn, and then a smaller cemetery containing the remains of lesser-known citizens.

Ace gently elbowed Nilsa. "You gonna start singing?"

She sometimes sang Christian hymns that she learned in childhood as they walked along the pike. It passed the time and gave them both a sense of comfort in the midst of all the pain. She smiled beneath the foggy moonlight. "You want me to?"

"You know I like your voice," he replied.

Her smooth, clear voice chimed like a bell into the darkness of the night:

O Lord my God, When I in awesome wonder,
Consider all the worlds Thy Hands have made;
I see the stars, I hear the rolling thunder,
Thy power throughout the universe displayed.

By the time they reached the parking lot of the Stop & Shop in Wethersfield, Ace had persuaded Nilsa to agree to the plan. Nilsa was worthy of a long and healthy life. After all, Ace needed her. Her mother needed her. *Her children needed her.* She vowed to never turn another trick again or inject poison into her veins. The party was over and fuck her if it had not been the party from Hell.

Nilsa eyed a lone vehicle parked in the far corner of the store's lot. "That's Devin's van."

"Let's get back to the motel," Ace said.

"I'm just gonna say hi."

Nilsa walked across the lot to the beat-up blue van owned by their mutual acquaintance, Devin Howell. They had met Howell a few months before. At the time, he was pumping gas at the Exxon gas station on the corner of Broad Street and New Britain Avenue. The rain was heavy and Ace and Nilsa were soaking wet as they approached Howell's van and asked for a ride to their motel room on the Berlin Turnpike in Wethersfield. "We'll give you five bucks," Ace said.

Howell had to go to Lowe's to price out some supplies for an upcoming job. He was driving in that direction anyway, so it was not a problem to assist two near-strangers who appeared down on their luck. "Yeah, sure. The door's unlocked."

Nilsa and Ace squeezed into the bucket seat on the passenger side. Nilsa used her street name, Maria, when she introduced herself to Howell. As they drove to The Almar Motel, Howell told the couple in his mild Southern drawl that he had a lawn-care business. Ace glanced over his shoulder at the back of the van. The space was large, with a long bench sofa littered with lawn service tools and clothing. The stench of body odor pervaded the vehicle's interior.

When they arrived at the motel, Ace and Nilsa invited Howell into their room to hang out. Howell brought some beer and marijuana. Nilsa and Ace offered to share a little crack, but Howell refused. He was a weed and booze guy. Together, the three got high on their poisons of choice. Howell told them that he was living in his van and he often parked it at the Stop & Shop parking lot in Wethersfield. He left the motel less than an hour later. As he drove back to the Stop & Shop lot to bed down for the night, he glanced at the open ashtray and saw that a $20 bill rolled up inside of it was gone. "No fucking good deed goes unpunished," he cynically thought. Ace and Nilsa had ripped him off.

In the months that followed, the occasional contact with Howell proved beneficial to Nilsa and Ace. The couple had lived on the Berlin Turnpike for the last 18 months or so, first at The Elm Motel and then at The Almar. Their daily routine involved walking from the motel on the pike to the familiar section of New Britain Avenue in Hartford where Nilsa turned tricks, about 1½ miles from The Almar. Ace had not worked a job for seven or eight months and he no longer had a vehicle of his own. Especially in the cold weather, Nilsa and Ace relied on acquaintances to spot them walking along the busy roadway and offer a lift. Occasionally, they had money for a cab, but that meant less money for drugs.

Howell also proved useful in assisting Nilsa and Ace to cop drugs. He did not mind driving them to local dealers living 15 to 20 minutes away. He would not get high with them when they scored. He seemed content to do them a favor by giving them a ride in exchange for a few dollars. All told, Howell served as the couple's makeshift Uber driver on about five occasions over the course of one month.

At approximately 2:45 a.m. on July 25, 2003, Ace watched Nilsa's skeletal form traipse across the empty parking lot. It was hard for him to believe that this was the same woman whose weight had sky-rocketed to 180 pounds when she was last released from federal prison—all beefed up by the cheap, starchy food. Nilsa stopped at the van and appeared to talk to Howell, who sat in the driver's seat. Then she walked around the van and got into the passenger side. Howell turned on the engine and slowly drove away. It was the last time Ace would see Nilsa alive.

*

When Christ shall come, with shout of acclamation,
And take me home, what joy shall fill my heart.
Then I shall bow, in humble adoration,
And then proclaim: "My God, how great Thou art!"

Nilsa "Coco" Arizmendi, Jan. 29, 1970–July 25, 2003
Rest In Peace

2.

It's a strange thing, writing letters to an alleged serial killer. Stranger still is reading the letters that he writes back.

When I first contacted William Devin Howell in July 2015, he was serving a 15-year sentence for the murder of Nilsa Arizmendi. Howell had yet to be charged with the murders of six other victims whose bones were found in the same wooded area behind the strip mall in New Britain. Nonetheless, the tone of his first letter to me indicated that he knew that the remaining charges were about to slam down upon him with the force of a sledgehammer.

Two months earlier, Howell's image had been smeared across local and national news channels when Chief State's Attorney Kevin Kane named him as the main suspect in the New Britain serial killings. Kane's announcement was a long time coming. Howell told me that two years earlier, he refused to speak with police officers about the accusations without a lawyer present. His refusal to speak resulted in Howell being stripped of his industry job in prison as a kind of punishment by the Department of Corrections (D.O.C.).

While not a big deal to a prison outsider, for an inmate who lives for a few extra dollars a week to purchase better quality soap or tinned spicy tuna at the prison commissary, it was a grave loss for Howell. He took pride in having an industry job. It paid a whopping $1 an hour compared to typical prison jobs that pay 75 cents a day. Howell explained to me that he had worked all his life, whether in lawn care or a pizza parlor or a 7-Eleven in Florida. No job was beneath him and it discouraged him to be sitting in isolation doing nothing.

In April 2015, after speaking with one of Howell's former cellmates, Jonathan Mills, who told investigators that Howell confessed many details of the crimes to him, police obtained a search warrant for Howell's cell at Garner Correctional Institution in Newtown, Conn., where he was being held at the time. The search warrant detailed items taken from the inmate's cell: a newspaper article about the death penalty in Florida; a notebook with handwritten entries that referenced darkvomit.com, a website that sold memorabilia associated with serial killers and other notorious murderers; and a cell phone bill from July 2003 with words written by Howell, "This just shows the day after I killed."[2]

The newspaper article about the death penalty in Florida prompted authorities to look into whether Howell was behind the unsolved murder of April Marie Stone, 21, who went missing on Jan. 14, 1991, after she was seen walking along a state highway in South Apopka, Fla. Her body was found two days later beside a dirt road in nearby Sanford. She had been stabbed to death and wrapped in a blanket. At the time of the killing, Howell was living about 15 miles away in a trailer in Casselberry with his girlfriend, Mandy, and their infant son. A few months after police found Stone, Howell was charged with soliciting prostitution in Altamonte Springs, the next town over from Casselberry. He had approached the undercover officer in a blue Ford pickup truck and offered her $15 for oral sex, according to the arrest report. He entered a plea of guilty and avoided jail time by paying a fine. It was not until 2015, after Howell was charged with murdering six more victims found behind the strip mall in New Britain, that law enforcement looked into the possibility that he may have been behind Stone's murder in Florida, years before. Investigators in Florida looked into the matter, but did not find any evidence linking Howell to Stone's murder.

I never thought that Howell was behind the slaying of April Stone. She was not part of what appeared to be his target group—prostitutes, many with substance abuse issues—and her body, though wrapped in a blanket, was not buried. Additionally, although Howell had been accused of grisly atrocities—including slicing the fingertips of one of his victims and dismantling her jaw, death by stabbing did not conform to his apparent modus operandi.

I took a deep breath before writing my first letter to Howell, fully aware that I was about to step aboard Ozzy's proverbial Crazy Train with no hope of escape in the years ahead. Here is my letter of introduction:

July 19, 2015
RE: Correspondence and Visitation

Dear Mr. Howell:

I am doing some research and writing about the unsolved murders in New Britain. Since you are the main suspect, I would very much like to correspond with you and meet with you to discuss the allegations. Juliana Holcomb, the daughter of your ex-girlfriend Dorothy, describes you as a "kind-hearted giant." In personal photos, you appear to be a friendly individual who would not harm a fly. I would like to hear your side of the story in this matter.

Please write to me and let me know if I can get on your visitation list. I am a practicing attorney. However, I have no desire to become involved in any of the legal aspects of your incarceration. In my capacity as a journalist, I simply want to hear your side of the story.

Sincerely:
Anne K. Howard
Attorney at Law

And so began my relationship with a man that I believed would one day take the title of Connecticut's most prolific serial killer.[3]

As a means of connecting with Howell's loneliness and need for human contact, I mentioned his ex-girlfriend, Dori, and the warm sentiments that her daughter conveyed to a local reporter.[4] I tossed in a little flattery and gave the impression that I was open to the idea of his innocence. My feigned concern was intended as something of a ruse, and it worked.[5] A few weeks passed and Howell wrote back. In his first letter, dated Aug. 9, 2015, he admitted that he had struggled about whether he should meet with me or even write back.

For reasons I do not understand, perhaps sheer friendlessness and a yearning for human connection, or possibly just to get me to send him money (likely, a combination of both), Howell decided that he did want a face-to-face meeting with me, but it would have to be in my professional status as an attorney. He explained that the D.O.C. had *made it very clear that they were granting no visits to reporters and the like.* He suggested that I answer a few of his legal questions regarding a civil matter that had nothing to do with the current murder charges. Doing so would permit us to have a private, unrecorded visit.

It would not be that easy. I had been practicing law long enough to know that putting myself on the attorney visitation list at Howell's current residential facility, MacDougal–Walker Correctional Institute (Walker C.I.), for the actual purpose of obtaining information for an upcoming true-crime book would be a misrepresentation that could result in sanctions from the Connecticut and Ohio bars and possibly the permanent loss of my law license. Also, providing him with legal advice, even in a small claims court case, without a written attorney/client contract would be equally reckless.

I told Howell as much in my next letter. Still, he continued to write. Interestingly, he always signed his letters with the name Bill, derived from the first name on his birth certificate, William, even though most of his friends and acquaintances knew him by his middle name, Devin. I would gradually come to realize that Bill was a man with many aliases reflecting his many sides. Fellow inmates in prisons across Connecticut called him Hillbilly because of his Southern accent. Others called him Wild Bill. The crew he worked with at the Big Y grocery store in Torrington prior to his current incarceration called him Billy. Now, in chiseling his name down to Bill, it seemed that he wanted to build some distance between his present and former self.

From the start, Howell's letters revealed an unbelievably lonesome and depressed man. I spoke at length on the phone with a former acquaintance of Howell's from Virginia and she described an adolescent Howell as being "starved for love." I could not have said it better. Howell was not just looking for love from me in his letters—he was *begging* for it. Being isolated from the opposite sex for several years gave that craving a somewhat sexual component. For all he knew, I was a blue-haired elderly woman. Nevertheless, he wrote these words in his first letter:

8/9/2015
... this may sound creepy, but I'd like a hug. Nothing creepy and not trying to cop a feel, but I haven't had a hug in almost 10 years and I'd just like simple hug if you don't mind A hug from you may be the only hug I get for the rest of my life. Like I said, nothing creepy, just a simple hug. I promise I'll be on my best behavior.

Howell's request for a hug gave me only modest pause. My main reaction was pity, coupled with the awareness that this was a very vulnerable man. The 1985 song by Aretha Franklin, "Who's Zoomin' Who," came to mind. Was he playing me? He must have been. Otherwise, how could a man accused of killing seven human beings illicit any feelings beyond my sheer contempt? It would not be the last time that I felt genuine sadness for Howell, nor would it be the last time that I rebuked myself for having that reaction while questioning his true motives.

Howell's subsequent written comments regarding his request for a hug helped me to understand why his alleged victims trusted him enough to get into his van.

8/29/2015

But I would like to meet with you. And there is a legal basis for your visit. And if you truly do want to get a feel for who I am that is the best way to do it. And the hug can be optional :). I see where that may have come across a little creepy in my first letter, but it wasn't meant to be. But it's just that its been so long (years) since I've had something as innocent as a friendly hug. And I felt like I had nothing to lose by asking. In fact, it could be my last chance to ever have a hug again for the rest of my life so I had to ask and I apologize if I creeped you out in any way.

I can also see why certain types of women become involved with men carrying life sentences for terrible crimes. Such individuals can possess the charm of a wounded little boy crying out for mommy's love. Stumble onto the scene a highly gullible, emotionally damaged woman with nurturing tendencies, and the monster-turned-little-boy becomes the object of sympathy and even romantic desire.

Needless to say, I felt zero romantic desire for Howell. His most recent mug shot brought to mind the name that he reportedly called himself to another prisoner: Sick Ripper. In that photo, he had all of the markings of a man requiring high-maximum supervision. His hulking figure was dressed in orange prison garb intended to alert the authorities in the event that he escaped. His mouth pressed grimly downward as his eyes stared straight into the camera lens with an unsettling mixture of sorrow and rage. And so entered another emotion that would occasionally invade my mental space in the earliest days of our written correspondence: terror.

Howell made no secret of asking me for money right away. He asked if I could deposit $30 or $40 to his inmate trust account. He was helpful enough to include a money order form in his first letter. Giving the suspect money felt wrong on every level, but I was open to the idea if it would result in him providing information for my future book. I even entertained the idea that he would someday confess his crimes to me—either before or after legal resolution occurred. I contacted a reporter friend from a local news channel and asked what he thought about it. His answer surprised me: "Sure, you're allowed to give him a little cash to go towards postage and writing materials."

Thirty dollars would cover a lot of paper and stamps. I knew that giving Howell the money would make his prison sentence the smallest bit easier and when readers found out that I had given him money, I would look like a crummy human being. Arguably, I would *be* a crummy human being. Was I willing to do it in order to get the inside scoop?

I sent him $30.

In his next letter, Howell included a sales receipt from the D.O.C. that documented his purchases. It seems that he felt a fiduciary responsibility in the face of my recent gift. With the money, he had purchased five pre-stamped envelopes, two bagels, a tube of Velveeta squeeze cheese and buffalo wing blue-cheese chips.

One week later, Bill phoned my law office to personally thank me for the gift. My paralegal, Heather, retrieved the voice mail. "He has a soft, Southern voice," she remarked. "He actually sounded kind of nice."

3.

The chatter of bush crickets sounded in waves: *Katy did, Katy didn't,* they called back and forth, *Katy did, Katy didn't.*

The rhythmic dialogue was accompanied by the low, throaty mating calls of male bullfrogs skipping about with peepers in the swampy soil. The 15 acres of state-owned, unadulterated forest was full of deer, with legions of fireflies lighting up through the trees at night. Remarkably, this tranquil place was located just more than 100 feet from a strip mall on a busy roadway cluttered with fast-food franchises and automotive shops offering low-rate oil changes. Diagonally across the way sat Westfarms Mall, a high-end indoor shopping center where privileged brides-to-be registered for china and crystal at Tiffany's and their mothers purchased monogrammed bags at the Louis Vuitton boutique.

The monster knew to move slowly; heedful, it crept into Howell's veins and shifted his nervous system into a state of high alert. He could see better, hear better and definitely *think* better. Earlier, he stripped the lifeless woman of her clothing and personal effects in the back of his van. He would dispose of those later, in random garbage cans located at gas stations or public parks. He duct taped the body into fetal position, wrapped it in three large plastic trash bags—two at the top and one at the bottom—and covered the grisly parcel with tarp in the back of the van. He mowed a few lawns later that afternoon, then drove to the edge of the strip mall's back parking lot at about 5 p.m., opened the side door of the van and threw the bagged body over the side of a sloping embankment. He watched it tumble down to the ravine.

Perfect. It landed in a pile of hedge trimmings and barrels. Safely concealed, until he could get to it the following day.

He had trouble falling to sleep that night. Nilsa was the only victim he actually knew before committing the crime in question and he worried about the resultant implications. Since he had not planned to rape and strangle her, as he had with the other female victims, he had not taken the usual precaution of changing the license tag on his van. Usually, he changed the tags beforehand to prevent a boyfriend, pimp or otherwise observant witness from writing the number down. Now, not only could Ace potentially give that information to authorities, he could also identify him by name as the last person to be seen with Nilsa.

Early the next morning, he returned to the strip mall. He drove around back, making sure that the door of the Subway sandwich shop was closed. Sometimes, employees went outside to dump trash in the garbage bins, but today, the coast was clear. He went to the guardrail that lined the steep, wooded embankment and tucked a small shovel into the brush; then he circled the van into the parking lot of the McDonald's located just a stone's throw from the woods and parked in a remote location of the large lot. He quickly left the vehicle, walked across a narrow cut-through that was inaccessible to cars and returned to the ravine.

Everything depended on this moment. Would he be seen by someone unexpectedly entering the parking lot? The foot of the ravine, where the body lay, was visible to the observer. He rushed up the hill at record speed, retrieved the spade and nervously carried it back into the ravine. Tool in hand, he dragged the body about 100 yards into the woods. The location was a little more concealed than the bottom of the ravine, but there was still the risk of being discovered by a hunter wandering in the woods, although hunting was illegal there, or a single engine, Piper cub plane flying just above the tree line. Dropping the spade, he placed his victim's remains beside the others.

Though the forest was deadly silent, a sense of panic threatened his ability to focus. "Calm down," he told himself. "No one's here." But the fear of being caught would not subside. He sat on a moss-covered rock the size of a small beanbag chair. "Breathe," he told himself, fighting off a dull ache swelling in his chest. The light rain that fell in the night had heightened the forest's pungent scent. He could almost taste the aromas of evergreen and birch in his midst. It helped to relax him.

He glanced over at the figure of Nilsa Arizmendi, enshrouded in trash bags. Man, she put up a fight. She was obviously stronger than she looked—skinny from the drugs, but big-boned and muscular at her core. When she had refused to submit to the first rape, he threatened her with a large, rusty wrench. In the past, the women he raped did what he said—just seeing the size and weight of that wrench had a way of smartening them up. But Nilsa was different. She did not submit. She fought back with the will of a warrior. He could not understand why. It was not like her life was worth a shit—a crack-whore on drugs. She mentioned once that she had children, three or four, at least. What kind of mother leaves her babies for the needle?

She had entered his van at the Stop & Shop parking lot two nights ago and asked if he could drive her to Hartford so she could purchase drugs. He said no. She offered to give him a blowjob for $30. He talked her down to $20. When she refused to finish the job, he grew angry and tried to rape her. "Do what I say or I'm gonna hit you with this wrench!" he warned, quite fairly, he thought. When she kept on fighting and screaming, he raised the wrench. "Shut up!" he shouted. He whacked her on the side of the head, just above the ear. It didn't knock her out, but it sure as hell got her to stop fighting so he could tie her up to the backbench of his van. Semiconscious from the blow, she slowly came to her senses as he drove to the back of the parking lot behind the Stop & Shop, where he quickly raped her for the first time.

He refastened the ropes and zip ties and secured her to the backbench of his van, making sure her mouth was covered in duct tape. He drove to the back of an empty business along Farmington Avenue and raped her two or three times. Morning came and he was getting tired. As with his other victims, he allowed himself to rest beside his captive, slipping into a kind of catnap—half awake, half asleep—but always ready to pounce. At dawn, he drove her to the parking lot of a Motel 6, removed the duct tape from her mouth and ordered her to perform oral sex so he would be stiff enough to assault her again. He raped her a few more times. Depleted of strength and sexually satisfied, he finally strangled her in the back lot of the Motel 6 later that morning.

Presently having regained his composure in the forest behind the mall, he got back to his feet to complete the task at hand. Burying the dead. The morning commute had begun. Cars and trucks sounded in the distance and a long line of cars waited at the McDonald's drive thru. He dug a shallow grave, simultaneously crushing mosquitoes that landed on his sweaty arms. He wanted to dig deeper, but the water table was high in that swampy earth and if he went below a foot and a half, mud emerged. He dug just low enough for the body to fit.[6] As with the others, before lowering the body into the earth, he removed the black trash bags and duct tape that bound them. He covered the grave with a loose layer of soil, leaves and sticks. As a landscaper, working with dirt was an activity that brought him a sense of satisfaction.

As he rushed out of the woods, the monster retreated to its cage, securely buried deep within his loins. In the hours that followed, life went on as usual. He ordered beef and Cheddar burgers and fries and brought them to his girlfriend Dori's house. After dinner, they watched an episode of "Forensic Files" on TV. A scientist was talking about how they identified the charred remains of a woman trapped inside of her car. Howell's thoughts turned to the naked corpse of Nilsa Arizmendi, concealed beneath only a modest layer of soil and twigs. Would someone eventually discover her corpse? Would *he* be the subject of a "Forensic Files" episode one day?[7]

Laying on the couch, he put his head on Dori's lap and she gave him a vigorous scalp scratch. She then removed his shirt and went about scratching his itchy skin and attacking the pimples on his back. Damn, it felt good.

He rolled over on the couch. Dori smiled when she saw the bulge in his jeans. He didn't have to ask Dori if she was in the mood. She was always hungry for sex—the more the better. She liked him to use sex toys, too, and no position was off the table. The couple had sex at least two or three times per day. Dori had no clue that her lover was simultaneously picking up several prostitutes a week on the side and even less of a clue regarding his nefarious activities in the back of the van where he lived when he was not spending time at her house.

"You're the best I ever had," she once told him.

"What makes me the best?" he asked.

"You're not a selfish lover. You please me first. You take your time."

Well, not always. Tonight he was in a rush—too horny to wait. Fully engaged, he glanced out the window and saw a cop car drive past, the siren wailing and lights flashing. Beneath him, Dori moaned with pleasure.

It was like nothing had happened only hours before.

4.

William Devin Howell came into the world at Sentara Hospital in Hampton, Va., on Feb. 11, 1970. His mother, Melissa Howell, was 40 years old, and his father, John Howell, was 45. Nowadays, increasing numbers of women delay childbirth until their late 30s or early 40s, but back in the Seventies, late pregnancy—more commonly known as geriatric pregnancy—was not only unusual, it was considered a medical risk to both mother and child.

Melissa Howell thought she was finished with having kids by her 20th birthday. First came Randy and then came Rocky. Now, they were both grown men with families of their own. Five years earlier, she was taken by surprise with the unexpected pregnancy of a third son, Kevin. Although her situation at that time was relatively stable—a house, a working husband, two older sons—it still could not have been easy carrying a third son to term in her mid-30s while holding down a night job at Whataburger to earn spending money for family birthdays and holidays. Making matters worse, she broke her leg working at the burger stand and had to hop around on crutches in her final trimester with Kevin. Her fourth pregnancy, also unplanned, was not much easier. When she gave birth to William, her son Rocky was fighting in Vietnam.

The respective childhoods of Howell's parents teemed with hardship. According to the serial killer suspect, his mother's parents died when she was young and she and her brothers were distributed to different families on farms in North Carolina. He wrote to me that both of his parents "*were raised poor.*" They had no electricity or indoor plumbing. "*I remember my mom telling me that when she was young she* had to heat a brick in the fireplace and wrap it in a blanket to carry to bed to stay warm. Back then, my dad said, indoor plumbing meant there was a hand powered water pump at the kitchen sink."

Howell's parents overcome poverty and lived a blue-collar version of the American Dream. John Howell was a hard-working machinist who left for work at the crack of dawn on weekdays and reliably returned by 5:30 each night. According to Howell, his parents were *"old-school with old school family values. They never did drugs or anything like that. I did hear that my parents threw a pretty nice Christmas party and pops would go to N.C. and bring back a bottle of moonshine. But that stopped well before I was ever born."*

Regarding his father's last drink, Howell wrote:

"As the story was told to me there was a Christmas party and my 2 oldest brothers were teenagers and drunk. One was streaking through the neighborhood and the other was puking his guts out in the bathroom, and as my dad told it to me, he (my dad) was too drunk to help either one of them. That was the last time he took a drink and the last alcohol fueled Christmas party they ever threw. I believe that was back in the 60s and I wasn't born until 1970."

His parents were good providers and Howell frequently reminded me to add that fact to the book that I was writing about him.

"There was always food on the table, clothes on our back, heat in the winter and A.C. in the summer. We never received Welfare or Food Stamps and I paid full price in the lunch line. We were far from rich, but we weren't poor either. My father was tight with money, but we always had what we needed."

Howell's mother worked two different jobs before she fell ill when he was 11 years old.

"My mom worked part-time at night at a little burger joint called 'What a Burger'. She worked that job over 20 years. I remember on Sat nights she'd bring home cheeseburgers

and french fries when she came home.... Those were some good burgers. My mom also worked as a school lunch lady during the day. But she didn't start that job until I was in 3rd or 4th grade."

Portions of Howell's early childhood in Virginia bring to mind "The Andy Griffith Show," with Howell in the role of Opie Taylor. His earliest memories involve catching tadpoles and crayfish in the ditch behind the family's three-bedroom bungalow. *"The ditch that runs behind my house, about a mile downstream it empties into a creek. I used to ride my bicycle to that creek and go fishing. All I'd catch were carp which were no good to eat but they got pretty big (2 to 3 foot long) so they were fun to catch and let go, especially when you're 8, 9, 10 years old."*

Thursday nights were special in the Howell house. That's when the oldest brother, who Howell claimed was more like an uncle, brought his family over to play pinochle with his parents. It gave Howell the chance to play with his nephews, who were actually his peers.

Howell proudly recalls watching his father make repairs in the family garage on weeknights and over the weekends. As a little boy, he would observe his father fix just about anything—from lawnmowers to car engines to miscellaneous kitchen gadgets. John Howell was a self-sufficient jack-of-all-trades, puffing away at his pipe full of Granger tobacco and focusing on solving the problem at hand. He was sometimes given to explosive outbursts—kicking the lawnmower with his boot when the repair went badly, swearing at the ceiling in frustration. The youngest Howell watched ... and learned.

It seemed leisure time in the Howell household often revolved around the completion of a task. When Howell's mother had nights off, she relaxed by crocheting big blankets that would take months to finish. Howell never learned how to crochet, but his mother did teach him to cross-stitch and make ceramics. Meals in the Howell household included items from the family garden: pickled beets, butter beans and squash, and also jams and jellies that his mother made from her annual summer venture at a place that let people pick their own strawberries for a minimal charge. *"Mom knew how to do all that stuff. And there was always dinner on the table when pops got home. And I'm talking a home-cooked meal not no 'throw a box in the microwave' type stuff…. back then, there were no microwaves."*

Nonetheless, there were times when the family cut loose and had some fun. Every summer, the Howell family purchased a season pass to Busch Gardens. Howell recalls, *"We'd go 2 or 3 times a week sometimes. A lot of time we'd go during the week in the evenings and there'd be hardly any lines. I remember having to stand on my tippy toes to make the height requirement to ride the Loch Ness Monster."* Although the ocean was just a short car drive away, most of Howell's swimming took place at a private pool located a block or so from his house. It was not *"an uppity type of place,"* he told me in one prison visit, but there were "rules" for getting a membership. A family had to be sponsored by another family in the neighborhood, and it was basically a way (he whispered into the phone), *"of keeping out black people."(8)*

Sometimes his Aunt Ann dressed him up and took him to Sunday school. Aunt Ann was married to Melissa Howell's brother, Mack. The couple lost their son, William Ray, when the boy was only 5 years old. Thereafter, they took to religion. "They were holy rollers," Howell told me. Decades later, when she learned about the murders that her nephew was accused of committing, Aunt Ann would tell a reporter, "I hope somewhere down the line, if he lives, he sees the need for calling on the Lord. He would still have his day in court and be punished, but he would have peace." And what would the elderly Christian woman do if the little boy, now a full-grown monster, paid her a visit? "If he would walk in my door right now," she told that reporter, "I would hug him just like I would hug anyone else. I know his mother would do the same for mine."[9]

Starting at the age of 5, Howell attended a Boys Club on Wednesday nights and every other Saturday. The counselors supervised the boys as they shot pool or engaged in various activities in the movie room, such as playing bingo, making model airplanes and magic classes. They also learned how to box and played dodgeball in the gym. Today, there are condominiums behind Aunt Ann's house, a short drive away from the home where Howell was raised, but in the '70s, it was all field and woods, and Howell used to ride his dirt bike back there.

"My mom was always active in my life. She knew all of the supervisors at the Boys Club on a first name basis and actively participated in fundraisers etc. All through elementry school she was always a room mother to my class. She attended P.T.A. meetings and all that stuff."

I was puzzled by Howell's descriptions of a stable early childhood. Something was not adding up. How did little Opie turn into a serial killer?[10]

5.

July 25–Aug. 14, 2003

Ace went back to The Almar Motel and stayed a few hours. Nilsa never showed up. It was not like her. She always returned. At about 6 a.m., just after the sun rose to announce another dismal summer day, Ace left and walked back to the Stop & Shop parking lot. Howell's van was not there. He wished he had not thrown away the lawn care flier that Howell had given them when they first met. It had his phone number on it, but now Ace had no way of contacting him.

Ace had no reason to think that he would not bump into Howell at the Stop & Shop parking lot in the near future. It was Howell's most common resting place. Walking back to New Britain Avenue, he breathed in the toxic fumes spewing from the flatbeds and semis that whooshed past and wondered where he could find his next fix. Without Nilsa beside him, there was no point in going to rehab. He asked around for Nilsa in all the familiar places, but no one had seen her. The following day, he contacted Nilsa's adult son, Jason, and told him that Nilsa was missing. Jason promised to let the family know.

Ace had considered contacting Nilsa's mother directly, but decided against it. Valeria Arizmendi took care of Nilsa's youngest child, Miguel, and though Ace's relationship with Nilsa's mother had always been close (he considered her his mother-in-law, even though he and Nilsa never married), he knew that she would be upset about Nilsa's disappearance and think badly of him. In recent months, Valeria had been very clear about her disapproval of Ace and Nilsa's lifestyle. When describing this chaotic period of time at his girlfriend's murder trial years later, Ace said, "Things were just crashing in."

A few more days passed and Ace's concern turned to dread. Where was she? He and Nilsa had been together, off and on, for more than 20 years, and they had hooked up for the last seven years without any physical separation whatsoever. That is not to say they never fought. Sometimes, their fights became violent. Once or twice, Ace hit Nilsa. Bold and fearless, she hit back. Both of them tried walking out of the relationship, but—without fail—neither of them could get farther than a street block away before turning the corner and coming back.

Ace phoned the Hartford Police Department to report Nilsa missing. The dispatcher did not even put him through to the detective bureau. He probably thought the missing woman was just another addict strung out under a bridge. Ace gave dispatch the contact information for Nilsa's mother and was told to wait three or four more days and that Nilsa would probably show up.

Ace knew that he was being blown off. If Nilsa were a missing middle-class soccer mom, the cops and media would be all over it like flies on shit.

Busting a repeat offender on a drug charge is far easier than finding a missing person, especially if that missing person is a prostitute who frequently falls off the radar for short periods of time. On Aug. 8, 2003, 14 days after Nilsa's disappearance, Ace was arrested for possession of narcotics. Once again, Ace Sanchez, also known as Raphael Sanchez, was prison bound. He had been in and out of prison since the mid-1980s. In 1997, he had served a lengthy sentence for possession of narcotics and conspiracy to distribute heroin. Nilsa was his codefendant in that case. They were caught selling 45 bundles (or 470 bags) of heroin.

When Ace entered lockup in August 2003, he spoke with authorities about Nilsa's disappearance. He went to the lieutenants and then the assistant warden, but he felt like he was getting the runaround from the higher-ups. No one seemed to care. Finally, he spoke with the prison chaplain, who gave him the address for the Connecticut State Police Department in Hartford. Ace wrote to it on Aug. 14, 2003.

Ace was not the only person who was worried about Nilsa's mysterious departure. In the days that followed the fateful events of July 25, 2003, Nilsa's mother and her oldest sister, Lauren, went to the area of New Britain Avenue in Hartford where Nilsa frequented and actively looked for her. In the past, Valeria would sometimes see Nilsa and Ace when she was driving from her home in East Hartford to church in Hartford. On those occasions, Nilsa and Ace would hide. They were well aware of Valeria's disapproval of their shared drug habits, along with Ace's failure to work an honest job and provide for Nilsa.

If only Valeria could drive past them now. She would express no recriminations, only immense relief that her beautiful daughter, her "Coco," was alive.

The extended Arizmendi family was a close-knit unit. Valeria arrived in New York from Puerto Rico at the age of 18. She gave birth to Nilsa in Patchogue, Long Island, at the age of 20, with Nilsa's father, Jorge Rodriguez. Valeria's future husband, Ricardo Santiago, had raised Nilsa and her two sisters since Nilsa was 4 years old. He was a good provider, working hard as a landscaper, while Valeria remained at home to care for the girls. The family settled and lived in a housing project in Hartford, Conn.

Nilsa grew into a beautiful girl, with dark eyes that sparkled and a compassionate spirit that put others at ease. A good student, she was well liked in school before she left at the age of 14 due to pregnancy. In a few short years, she had two more children, 18 months apart. It was not easy for her to face that level of responsibility before her 20th birthday, but she embraced her role as a very young mother and loved her children dearly. Christmas was her favorite holiday. She enjoyed decorating the tree and wrapping gifts with her children and parents. For Easter, she purchased her children the biggest and most extravagant baskets that she could find; comically over the top, they were full of stuffed animals, chocolate bunnies and plastic eggs containing jellybeans.

At the age of 18, following the birth of her third child, Nilsa started doing heroin. Years later, when she found out that she was pregnant again, she stopped using heroin and sought the assistance of a methadone treatment program so as not to injure the unborn baby. When she was five months along in that pregnancy, she reconnected with her childhood sweetheart, Ace Sanchez, at a methadone clinic. Sanchez encouraged Arizmendi to stay clean during her pregnancy, but after Miguel was born, the two relapsed and returned to injecting the demonic poison into their veins.

By August of 2003, the Arizmendi family members were also troubled when remembering things that Nilsa had said to them in the weeks leading up to her mysterious disappearance. They tried to shake the feeling, but it was as if Nilsa *knew* that she was not long for this world, and she was saying her final goodbyes to the ones she loved.

On July 30, 2003, Valeria and Lauren went to the Wethersfield Police Department to officially report Nilsa as missing. A dispatcher entered Nilsa's name into the National Crime Information (N.C.I.) computer system the following day. Mother and sister then assisted the police in distributing missing person's posters along New Britain Avenue headed in the direction of Wethersfield. The poster's photo came from Connecticut's motor vehicle department and was more than seven years old. At the time, Nilsa had been released from the penitentiary. After months of sobriety from crack, combined with a high-carb prison diet, she appeared as a pudgy-cheeked, attractive female. That dated image bore little resemblance to the drug-ravaged waif who had been last seen with Devin Howell.

Days turned into weeks and the Arizmendi family's anxiety escalated to outright fear. Valeria had raised Nilsa's four children, all of them at times, when Nilsa was in jail, or when Nilsa had succumbed again to the throes of her addiction. Miguel had lived with his grandmother since he was 18 months old. At age 6, he remained in Valeria's care.

Although drugs may have destroyed Nilsa's ability to responsibly care for her four children, she always attempted to stay in touch and she was especially close to Miguel. She visited her mother and Miguel throughout the months of February, March, April and May of 2003, sometimes taking Miguel to the park. She usually phoned Valeria every two to three weeks.

Valeria knew that if Nilsa were absent because of another incarceration, she would have phoned her mother to inform her, or had someone else phone her, as she had always done in the past. But the last phone call Valeria received from her daughter had occurred a few weeks before Nilsa stepped into Howell's parked vehicle at the Stop & Shop parking lot. The last time Valeria actually saw her daughter had been one month earlier, on Father's Day. Nilsa and Ace were idly walking down New Britain Avenue and Valeria had passed them in her van. It all seemed so ordinary at the time.

6.

Theories on why an individual becomes a serial rapist and killer are a dime a dozen. They include the nature vs. nurture debate and the possibility of traumatic brain injury in early childhood.[11] While Howell reports having no history of brain trauma in childhood, I did ask him about a scar, about two inches in length, above his left eyebrow. He told me that it is the result of being hit by a ball while serving a prison sentence in Virginia in 1998. He was playing softball with other inmates and attempted to catch a pop-up coming his way. The sun got in his eyes and the softball hit him hard, directly above the temple. In the days that followed, a knot the size of a goose egg slowly reduced in size, but a bump remained that resembled a large pimple. He tried to squeeze it, as he would do with a pimple, but the skin would not break. He even placed staples into the erasers of pencils to try to puncture the bump, to no avail.

He finally saw the prison doctor, who cut open the skin to lance the wound. However, the doctor quickly stitched the laceration back up and said that he could do irreparable harm because the problem did not involve an infection. It looked like a blood clot. Howell was taken to the hospital and diagnosed with a pseudo aneurism. If Howell, or the first doctor, had punctured the large pocket of air, it would have resulted in excess bleeding that could have led to death.

Excluding the possibility of brain trauma, the nurture element of the equation can be further explored. According to FBI profiler Roy Hazelwood, a large number of sexual criminals have been childhood victims of physical, sexual, or psychological abuse.[12] One imagines William Devin Howell stretched out on a leather settee, his enormous body clad in loose-fitting khaki prison garb and Sigmund Freud drily requesting in a thick, Moravian accent: "Tell me about your *mother.*"

Howell thoughtfully replies:

My mom had a little bit of Indian in her blood and you could see a little of it in her features. (I think one of her grandparents was Indian. I know she told me one time that I'm like 1/16 Indian or something like that.) Mom had black hair and brown eyes and was on the heavy side...

My mom was old school and raised me as such. When I did wrong I got spanked. She'd spank me with flyswatters, the old wooden paddles that came with a rubber ball attached to it with a rubber band. I remember hiding those under the couch cushions, or she'd make me go get a switch... and don't bring back any rinky-dink stuff either, she'd say, or she'd go get a bigger switch.

She'd told the neighbors that if I were at their house playing and got out of line that they had her permission to spank me and send me home. None ever did, but the message was sent for me to be on point.

If I was really bad mom would tell dad and he'd spank me with the belt when he got home. But with all that said, I don't feel I was ever abused in any way. My parents never hit me with their fists and never beat me just for shits and giggles or because they had a bad day. I never got a spanking I didn't earn and I have no marks or scars from them.

Again, Mom was old school.

Some people would equate the frequency of Howell's spankings with child abuse, others might say it was not out of the ordinary for a child living in that region of the country during that era and others might argue that poorly behaved children nowadays need to get spanked like that more often. Howell agrees with the latter opinion, stating: "*Mom did not spank me just to spank me ... I earned every one I got. Mom's spankings did not make me a serial killer.*" One of Howell's brothers mentioned in an online chat room that, if anything, Howell's parents were too easy on their youngest son. They were old and tired and let him get away with a lot in his adolescence.[13]

Possible physical abuse aside (some criminologists posit that a brutal or excessively controlling mother creates a serial killer), what interests me more about Howell's background is what happened to him at the age of 11 or 12. His mother was diagnosed with breast cancer and then suffered a series of strokes. Melissa Howell's prolonged illness had a cataclysmic effect on her youngest son's life. Though not a physically demonstrative woman, she provided Howell with a sense of stability and routine and that foundation was lost when her illness set in.

In her early 50s, Melissa Howell underwent a mastectomy followed by radiation and chemotherapy, which left her weak and ill and out of work "*for a little while*," according to Howell. When she was well enough, she attempted to return to work, but after only a few weeks, she had a stroke on the job. In the days that followed, she had a series of additional strokes that left her paralyzed on her left side. The family set up a hospital bed in the living room in front of the window and Mrs. Howell passed the remainder of her days on Earth, three more years to be exact, propped up in that bed gazing out at the neighborhood.

Then came the morning when she would not wake up. John Howell called an ambulance for his wife to be taken to Sentara Hospital, but it was too late for recovery. She had slipped into a coma and hospital staff prepared the family for imminent death.

Howell spent the first two nights in the hospital with the rest of the family. They wanted him to stay over on the third night, but he insisted on going home because he wanted to see his girlfriend.

"While I was at my girlfriends getting laid and trying to forget my problems, my mother died... I was 15.

"It was a relief to me when she passed away because I knew she was no longer suffering. I couldn't stand to see her like that. She asked me on more than one occasion to get her my father's pistol and go outside and play. I couldn't stand to see her suffer, nor could I give her my father's gun, and it really fucked me up inside not being able to help her. It still stirs up a lot of emotions just remembering those times. My father passed away 5 years later after I turned 20. I've been pretty much on my own since then. I got an inheritance in bits & pieces that I rapidly pissed away followed shortly by a jail sentence."

Howell still mourns the loss of his parents. *"I was raised in a home where family stuck together,"* he once wrote me, *"and here I sit alone in prison for the rest of my life."*

7.

August 2003

Wethersfield is considered to be the oldest town in Connecticut. Founded in 1634, the community contains an unusual mix of handsome colonial homes, modest bungalows and, of course, a portion of the infamous Berlin Turnpike.

Prostitution and drug trafficking are currently active industries along the long strip of highway that stretches through the central Connecticut towns of Berlin, Newington and Wethersfield. Known as "Gasoline Alley" in the 1950s, the 12-mile strip was once a stopping ground for tourists and business travelers coming from the larger cities of Washington, D.C.; New York; Boston and Philadelphia. Most of the businesses that sprouted along the strip reflected the wholesome demands of post-World War II Americans: ice cream parlors, fuel stations, bowling alleys, hamburger stands and *scores* of mom-and-pop style motels hosting more than 1,000 rooms.

A lot changed in 1965 with the opening of Interstate 91, a busy freeway running parallel to the Berlin Turnpike. Many businesses along the strip folded and the ones that survived were forced to cater to a new and considerably seedier clientele. The tourists were gone and businessmen traveling to Hartford, the insurance capital of America, were opting for newer chain hotels located along Interstate 91. Almost overnight, the Berlin Turnpike became the suburban version of Boston's Combat Zone. One of the Pike's three drive-in movie theaters showed X-rated films and there was no shortage of strip clubs, massage parlors and adult shops selling sex toys and low-quality lingerie. Conveniently, many of the motels nearby offered cheap daily, and even hourly, rates.[14]

The Almar Motel, where Nilsa Arizmendi spent the last six months of her life, was one such establishment. It did not have the reputation of being the worst motel on the strip, but it certainly was not a place that guaranteed its occupants physical safety and bug-free beds. Perched on a hilly road about 50 feet from the strip, The Almar reflects a bygone era when roadside motels were considered one step up from the auto camps of the 1920s where travelers pitched their tents.

From the outside, it does not look so bad. A two-story manager's building is attached to an I-shaped, low-rise row of individual rooms. The door of each unit faces the parking lot—a throwback to a time when guests backed their cars up to the room's door and brought their luggage in from their gas guzzler's trunk. The stucco exterior is colored an orangey-peach, more common to architecture in the Southwest. The red-and-white sign at the motel's entrance has a classic style, like signs that appeared on Route 66 in the late 1970s. An arrow below it boasts "cable TV, HBO, Phone and Jacuzzi." Beneath it is a blue-and-white sign advertising "Daily/Weekly Rates, Micro and Fridge." Nowadays, such accommodations attract a very particular base of customers: mostly drifters and transients who cannot come up with a deposit and first month's rent on an apartment in the area, or cheating spouses looking for a place to bring their side pieces for an afternoon quickie.

Det. Robert DeRoehn of the Wethersfield Police Department was assigned to investigate the disappearance of Nilsa Arizmendi. He visited The Almar in August 2003. The motel's manager took him to the back of the motel and showed him Room 123, where Nilsa had once lived with Ace. By then, the motel's owner had removed all of the couple's belongings and the room had been thoroughly cleaned. DeRoehn could have applied Luminal, a chemical that illuminates liquids such as blood and other substances to the walls, floors and furniture. Instead, he chose not to search the room in any manner.

From the start, the investigation into the disappearance of Nilsa Arizmendi contained flaws. For example, DeRoehn and others from the Wethersfield Police Department forwarded fliers to Hartford area police departments with the request that they be distributed in areas frequented by Arizmendi. Unfortunately, the fliers said that Nilsa was 5'2" and weighed 140 pounds. In fact, she weighed about 90 pounds at the time of her disappearance. Also, they incorrectly stated that Nilsa went missing on July 24, 2003, rather than a day later, and failed to provide Nilsa's alias, "Maria," which she used on the street.

Errors aside, DeRoehn focused a lot of time and energy working the case from day one. He spent many early-morning hours touring the side streets and neighborhoods in and around Washington Street, Broad Street and New Britain Avenue. It was the time of day when blue-collar workers solicited prostitutes for "morning wood" or prostitutes would be returning to their lodgings after a long night of turning tricks. Ironically, the seedy district surrounded Trinity College, where students from well-off Connecticut families learned in luxury.

Additionally, DeRoehn entered Arizmendi's information into the FBI missing person's database and included descriptive details of her jewelry and past medical and dental procedures. He also contacted correctional facilities to see if she was an inmate and plowed through National Deceased Persons reports, all to no avail.

Almost a month following Arizmendi's disappearance, on Aug. 24, 2003, DeRoehn saw Devin Howell's blue van parked in the Stop & Shop parking lot in Wethersfield. He drove past, not giving it much thought. At that point, Ace Sanchez was at the top of his suspect list. No doubt, years of training and experience had taught DeRoehn to always look to the husband or boyfriend before wasting time on other leads.[15]

∗

Howell continued to park his van at the Stop & Shop parking lot. It would be a mindless decision that he would later kick himself for making. Doing so was not out of keeping for a serial killer with a trail of victims, however. For many, as the killings continue, a sense of over-confidence sets in and the killers begin to take shortcuts when committing their crimes. This, in turn, results in serial killers taking more chances over time that lead to identification by law enforcement.[16] About a month or so after Howell killed his fourth victim, Nilsa Arizmendi, a police car drove up to the back of his van. A female officer got out and shone a flashlight into the windows of the van. Howell's heart raced as he lay beneath the blankets strewn across the backbench. The officer walked to the back of the van and wrote down the license plate number. Sweat formed on Howell's brow; he pulled the covers over his head like a child hiding from the bogie man. He sat up and anxiously watched as the female officer walked into the Stop & Shop grocery store; then he jumped from the bench and went to the driver's seat. Time to get the hell out of that parking lot—and fast!

8.

It is difficult to lose a mother at any age, but especially when you are young. On the subject of his mother's illness, Howell writes:

It was very hard on me and I didn't know how to deal with it so at age 12 or 13. I started drinking and staying away from home as much as possible. I was in Jr. High School and began dating Mandy. I used Mandy, alcohol, and weed to escape my problems at home. I couldn't stand to see my mom suffering knowing I couldn't help her and knowing she'd never get better. I remember a couple of times she had asked me to get her my father's gun from the dresser drawer and to go out and play. It killed me inside because I didn't want her to suffer... but I couldn't put a gun in her hand either.

So I dealt with it by not dealing with it. I used alcohol, weed, and my girlfriend to escape my problems.

I had a paper route after school and after I delivered my papers I took care of my mom until my dad got home. As soon as my dad got home I'd be gone. I had to be home between 9:30–10:00 p.m. My dad went to bed by 11–11:30 and by midnight I had sneaken out and was crawling through Mandy's window. I'd get back home around 4:30 a.m. or so, so I'd be in my room when dad got up for work.

By then, I had moved my room to what was formerly the den before mom had gotten sick. The den being a single car attached garage that had been converted to living space. So when I made it into my room I had 2 doors. One led up into the house, the other led directly outside. So sneaking out was no problem.

Dad was busy trying to work and take care of mom and didn't really have the time or energy to deal with and control a defiant teen (me). So I pretty much just did what I wanted. And back then, it seemed that all I wanted was to drink and spend time with Mandy.

Howell used more than alcohol and the comfort of his girlfriend to cope with his mother's prolonged illness. It was at the height of his mother's medical drama that he engaged in his first transaction with a prostitute. At the age of 14, when a young man's hormones are raging, he stole off with his father's car at 1 o'clock in the morning. He wrote that he *"was sneaky"* when taking his father's car out at night, something he did a lot in the years that followed, *"even down to disconnecting the speedometer cable so as not to put miles on the car and unlocking the steering wheel and rolling the window down and placing it in neutrual and pushing it out of the driveway before starting it and 'ghost-riding' it back in the driveway (Lights out, engine off)."* On the drive back home, he would replenish the fuel that he had burned. Usually he took Mandy or another girl out for a drive. *"A lot of times we'd go to York Town or to that little nature park across the James River Bridge."* But on that particular night, none of them could get out, so he *"went cruising"* to the red light district.

"I picked up a prostitute and got my first blow-job from a prostitute. I was 14 or 15 at the time. After that, I was hooked and picked up prostitutes for blow-jobs whenever I had the chance and the means. It was my secret addiction. If I had the money and was by myself and passed a whore on the street I picked her up. Going rate was 20 bucks and I've probably picked up hundreds over the years."

As the years passed, picking up prostitutes for blowjobs became an outlet into which Howell vented his emotional distress—a raging storm of feelings that he was not prepared to face or understand. Although consumed with that desire, Howell also dated Mandy off and on from ages 13 to 22.

Mandy had no idea that Bill solicited prostitutes and his voracious sexual appetite did not keep him from enjoying an active sex life with her. He wistfully recalls their time together:

"She was my shoulder and my crutch. She saw me through the hardest times of my life. But I was hell bound on being a screw up and not even her or the love I had for her could save me from myself."

Men who randomly rape and murder women are sometimes taught by their mothers to degrade women for their sexuality or clothing and engage in "slut shaming" behavior. With this in mind, I asked Howell about his mother's relationship to Mandy. His answer further defined the immense schism between his pain-filled home life in early adolescence and his escape from reality during that time.

"As far as how my mom liked Mandy. I don't even know if they ever met. None of my friends ever came to my house. I was always trying to stay away from home. Not bring people home. It was very rare that my friends came to my house."

To this day, Howell pines for his first love.

"Mandy is a good girl. She doesn't drink or use drugs. She was one of the best things that ever happened to me and I wish that back then I would have had enough sense to be more responsible and do what I needed to do to keep her in my life. I took her for granted and didn't treat her as good as I should have. And I don't blame her for leaving me because I was a wreck."

Given their frequent midnight rendezvous in Mandy's bedroom, it comes as no surprise that Mandy got pregnant with Howell's child. She went on to give him another child. When they broke up, Mandy married another man and took the children out of state. At Howell's request, I am not going to write about his children, except to say that he has not seen either of them for decades. When Mandy took the children out of state and would not allow him to visit them, it left a hole in his heart and a simmering rage that festered in the years that followed.

"I don't want anything brought down on them because of who I am. So whenever I'm asked if I have kids, I just say no. I think it's just easier for everyone. But the truth is that I miss them everyday and they are trapped in time in my mind as the 7 and 2 year olds I last saw, and it's still as fresh in my mind as if it were yesterday."

Howell stopped attending the Boys Club when his mother fell ill. It was all downhill after that. About the time of his mother's death, he was charged with burglary. He and a friend were riding bikes around the parking lot at the local mall when they noticed that Sears had failed to lock the gate to the outside of the gardening department. The teenagers could not resist the temptation to step inside. They first poked around the rows of hardware and potted plants, but it was not until they set eyes on a chainsaw that they formed the intent to steal. Little did they know that they had tripped a silent alarm minutes before and the police were on their way.

Not long after, Howell got a call from a friend who was "feuding" with his neighbors. "They got a dirt bike motorcycle just sitting in their yard right now," he said. "Come on over and take it!"

Howell had been drinking that night; he states that there was *"hardly ever a time"* when he wasn't drinking during his adolescence. He stole the bike and got away with it—for a few weeks. Then another friend was caught riding the dirt bike and told the police that Howell was the one who gave it to him. Howell was charged with the crime, which didn't make much sense to him. Since he was not the one riding the dirt bike when the cops arrived, he reasoned that the other kid should have been charged. He emphasizes that it was the only time that he ever stole, except for taking license plates from cars so he could drive under suspension.

A recurrent theme in Howell's story is that of powerlessness, mainly experienced in the face of not being able to maintain a valid driver's license. By age 19, Howell had two DUIs on his record and one driving under suspension. Virginia courts used the combination of those offenses to declare him a habitual offender, which resulted in Howell having his license taken from him for 10 years. Any subsequent charges would be automatically labeled as habitual offenses and, as felonies, would carry one- to five-year sentences. In short, Howell risked spending his entire adulthood in and out of prison by refusing to take public transit instead driving himself around.

Nonetheless, Howell could not resist the urge to drive. He had a pattern of buying cheap *"hoopties"* for $300 to $400 and licensing them with out-of-state tags that he stole off cars in motel parking lots. He tried to find Florida tags because Florida drivers were not required to have inspection, city tax or emission stickers on their windshields. Without fail, he always got busted.

The child wounded by his mother's long illness and sudden death continually chose to self-medicate to numb the pain. He blames alcohol for contributing to his disastrous life.

I know I'm accused of monsterous crimes, and because of those charges I must be some evil spirited monster that thinks of nothing but evil malicious acts or intent. But that's just not the case. I wasn't a con artist or scammer or thief. If I could help someone I would. I didn't and don't plot or scheme against anyone. I was raised with good morals and values and in spite of my charges, I try to live by those.

I screwed my life up at an early age. I've pondered many hours at what point it was that my life went wrong. And after all of that I've concluded that my life went wrong when I started drinking. I always thought that losing my liscense for 10 years at the age of 18 is where my life went wrong. But it goes back further than that. If it hadn't been for my drinking I'd never lost my liscense.

Don't get me wrong. I'm not an asshole who does stupid shit every time I drink. But most of the trouble I've been in happened while drinking. And I wasn't the type that went 'looking' for trouble when I drank. For the most part I was a 'happy' drunk. But drinking did make me less likely to avoid or walk away from trouble that came my way. Shit I was likely to let go if I was sober and was less likely to let go if I had been drinking. So it's not that I went looking for trouble when I drank, I was just less likely to run away from it.

I should have stuck to smoking pot and left the alcohol alone!!

9.

September–November 2003

Detectives DeRoehn and Davis visited Valeria Arizmendi's home on Sept. 20, 2003, and asked Nilsa's mother and sister questions about Ace. On Oct. 2, DeRoehn furnished a request to monitor Ace's telephone calls and written correspondence during the length of his incarceration. Apparently, DeRoehn had not ruled Sanchez out as a suspect as of Nov. 17. At that time, he remarked in a police report that Sanchez had been released from prison on Nov. 10 and went on to incorrectly state, "as of this write up, has not made effort to contact the Wethersfield Police Department."

By Sept. 13, Howell had entered the equation as a possible suspect. DeRoehn was notified that Nilsa Arizmendi was last seen as a passenger in the 1985 blue Ford Econoline van driven by Howell. He also learned that the van was actually registered in the name of Howell's girlfriend, Dorothy Holcomb.

DeRoehn let his investigative zeal get the best of him. In an attempt to efficiently locate Holcomb and thereby locate the blue van, he completed a form with the State of Connecticut Department of Social Services (D.S.S.) requesting the release of information about a member of a household requiring food stamps (T.F.A.) or cash assistance (A.F.D.C.). To DeRoehn's knowledge, Howell's girlfriend was not in violation of probation or parole under any federal, state or local authority. Nevertheless, he checked a box on the form indicating that he, as a law enforcement officer, was making this request in his official duty "to locate or apprehend the individual named in this request."

Two months later, DeRoehn furthered his ruse, this time in a way that is not only permissible, but also commonly employed by law enforcement officers. When he found out where Holcomb lived, DeRoehn went to the house on Washington Street in New Britain with Det. Michael Godart of the Wethersfield Police Department and told a bold-faced lie.

The officers knocked on the front door. No one answered. All of the lights were turned off inside. They walked to the side of the house and saw the dim figure of a white male with longish blond hair standing over the sink in the kitchen. The men went to the rear door and knocked. Holcomb, a stout, middle-aged woman, opened the door. DeRoehn and Godart presented their IDs as law enforcement officers. Holcomb crossed her forearms over her ample bosom. "What do you want?" she asked.

Maybe Holcomb would have reacted differently to DeRoehn if she met him at a bar or bumped into him on the street. In his 40s, the good-looking detective possessed a full head of brown hair and sparkling brown eyes, although his complexion was rough—as though he had bad acne in adolescence. Many thought he was an exact look-alike of the actor Ray Liotta. In these circumstances, however, Holcomb was not pleased with either of her guests.

DeRoehn asked if Holcomb owned the blue Ford Econoline van parked in front of the property's two-car detached garage.

"Why?" Holcomb defensively asked.

DeRoehn explained that he was looking for the van because it was connected to the thefts of some lawn care equipment in the area. It was not true, but if he told Holcomb he was interested in the van in relation to a missing person's case, she would no doubt inform Howell as soon as they left and Howell would flee.

Holcomb told the detectives that she owned the van, but she did not drive it much. She escorted them to the vehicle.

It truly brought new meaning to the word "jalopy." The windows on each side were broken and covered by dark-blue painted plywood. Patches of rust lined the bottom of the doors and the tires were almost treadless. On the side of the van, a white sign advertised "Quality Lawn Service, Call Devin" with a phone number below.

"Who drives the van other than you?"

"Why do you want to know?"

DeRoehn patiently repeated the question. Holcomb said that a friend named Thomas sometimes drove the van, but she did not even know where he lived.

"I think the operator of the van lives with you," DeRoehn said. "I think he is in the home right now."

"I don't know what you're talking about. I only live with my two kids. I don't know anything about stolen lawn care equipment. Are you saying someone told you I know about it? When did it get stolen? Who said they saw my van?"

The detectives refused to give Holcomb details about the fictitious theft. Holcomb grew belligerent. She rushed back to the house and phoned the New Britain Police Department. Furious and flustered, she gave the dispatch officer on the other end the verbal impression that the Nazi Gestapo had just stormed into her home with pistols drawn. Simultaneously, DeRoehn phoned the New Britain police and calmly explained that everything was fine. He and Godart were only looking for a van in connection with some local thefts.

Her pudgy arms akimbo, Holcomb seethed in DeRoehn's direction.

DeRoehn visually scanned the property one last time. He glanced at Holcomb, though refused to meet her eyes, and settled his gaze on the window right above the kitchen sink. The man he had seen when he first arrived was no longer visible. There was no sense hanging around any longer. They had found the van. The detectives left, but not before bidding Holcomb a good day.

In a country without a Constitution that protects the rights of its citizens, DeRoehn and Godart could have seized the van right at that time, taken it back for forensic processing and arrested Howell for the murder of Nilsa Arizmendi. It would all have taken a matter of weeks. Possibly, the murder of Joyvaline Martinez, which took place in mid-October, may not have occurred. But alas, the rules of that pesky document must be followed with fastidious resolve by members of law enforcement and the courts.

A search warrant of the van was later issued by a court magistrate. By then, Howell had driven the vehicle in question over several state lines and safely arrived in his home state of Virginia.

*

Authorities may have been suspicious of Howell at that point in time, but they were also still wondering if Ace Sanchez killed Nilsa Arizmendi in a domestic dispute. Even Arizmendi's family wondered if Sanchez were somehow responsible for her disappearance, or had information about it that he was not sharing. In an Incident Report from the Wethersfield Police Department dated Dec. 2, 2003, Det. DeRoehn relayed that suspicion. It appears that he even tried to coax a confession from Sanchez:

About 930 hours I arrived at the Manchester Adult Probation Office where the clerical staff notified PO Lawrence that I was there. Lawrence escorted me to his office where I met Sanchez. I asked Sanchez where he had been further stating that I thought he would up at the Wethersfield Police Department to speak to me about Arizmendi. Sanchez stated that he thought I would go to his house and speak to him. I told him that I wasn't missing my wife and it been three (3) weeks since he was released from prison and he had made not attempts to contact me.

Lawrence allowed me to use the office next door to him, another Probation Officer's (sic office.) That PO is currently deployed in Iraq. I advised Sanchez that he was not under arrest and was free to leave at anytime. I removed a national Crime Information Center (NCIC) Missing Person File from my notebook and asked Sanchez to assist me with details of Arizmendi that he would know better than her family such as scarring, clothing last worn, jewelry etc. Sanchez provided me with many of the answers I needed.

During our conversation I asked Sanchez what he thought happened to Arizmendi. He stated that he feared the worst and thought she was dead. Sanchez stated that Arizmendi could not just walk away from her life in the Hartford area. She had him, family in the area which included children, and at least a bundle a day up to three bundles a day heroin habit depending on how much crack cocaine she was smoking. He stated that he looked everywhere for her including all of the places in Hartford where he knew she purchased narcotics. I told him that the word on the streets was that he killed her. Sanchez stated, "I'll take a polygraph right now." I told Sanchez that I could arrange a polygraph appointment in West Hartford at the West Hartford Police Department. Sic Would he be interested? Sanchez stated, "Yeah, let's do this." Sanchez maintained that the last person he saw Arizmendi with was a guy named "Devon" who drove an old blue van that he lived in at the Super Stop & Shop on the Berlin Turnpike in Wethersfield. Sanchez stated that he and Arizmendi had partied with "Devon" a few times and even allowed him to stay in their motel room previously. I showed Sanchez a picture of William Howell DOB 02/11/1970 and he stated that the DOC photo was Devon. I told him that I had already spoken to him and would be speaking to him again.

Later that day, Sanchez took the polygraph test. At the conclusion of the examination, the sergeant administering the test found that Sanchez was deceptive. Det. DeRoehn's report went on to state:

Following the polygraph examination I drove Sanchez to a retirement home on Charter Oak Avenue in the City of Hartford. Sanchez stated that his father was there and was leaving for Puerto Rico soon. Sanchez stated that he wanted to see his father before he left. During the ride from the West Hartford Police Department to Charter Oak Avenue I told Sanchez that initially the case was not assigned to me. I requested the case because I believe that Nilsa Arizmendi died a horrible death and I wanted her family to have some closure. I further stated that since starting this case I couldn't shake from my mind the thought of wild animals biting, gnawing, and pulling at Nilsa's body from her shallow grave. I told Sanchez that I felt for his "Son" Arizmendi's son Miguel who does not know why his mother left him without ever saying goodbye. Sanchez started to cry as I stopped the car in front of the retirement home on Charter Oak Avenue. Sanchez continued to cry and wipe tears as I looked through my maroon folder to make sure I had his home phone number. As I thumbed through my folder I came across Sanchez's Department of Corrections photo. I showed it to Sanchez and he stated, "I don't even know who that is anymore." Sanchez exited my unmarked cruiser and walked towards the front door of the retirement home. I told him that I would be in touch.

DeRoehn did get back in touch with Sanchez on Dec. 19, when he asked Sanchez to take another polygraph examination and Sanchez agreed. The results of the second examination were "inconclusive."[17] This development prompted DeRoehn to focus more of his energies on pursuing William Devin Howell.

10.

When through the woods, and forest glades I wander,
And hear the birds sing sweetly in the trees.
When I look down, from lofty mountain grandeur
And see the brook, and feel the gentle breeze.

"How Great Thou Art"

Late autumn, 2003. Nature went about its usual activities behind the strip mall in New Britain. A single, dried-up maple leaf tumbled from a naked tree branch. The shimmering red form danced like a fairy angel in the early morning sunlight, fluttered and turned in the cold breeze and lightly fell to rest on the frosty ground. In the distance, white-tailed deer fed on acorns, twigs, and buds from the hardwood trees in preparation for the long, cold winter ahead. A lone hawk soared peacefully through the clear-blue sky as squirrels pounced across the forest's floor, skirting up and down the trees, darting from roots to stones, utterly oblivious to the busy commercial strip close by—and the remains of seven human beings buried in their midst ...

11.

A little under six months into our written correspondence, on Dec. 21, 2015, my relationship with Howell, hereinafter, Bill, took a dramatic turn. To my surprise, Capt. Scott Salace, a higher up at the correctional institute where Bill was housed, granted my request to phone the inmate, despite knowing my intentions to write a book about the six remaining murders that Bill was alleged to have committed. (According to Bill, the captain once delivered one of my sealed letters to his cell and opened it up in front of him, grumbling as he scanned its contents: "Let's see if Howard is on the up and up.")

Our first phone call lasted for 21 minutes and 42 seconds.

My thoughts tossed about in a sea of nervous energy as I waited for the phone to ring at my law office with my paralegal, Heather, sitting across from me, also anxiously waiting for the phone to ring. Before his identity as the serial killer suspect was revealed to the public, I envisioned the culprit of the horrible crimes that I read about online as some kind of modern-day Jack the Ripper—a shadowy force of evil trolling the commercial district of New Britain, hunting for vulnerable prey. Never in my wildest imaginings did I think that I would someday speak with that same man.

The state of Connecticut listing showed up on my phone. I waited for the second ring, so as not to appear too eager, and picked up. "This is Anne Howard."

The low voice on the other end was gruff and intimidating. "William Devin Howell."

"Bill? Is that you?"

"Howard!" the voice shouted into the receiver.

Yikes, I thought. He sounds like a pissed-off coach in the locker room at halftime.

"I meant *Howell*," he shouted. "Howell!"

Some scuffling noises. A clumsy transfer of the phone receiver between hands … then a far gentler voice came on the line. "Anne? It's Bill."

Hearing him for the first time set my mind at ease. In a letter dated two days before, in which he drew me a Snoopy wearing a Christmas cap followed by a line of Woodstocks holding Snoopy's scarf, he indicated that without my presence in his life, he would have committed suicide. I wondered if it was a con when I read it, but his voice on the phone told me otherwise. His lawyers were right. Some kind of psychological dynamic was taking place between the two of us.

We talked about the small claims case that he had lost against Dori's sister, Trudy Hackler. Bill had saved up $2,242 working at the prison and sent the money to Dori's sister with the agreement that she would put the funds into a savings account for Bill's use upon his release. Instead, Bill claims that the woman he trusted drained the funds for her own use and went on a cruise. Based on the legal paperwork that I reviewed at the courthouse, it appears that Trudy did take most, if not all of the money and spent it. Still, the small claims magistrate ruled in Defendant Hackler's favor, obviously having no desire to side with a serial killer suspect regardless of the fact that the law was on his side in that particular dispute.[18]

Again, Bill requested my legal representation in the matter and again, I demurred. I did promise to pull the legal documents that he needed from the clerk's office at the courthouse and mail them to him the following week as he planned to file a grievance against the magistrate that made the ruling. "Good luck with that," I told him.

I asked him more about his childhood acquaintances and wondered what kind of music he liked. Heavy metal, he told me. Ozzy and Black Sabbath.

"What's the best concert that you've ever been to?" I asked.

"I haven't gone to many concerts. Mostly when I was a teenager ... Ronny James Dio was good. He's one of my favorites—and Metallica."

My reason for keeping the conversation light was twofold: I did not want to scare him off with a Nancy Grace-style interrogation, and I knew that our call was being recorded. The captain's cooperation in allowing the call was likely condoned by the prosecution in hopes that Howell would provide information to me that would injure his case.

"Have you heard from your Aunt Ann lately?" I asked.

"No, she used to send Christmas cards." His voice cracked with sadness. "She hasn't done that lately. She is really old and she had back surgery. Aunt Ann is a Christian lady. She took me to Sunday school when I was a kid. Behind her house in Hampton, it's all condominiums now, but when I was a teenager, it used to be all fields and woods back there and I'd drive my motorcycle on a BMX track that people had built."

"You miss Virginia, don't you?"

"Yeah ... yeah, I do."

"Ever wish you never came to Connecticut in the first place?"

He laughed. "Hell yeah! All the time!"

"So tell me about your life in high max ..."

He described his day-to-day existence in the protective custody (P.C.) unit at Walker C.I. He was housed with six other inmates who were assigned to that unit due to the high-profile nature of their crimes. His "neighbor," whom Bill referred to as a "kid," jumped off a bridge holding his baby, but claimed it was by accident. The baby died. The father survived. He recently rejected a plea deal for a 50-year sentence—basically life. The jury gave him 65 years. There were also a few former cops in the unit who required separation from the general population for obvious reasons.

Most days, the clock seemed to move in slow motion. For 90 minutes every morning, the men could congregate in a dayroom to watch TV and play cards and they were given another 90 minutes before dinner. Weather permitting, they could step outside into a small cage affixed to a concrete slab. "Be careful what you say to those men," I told him, remembering DeRoehn's affidavits describing his alleged conversations with jailhouse snitches.

"Oh, yeah. I'm careful."

I had read online that prosecutors recently handed over a daunting amount of evidence to Bill's lawyers, resulting in a continuance of his probable cause hearing. According to the arrest warrant, the prosecution's evidence included "thousands and thousands" of pages of DNA testing reports and those reports indicated that the DNA of all the victims, except Mary Jane Menard, was found in Bill's van. "How do you feel about that discovery?" I asked. "Do you have any hope of being acquitted?"

"No," he said. "People have already determined that I am guilty. It's not just what you say, but what you don't say. You ask for a lawyer and they say you're guilty because you asked. You answer one of their questions and they twist it around against you."

"Do you think it is worth it then, to go through the stress of a long trial?"

"I don't know. My attorneys say it will take two or three years. I just don't know."

"Well at least you don't have to worry about the death penalty in Connecticut."

"I'm not relieved about that. I wish I could just close my eyes and never wake up. That would be better than having to sit in prison and rot to death someday of a disease like cancer."

A metal door slammed shut and the captain was back in the room, ordering Bill to hang up. We said our goodbyes and I promised to meet with him soon since I was now approved as a social visitor on his visitation list.

The next day, correction officers raided Bill's cell. He was removed to another location so he could not see what they were looking at for more than an hour. He thought that they were reading the letters that I had sent to him, along with a journal that he had been keeping in which he had written "sometimes I just feel like hanging up." That written sentiment, along with his words about wanting to die at the end of our phone call the day before, was enough to result in his being placed on suicide watch over the holidays.

12.

So hoist up the John B's sail
See how the mainsail sets
Call for the Captain ashore
Let me go home, let me go home
I wanna go home, yeah, yeah
Well I feel so broke up
I wanna go home

Sloop John B, The Beach Boys
November 2003–February 2004

The city of Hampton is located at the southeastern end of the Virginia peninsula. Hampton boasts the world's first bridge tunnel, opened in 1957. It crosses the mouth of the ice-free Hampton Roads harbor, which serves as a gateway to the Chesapeake Bay and Atlantic Ocean. Visit Hampton and you will be immediately struck by its abundant military and nautical history. Home of Langley Air Force Base, the nation's first military installation dedicated solely to airpower, it has been the epicenter of military aviation training, research and development in the last century. The Hampton Road's area, with Norfolk hosting the world's largest naval base, and the U.S. Coast Guard headquartered in Portsmouth, makes it America's most heavily populated home to military families, with nearly a fourth of the nation's active-duty military personnel stationed there. In the civilian sector, many residents in Hampton are employed at the expansive Newport News Shipbuilding, located at the foot of the majestic James River Bridge.

Additionally known for its miles of beautiful beaches and waterfront homes, Hampton has been home to many notable people in history, including James Armistead, America's first African-American spy during the Revolutionary War; Jefferson Davis, president of the Confederate States of America; and African-American statesman Booker T. Washington.

Hampton is also where William Devin Howell grew up.

Having been raised in a milder climate, Bill was averse to Connecticut's harsh winters. Following his initial arrival to Connecticut in 2001, it was his routine to leave New England in the late fall and move south to Virginia or North Carolina. It also made sense to go south for the winter if he wanted to earn a living in lawn care. Being apart from his then girlfriend, Dori, was not a big deal. The two were comfortable living independently for months at a time.

In 2003, Bill spent Thanksgiving at the home of his longtime friend, Joseph Ashley Martin, who went by his middle name, Ashley. He had promised Martin that he would also attend his wedding to Cynthia later in the week. Bill arrived at the well-maintained brick ranch four or five days before the holiday. Martin was glad to see his old friend, who was known by others in Hampton by his middle name, Devin. The two had grown up in the same neighborhood and it was not unusual for Bill to visit during the winter months. In addition to childhood memories, the friends shared a few other common bonds. According to a mutual acquaintance, Devin and Ashley were viewed by their peers as quiet, beer-drinking country boys at heart.

A big difference between the two men had always involved physical attractiveness. Martin had dark, shoulder-length hair, friendly brown eyes and a sweet, mama's boy quality that attracted the opposite sex. In contrast, Bill was always a little overweight and scruffy in appearance, although his easygoing demeanor was enough to set the girls at ease.

"Hey, Hound Dog." Bill gave Martin a playful punch in the stomach at the front steps. Hound Dog was the pet name given to Martin by a crew of carpet layers when the two friends worked together. Bill had no idea why Martin got that name, but he couldn't deny that it suited his easygoing buddy.

Martin led Bill into the kitchen and cracked open two beers. He handed one to Bill. "You got here early," he remarked, sitting at the kitchen table.

Bill took a big gulp of beer and remained standing. The last thing he wanted was to sit down after driving for nine hours straight. "Not really. Last time it took longer 'cause I caught D.C. at rush hour and the construction on the New Jersey Turnpike was a bitch."

"Why do you go I-95 South to I-64 East, Devin?" Martin asked. "You should go the back way."

"Nope," Bill firmly replied. "It might be faster, I don't know, but there's like a 10- to 15-dollar toll to get across the Chesapeake Bay Bridge Tunnel and then tons of stoplights along that route."

Bill made quick work of his beer and went to the fridge for another. He looked back at Martin. "I need to get you fattened up tonight with some of my famous cheeseburgers, Hound Dog. Y'all skin and bones."

Martin chuckled. He was used to Bill teasing him, having lived with him and another friend, Harry, in a townhouse apartment in the past. And he couldn't deny that Bill made the best cheeseburgers he ever tasted—better than anything you buy at Whataburger.

"Shit, I can't believe how congested Hampton has gotten," Bill lamented. "I remember when Target and Walmart were nothing but woods."

"Yeah, it's getting bad," Martin agreed.

"Remember that amusement park at Buckroe Beach? That old rickety wooden roller coaster? You could feel it come off the tracks at the tops of the hills!"

Martin smiled, sipping his beer. "Wouldn't of been fun if you didn't think you might die …"

"Exactly!" Bill exclaimed. "Like at any moment, you were going to go flying off the tracks and lose your fucking head!"

Fresh beer in hand, Bill stood staring into the open fridge. "Your mom got any Krispy Kremes around here?" Martin's mother, Ann, was a sweet Christian woman who kept the kitchen well stocked, not unlike Bill's Aunt Ann. She could not have been more opposite to her husband, John, who was a crusty old Southerner chronically bent on giving people a piece of his irritable mind.

"Nope. We can go get some, if you want." The Krispy Kreme doughnut shop was just around the corner, located on Mercury Boulevard alongside all of Bill's favorite culinary haunts: Arby's, Burger King, McDonald's and Pizza Hut. Driving along that strip was a proverbial "blast from the past"—most of the business establishments maintained their outdated appearances. The Burger King was a cube-shaped building with "Home of the Whopper" still posted over the side door and the Arby's sign was shaped as an over-sized 10-gallon rancher's hat. The Pizza Hut also maintained its original architecture, shaped like a Tahitian hut with a bright-red shingled roof in place of thatch.

During the weeklong visit, Bill asked Martin to help him clean out the blue van that he had parked in the driveway. According to subsequent police reports, what first struck Martin upon entering the van through the sliding door was the foul stench, which Martin assumed was body odor. It was only slightly reduced by the competing aromas of grass, oil and gasoline. The two friends emptied the van's contents, including a weed whacker, lawn mower and bags of clothing that littered the light-blue rug on the van's floor. The blue bench near the van's sliding doors was intact, with both a bottom cushion and a matching back cushion, according to those same reports. Martin watched as Bill removed the stained cushion that lined the bottom bench, rolled it up, and put it in a large plastic bag. Bill walked to the curb and left it there for trash pickup.[19]

Martin thought nothing of it.

A few days later, Bill said his goodbyes and was headed for North Carolina to visit his other longtime friend, Harry.

13.

Call it woman's intuition, but I sensed that Bill was having a hard time of it while I was baking cookies, wrapping presents and watching "It's a Wonderful Life" in the week that followed our first phone call. My suspicions were confirmed in his next letter.

January 11, 2016
Dear Anne,
Please excuse the writing. I am using a 'seg' pen which is nothing more than the plastic ink cartridge from a cheap pen. I have had a rough few weeks. I spent the first 2 weeks (on suicide watch) in what I call 'the butt naked cell' because that's how they house you. They give you what's called a 'Ferguson gown' and a blanket. Both are made from a heavy nylon type of material that can't be knotted. Kind of like a heavy duty moving blanket or a horse blanket if you know the type I'm talking about. And you are allowed no property whatsoever. Not a T-shirt, not underwear. No food other than the provided meals and even those don't come with a plastic spork. You must tear off a corner of the Styrofoam tray and use that as a spoon.
So that is how I spent my Christmas and New Year's. The following Monday they brought me here to Garner (another prison in Connecticut.) Today makes a week I've been here. Still on suicide watch but at a reduced level. I can now have a regular 'jumpsuit' with a T-shirt, socks, and underwear, as well as a book and this 'safety pen' I'm using and paper. But that's it.

He was exhausted from insomnia, bored and hungry all of the time. He had lost about 15 pounds—*"not that I can't afford to lose the weight, but I sure don't like it,"* he wrote and he had not been allowed to shave in three weeks. He longed to return to his cell at Walker C.I., which had a window that allowed him to receive sunlight, radio stations, and over the air TV stations. *"I was laying here thinking how I couldn't wait to get home when it dawned on me that I'm thinking of another 'prison' as home. How screwed up is that???"*

"It is an odd sentiment," I thought, "but not exactly screwed up. Killing seven people and burying them in shallow graves behind a strip mall—now *that* is screwed up."

Thursday, January 14, 2016
Still stuck at Garner. I am off of suicide watch and they have now moved me to seg pending transfer back to Walker. I've been in the seg unit for 2 days now. The staff here are real dicks. I have none of my property and no commissary. All they will tell me is that I am pending transfer and they are just waiting for a bed to open. But hell, my bed should have been 'saved.' They knew me coming here was only temporary and that the P.C. section at Walker is the only place that they can really house me. I'm really pissed over the whole predicament. But really I only have myself to blame. I knew that the psych doctor at Walker was a snake in the grass and I am the one that wrote what I wrote that gave him the opportunity to strike. And strike he did.

In that letter, he asked if I could set up an online "Go Fund Me Page" for him and install a link to J-Pay for people to make donations to his inmate trust account. The proposal was absurd. Who on Earth would give money to an alleged serial killer?

Oh wait, that would be me.

I really hope you will continue to write and support me here and there after your book is finished. I sort of feel a kind of friendship with you and when you are an Alleged Serial Killer, friendships are hard to come by. Especially lasting ones.

Truer words were never spoken.

A few days later, Bill was sent back to the P.C. unit at Walker C.I.

"I've never been so happy to come back to a 'prison!' I got my old cell back at Walker and am still on 'single cell' status and all the guys were happy to see me back. The first thing I did when I got here is yell down the Hall, 'What's up Bitches!!.. I'm baaack. And IIII'm pissed.

They were all like, yeap, Hill-Billie is back.

I make prison fun for these guys.

Safely caged in his cell at Walker C.I., Bill made paper flowers for a female counselor and sent his letters to me on stationery with hand-sketched floral patterns around the borders. His hot pot had been returned from inventory and he threw himself into creating his own dishes using leftovers from recent meals and items purchased in the prison commissary. His specialties included angelhair spaghetti with one half of a spicy beef sausage sliced up into pizza sauce—seasoned with Italian herbs, salt and pepper—and cheese and pepperoni bagel sandwiches. It took about 15 to 17 minutes to make the pasta because his hot pot only heated up to 151 degrees. That wasn't a big problem, however, since he had nowhere else to go.

He could make Rice Krispie treats *"better in here than I can on the street."* The ingredients took time to gather: a jar of marshmallow fluff and a Hershey bar purchased from the commissary along with a few boxes of cereal, peanut butter rationed from the tray he received on Peanut Butter and Jelly day (every other Friday) and cubes of butter saved from baked potato trays. By melting the Hershey bar on the hot pot and clipping a very small hole in the corner of the wrapper, he was able to drizzle chocolate across the top of each square "*and it comes out looking like it came from a Bakery.*"

He didn't like one of the new inmates who arrived when he was on what he described as "*my little vacation at Garner C.I.*" He sensed the man was "*a rat,*" and was glad that he would be transferring out the next week. He still got along with the other inmates, though. Most were former corrections officers or cops who had been convicted of rapes, drug use or possession of "*kiddie porn.*" Others had "*got mixed up in some type of domestic shit.*"

Insightfully, he wrote: "*If you took everyone's story in here you'd have a whole freakin news paper ☺.*"

He harbored resentment toward the inmate who was given the only job available to P.C. inmates, as a janitor. The man had recently been sentenced to 20 years for murder, and so Bill could "*kiss goodbye*" any hope of ever getting that coveted job. It paid $20 a month.

As the weather warmed in the month of March, he spent most of his rec time outside. There wasn't much to do in a 20 x 20 dog pen except feed bread to the birds through the fence and "*enjoy the fresh air.*" He had a "*little bird book*" given to him by another inmate the year before, and he used it to identify the birds that flew to the fence: sparrows, dark-eye juncos and tufted titmice. One red-winged bird came by every day and he saw a blue jay the year before. By May, the yard was crawling with "*chiggers,*" which he described as "*little red bugs about the size of a pin head.*" He warned the other inmates not to lean against the brick wall because the bugs bore into the pores of your skin causing "*a very itchy zit like type of sore,*" but they were "*real dismissive about it.*"

Never let it be said that a serial killer suspect cannot have a sense of humor:

"*Sometimes when we get a new officer on post I'll sit in my cell and 'blow Bubbles' just to see the look I get when he walks by and sees me. Or when we get a new co (corrections officer) and he asks if I want a razor on razor day and I say, 'No, I did my bikini line yesterday.' The look on their face and that moment of them not knowing what to say is priceless."*

Bill wrote more to me than I wrote to him. I was juggling the responsibilities of an active law practice, family obligations and writing this book, and my days passed quickly. In contrast, Bill felt that he was in a time warp where *"weeks can feel like months."* To stay sane or perhaps, more accurately, to distract himself from the insanity that put him there in the first place, he kept busy playing video games. His favorite one resembled his purported misdeeds in his 1985 Ford Econoline and follow-up trips to the back of the strip mall:

"I got the property guy to give me a couple of loaner games and I have 220 hours logged into one of them. It's like a never ending 'roll playing game.' You combine different monsters with different attributes to create new and more powerful monsters which can then combine again and it just goes on and on. And before you combine them you have to build them up to a certain level which takes a lot of time, and once you combine 2 monsters you have to start over again then build up the newly created monster."

He read books by authors including John Saul and Dean Koontz.

"You should read 'The Homing,'" he recommended. *"All Saul's books are good, but 'The Homing' is real scary."*

In an attempt to get inside my subject's mind, I ordered the used paperback on Amazon and read it while on vacation in Cancun, Mexico.

The first chapter provided immense insight into Bill's mental landscape:

Don't! he told himself. Don't go near her. Don't touch her. Don't even look at her!

Yet he couldn't keep himself from looking at her.

His eyes fastened on her, and in the deep recesses of his mind, darkness began to close around him.

A terrifying darkness—a darkness filled with nameless horrors that were reaching out to him.

He could already feel talons of fear sinking deeply into his soul, and hear a mocking laughter in his ears.

"The Homing," John Saul.

"What did you think of 'The Homing?'" he later asked.

"It was a page turner," I wrote back. "But I didn't find it that scary."

"What about the werewolves?"

"There weren't any werewolves in 'The Homing,'" I wrote. "Just a deranged psychopath who liked to torture people with killer bees and scorpions."

He was disappointed. *"Then I gave you the wrong title. That's another one by John Saul. It was good too. I think the one I'm talking about is 'Guardian.' You need to get that one."*

He also listened to the radio and watched television all day long and deep into the night. He tried to read "A Tale of Two Cities" by Charles Dickens, but couldn't get past the first five pages. I sent him the Stephen King novel, "Salem's Lot," but he found King's writing too intricate and complicated, although he said that he liked some of King's movies. He frequently made a point of apologizing for his handwriting, which I found to be quite neat compared to mine. He was also self-conscious of his poor spelling and grammar. *"Personally, I don't care about 'double negative' or other gramar skills I lack. I write it as I'd say it and it ain't ☺ allways (oops always only has one l) proper."*

His explanations were not necessary. I could see in his letters and during our meetings that he likely had an average, if not above average, IQ, with strong reasoning skills that were not reflected in his deficient writing skills.

What he lacked in formal education, he made up for in street smarts. Moreover, some of the books that he recommended were quite good. *"Did you ever get 'Wicked Intentions' by Kevin Flynn?? I just finished reading it. That's the 'true crime' book about the Labarre lady. That Chick was crazy For Real."*

He told me that he struggled with insomnia at night, mainly because his thoughts raced with past regrets in the darkness of his cell, and he was wracked by depression. Consequently, he slept off and on throughout the day with the television droning in the background. His list of favorite shows was almost as long as his recipe list: "Crime Watch Daily," local news, "Family Guy," "TM2," "Good Morning America," "The Steve Wilkos Show," "Raising Hope," "The People's Court," "Judge Judy," "Survivor," "Hunted," "American Housewife," "Big Brother," "Life in Pieces" "American Greed," "Amazing Race," "America's Funniest Home Videos" and "America's Got Talent," to name just a few.

I sometimes thought that his lifestyle was too cushy at Walker C.I. It seemed more like a government-imposed retreat. Over time, however, I came to understand that the hardship of lifelong incarceration in a segregated atmosphere can be mitigated by outside distractions such as television and hot pot menus, but no amount of entertainment can detract from the inner torment of being isolated, unwanted and reviled.

Meanwhile, the followers of my "Serial Murders in Connecticut" Facebook page routinely cried out for him to receive lethal injection. Underlying that demand was the presumption that death is the worst scenario because it not only deprives the killer of the pleasure of being alive, it hopefully leads him on a direct path to the fires of eternal Hell. Bill differs with that outlook. Lethal injection would be a welcome relief, he told me on more than one occasion. The shows that he watched on the small TV in his cell weren't that great and prison food was awful. His day-to-day life was miserable beyond what anyone on the outside could imagine; he was, for all intents and purposes, residing in Hell on Earth. Since he did not believe in God—and therefore rejected the notion of an otherworldly Hell—he could not conceive of anything worse than his current existence.

I could imagine darker things. For example, the terror that his victims experienced as he hit, raped and strangled them in the back of his van, or the ongoing emotional torment of the victims' families as they replayed the gruesome facts in their minds day after day. Without a doubt, the mothers of the victims were anguished by the notion that the man who killed their baby is still alive today. That suffering seems like a far greater hardship than living in a cell and watching television every day.

14.

Det. DeRoehn must have been frustrated. It had been weeks since his visit with Dorothy Holcomb. Since then, he searched relentlessly for Bill driving the highly identifiable van. If only he or Godart could find Bill, they could stop him as a suspended motor vehicle operator and take him in for questioning.

After contacting Holcomb, DeRoehn did a National Criminal Information Center (N.C.I.C.) computer check of Bill and found that the New Britain Police Department had an outstanding warrant out on Bill for a charge of assault in the third degree. According to the records, the victim of the assault was none other than Bill's biggest advocate, Dorothy Holcomb. It seemed the couple recently had a quarrel. During the fight, he ripped the telephone from the wall to prevent Holcomb from calling the police. She tried to run upstairs, but he physically restrained her and punched her in the stomach. He also punched the back of her head and her left eye.

DeRoehn downloaded a state of Connecticut photo of Bill and showed it to Godart. "Recognize him?"

Godart nodded. "The guy standing in Holcomb's kitchen."

Obviously, Holcomb was running interference for her boyfriend on the day of their visit. She probably knew that her boyfriend had a lengthy criminal history along the East Coast consisting of numerous traffic violations and that he was wanted for violation of probation. It was also possible that she was afraid of Bill's volatile reaction if she alerted the visiting detectives to his presence at the house that day, given the couple's past allegations of domestic violence.

A break finally came in the case on the following day when DeRoehn checked the N.C.I.C. database for the Connecticut registration number on Holcomb's van. It revealed that the van was in North Carolina. Evidently, Bill had been stopped and arrested for a motor vehicle violation by a sheriff's deputy of Dare County the day after Thanksgiving at 11:46 p.m. At the time, Bill provided false photo identification with the name of his nephew and a false date of birth, March 17, 1971. Bill posted bond and was scheduled to appear at the Manteo County Courthouse in North Carolina on Jan. 30, 2004. Fortunately for DeRoehn, Bill dutifully appeared in court on the day of his arraignment.

It took some work, but DeRoehn was able to convince North Carolina authorities to detain Bill at the Manteo County Correctional Center to await extradition to Connecticut in light of Sanchez's most recent polygraph results being inconclusive.

Who can explain the juxtaposition between an alleged serial killer's grisly deeds and the way that he presents to friends, acquaintances and the public at large? After making the 800-mile trek from Connecticut to North Carolina on Feb. 19, 2004, DeRoehn and his associates, Det. Davis and Police Officer Gagne, met with a hefty and courteous baby-faced man. At 5'9" and 220 pounds, Bill seemed harmless, albeit shackled and handcuffed via belly chain.

Bill's meager belongings, contained in an orange Manteo Correctional Center plastic bag, were deposited into the trunk of the unmarked police cruiser. Gagne read Bill his

Miranda rights. He arrested him for two counts of violation of probation. He was escorted to the cruiser and belted into the rear seat behind Davis, who drove. On the trip back to New England, Bill made it clear to the officers that he would only talk about the scenery. He also did not mind discussing his upbringing in Virginia. However, he did not want to talk about any of the outstanding probation violations against him.

DeRoehn sat beside Bill in the back seat. About three hours into the drive, Bill asked why the men had traveled 800 miles one way for a mere misdemeanor warrant.

"Do you really want to know why?" DeRoehn asked.

Bill nodded.

DeRoehn pulled out a folder and removed a picture of Nilsa Arizmendi. In a subsequent statement, DeRoehn said that Bill's eyes widened. The color drained from his face.

Det. DeRoehn,
Why don't you leave me alone? Yeah, yeah…
This is the worst trip
I've ever been on

Bill moved away from the detective and leaned back in the seat. Gazing out the window at the passing scenery, he expressly told DeRoehn that he would not speak without his attorney present. He was provided lunch and dinner on the road, and dropped off with Troop L in Litchfield, Conn., later that evening, where he continued to remain silent. He appeared in Superior Court in Litchfield on Friday, Feb. 20. He was thereafter detained at the New Haven Correctional Center on $100,000 bond.

Bill would not remain silent much longer, however. In fact, in the months and years to come, he would demonstrate a self-destructive habit of confiding in all the wrong people at all the wrong times.

15.

I drive along Route 219 North and enter the scenic town of Barkhamsted, Conn. Donna Summer's song, "Bad Girls" comes on the '70s satellite station:

Toot toot, Hey
Beep, beep

Bad Girls,
Talking about the sad girls
Sad girls
Talking about baaa'ad girls, yeah

I glance over at the reservoir just past the entrance to Ski Sundown and think about Bill's purported victims. They were sad girls. They met tragic ends. Their drug addictions placed them in a degrading lifestyle that exposed them to a monster. But for the drugs, they would never have sold their bodies on the streets.

Now your mama won't like it when she finds out
Girl is out at night.

My thoughts turn to Valeria Arizmendi. What pain she must have felt, driving to church on Sundays and seeing Nilsa and Ace hiding in the alleyways along New Britain Avenue. And yet, she kept the faith, bended to her knees during the service and beseeched a loving God to intervene. "Please leave that dangerous lifestyle!" she pled in Spanish to her eldest daughter.

When she returned home from her Pentecostal church every Sunday, Valeria cared for Nilsa's children, which is no small burden. How does she feel today when she looks at the youngest, Miguel, now a grown man? What kind of heartbreak does she endure?

It is May 2016, less than one year into my correspondence with Bill, and I am traveling to Suffield for our first prison visit. I think about the rage that the family members of the victims must feel toward Bill. I recall the photo taken of Joyvaline Martinez's extended family at a press conference several years earlier, when police identified their loved one as "Jane Doe Number One." They sit in a row beside Joyvaline's enlarged photo. She looks like a young R & B star—simply beautiful. The family members wear uniform T-shirts in support of Joy. The women wear sunglasses to hide the tears. An older Hispanic man's quivering hands are raised to his face. His anguish is beyond words.

Workers are clearing brush from the side of the road. I slow down and pass a flagger wearing a bright orange vest. He looks a bit like Bill, just a normal, 40-something Joe making a living, hoping for a little extra juice money on Friday night.

In the lobby at Walker C.I., I sit in a row of hardback chairs. The legs of the table beside the metal detector are wrapped with layer upon layer of medical tape, probably to reduce interference with the sensitivity of the machine. There is a poster on the wall instructing visitors on how to deposit money into inmate accounts using J-Pay. On the back of the seat before me, someone has carved the message: "Free Marash."

A set of metal doors rolls sideways to let me in. I step into the enclosed space and press the buzzer for the next set of doors to slide open. Through the glass panel, I see Bill standing behind the Plexiglas at the end of a long room containing two other visitors there to see prisoners. He is smiling my way, obviously eager to meet me.

Approaching the line of counters and phones, we do the same musical chair routine that I did with Steven Hayes on Connecticut's death row at Northern Correctional Institute when I interviewed him one year before.[20] Bill starts to take one seat and I simultaneously take another in the next cubicle. We quickly realize the mix-up and settle on the same cubicle. Bill picks up the phone and dials some numbers. I press 1 to accept his call in English.

He gives me a big, affable smile. His teeth are yellow and crooked, with big gaping spaces in between.[21] I smile back. "You've lost weight since your mug shot was taken."

Are those tears in his eyes? "Yeah, maybe."

"What are the small tattoos on your arm?" I ask. It seems like a good conversation starter. Who doesn't like to talk about their tattoos? He tells me that he gave them to himself in the sixth grade by plunging an ink pen through his skin and writing the name of a girl that he had fallen in love with for the purpose of proving that he would stay with her forever. That would have been about the same time his mother had been diagnosed with breast cancer. Other than those markings, he has no actual tattoos.

"Was the girl Mandy?" I ask.

"No. Another girl. I met Mandy in junior high and we started going out in high school. We went out for eight years. We were engaged, too." There is no longer a question about the tears in his eyes. They rise to the surface at the mention of Mandy and are about to trickle over the wet, pink rims.

"Tell me about Dori ..."

The dam bursts. Wide tears roll down his cheeks. "Me and Dori went out for three years. She didn't have a drinking problem back then, but when we broke up, she got involved with a guy in Litchfield and they spent all day at the bars drinking. The last time I saw her, it was eight months before she died. She visited me in prison, but by then, we were just best friends. We were always honest with each other and she was always on my side. She believed I was innocent."

As he speaks, I study his eyes. They have a very peculiar shape, like half moons turned upside down, and the bloodshot globes are enormous. "I need to say this, Bill. Don't assume that I think you are innocent. I don't want to give you that impression. I mean, I am open to the idea that you may be innocent, but I just don't want to mislead you during our visits." I say all this, thinking about the true-crime author, Joe McGinniss, who was successfully sued for fraud and breach of contract by convicted family killer Dr. Jeffrey MacDonald in a case that took decades to resolve. McGinniss was clear with MacDonald that he would not necessarily portray MacDonald as innocent in his upcoming book and yet, when he concluded at the end of the book that MacDonald's conviction was supported by the evidence, the killer claimed that the author was deceptive about his intentions. Such is the plight of transacting with a sociopath.

"That's fine," Bill says with a congenial smile.

I gaze at him. He gazes back. He knows that I believe he is guilty. I am sure of it. Still, he goes on to play the part of a man wrongly accused. "You know why there were three drops of Nilsa Arizmendi's blood in the back of my van? Her and her boyfriend, Ace, had a violent relationship and he hit her. Ace claimed he never went into the back of the van, but then how come he said he knew what it looked like and there were power tools back there?"

Well, Ace testified at trial in 2007 that he sat in the passenger seat up front and turned his head to see a bunch of power tools; that's not a far-fetched concept, turning around and seeing the contents of the van. Nevertheless, I say nothing. I am not about to split hairs on our first visit.

"And another thing," Bill argues, "why would I have the two of them sit crammed into the bucket seat up front at all times when I did not have a valid license and that would have attracted the cops? I used to do everything possible to not get pulled over by cops because it meant going back to prison. So I always drove five miles above the speed limit because if you drive at the limit or lower, it looks too obvious and if you drive too fast you get pulled over." He clutches an imaginary steering wheel in front of him, "So always go slow ..." he tilts the wheel, his bulging eyes flashing with boyish mischief, "slow and careful, just five miles over and with the seat belt on ..."

Seeing the happiness on his face as he mimics driving his van, it occurs to me that Bill *loves* to drive, for miles and miles and miles. When living on the outside, he existed as a nomad and reveled in the freedom that came with it. Illegally sitting behind the wheel of his many "hoopties" over the years and the infamous "murder mobile" in which he killed one person and allegedly killed six more, gave him a sense of mastery over an existence that otherwise made no sense. This was no more evident than when he inquired about the routes that I took to the various prisons where he resided during our future visits. I rarely remembered the highways and various exits; I simply relied on my GPS to get me to where I needed to be. My ignorance seemed to disappoint and even frustrate him. He wanted more details. Directions fascinated him.

This character trait comports with the findings of FBI profiler John Douglas, who states that sexual sadists drive a lot. The reasons are obvious: traveling long distances allows for greater opportunities to find victims and dispose of their remains, if necessary.[22] On the other hand, while Bill loves to drive, he is like most serial killers in that his geographic area of operation was narrowly defined to certain cities—in his case, the cities of Hartford, New Britain, Torrington and Waterbury, Conn.—all within an hour's drive.[23]

"If you were at the table in Vegas, how much would you be willing to bet on being acquitted when this is all done with?" I ask.

He presses his lips together and shrugs. "I'm probably here for life. But life for me is 15 more years with all my health problems and the stress and the bad food. I get my insulin shots twice a day, but my A1C levels are still high."

I listen to him angrily rant about the actions of the "snitch," Jonathan Mills. "Well, snitches aside," I remark, "the outcome in this case is going to come down to the DNA they found in the van, don't you think?"

His demeanor changes. As much as he wants to see me as a friend, he knows why I am there—to write a book about a serial killer suspect who will ultimately be convicted as not just a serial killer, but Connecticut's most prolific serial killer.

"My lawyers have shown me some of the stuff they have on me and, yeah," he sighs, "it's not looking good. I should never have taken that Alford plea in the Arizmendi case. That case was much weaker than the ones ahead of me. I could have beat it."

"Or you could have rejected the plea deal and gotten 65 years," I remind him.

He says nothing. It is clear that he is not willing to concede that his former attorney, Ken Simon, was right. "They found Arizmendi's DNA in your van," I remarked, "That was pretty damning evidence."

He looks away. Time to change the subject.

"I visited Steven Hayes on death row last year," I am referring to the man who, along with Joshua Komisarjevsky, invaded a Connecticut doctor's home in 2007 and committed unspeakable acts including burning the house to the ground with the doctor's two daughters tied to their beds. "He still writes to me. He said that he might get transferred to Walker, so I assume that means he'll be in your P.C. unit."

"I saw him at Cheshire once. He was in holdover before a hearing because he tried to commit suicide. He looked awful."

"I asked him about raping and strangling Mrs. Petit ..."

Bill looks at me with surprise, as if to say, "Are you really taking the conversation in this direction? You know I am accused of multiple rapes, right?"

"He told me that he blacked out," I say. "He doesn't remember doing it."

"He raped that doctor's wife?" He asks this in the most casual and objective of tones, like he is asking about the weather. "Huh. I didn't know that."

It dawns on me in that moment—this man is not a fool. He may have dropped out of high school, where he was enrolled in vocational and special education programs, and his letters may contain a lot of spelling errors, but he is by no means dumb. He plans to play by the rules and cover his ass in all of our future conversations.

The security guard shouts out that visiting time is almost over. We end on a positive note. "You seem to be in really good spirits, Bill."

The warmth instantly returns. He is that friendly Southerner once more. "No way am I going to let them lock me up on suicide watch at Garner again!" he says, laughing. "Every day, the shrink stops by and says, 'How are you doing today?' and I always put on this big happy face and say, 'Great. I feel calm. My mood is stable. I have no plan to hurt myself.' I do it like a robot. 'Yes sir, I'm calm. My mood is stable. I have no plan to hurt myself.'"[24]

As it turned out, Bill would try to kill himself a few months later.

After our first visit, I dreamt that Bill escaped from prison and came to see me. I was at the foot of my driveway and a flatbed truck drove slowly past. Bill was hidden from the driver's view. He lay face up, amidst burlap bags of mulch, and when he saw the number on my mailbox, he rolled off of that flatbed like Humpty Dumpty falling from the wall. I ran back to the house and bolted the side door behind me. He climbed to the second floor and banged his fists against the window. In the kitchen below, a group of security guards casually conversed over coffee and doughnuts.

I recalled the dream in waking hours and took comfort in the reality that Bill would not be going anywhere anytime soon. The protective custody unit in which he was housed was barricaded by high brick walls covered in swirling cylinders of electric barbed wire. The guards watched him from morning until night. When I visited, we spoke on blue phones with thick Plexiglas separating us. He was not shackled like a death row inmate, but he might as well have been in terms of his ability to move in any direction without immediate restraint.

And yet I sometimes wondered, even if Bill could escape, or if he knew me on the outside before his present-day incarceration, would he even consider me as a target? I suggested something to that effect in a "Serial Murders in Connecticut" blog post that his lawyers later showed him in one of their many efforts to dissuade him from trusting, and therefore opening up, to me. At the following visit, he appeared deeply insulted. "I would never hurt you, Anne," he softly said. "You don't actually think that I would hurt you, do you?"

"I just wrote that for dramatic effect," I replied, mostly believing my own words. "I know you wouldn't hurt me, Bill. If anything, I think you would protect me, if push came to shove." I was not lying about that, either. Perhaps Mandy once felt the same way, before seeing Bill's darker side? He was quite convincing in presentation, and I also surmised that a sober version of Bill was very different than a drunken one.

16.

April 2004

A former cellmate, Jonathan Mills, would one day tell detectives that Bill had a pet name for the van registered in his girlfriend's name. According to that source, Bill called it The Murder Mobile. I cannot help but wonder if that was a spin-off of the name he once gave a black car that he owned in Virginia: The Bat Mobile. Strangely, Bill's former friends from Torrington have told me that they used to call the ghastly Ford Econoline van The Murder Mobile back in 2002, one year *before* the murders took place.

Bill asserts that he never called the van The Murder Mobile. That was a lie made up by Mills, along with a slew of other lies.

Regardless of whether Bill called the van The Murder Mobile, back in April 2004, the vehicle was simply known to Connecticut police as a crucial piece of evidence requiring a detailed search. It took some work to locate the van. It was eventually found in the possession of Bill's friend, Harry, who lived in Windsor, N.C.

Tom Northcott, a detective at the Bertie County Sheriff's Office located at the northeastern tip of North Carolina, seized the vehicle on April 22, 2004. He knew not to enter the van and risk the contamination of any evidence, but he did peer through the front windshield and side windows. Inside were items typical to the driver of a beat-up old vehicle who also happened to own a landscaping business: a hedge trimmer and set of jumper cables on the floorboard of the passenger side, an orange extension cord reel between the driver and passenger seat and plastic gas jugs littered in the back.

The van was temporarily stored at the impound yard of the Bertie County Sheriff's Office. While not containing a bloodthirsty junkyard dog, the lot was secure. A chain-link fence topped with barbed wire enclosed the entire space, and the two opening gates were heavily padlocked. Only high-ranking officers had a key to them.

Two days later, DeRoehn and Davis arrived in Windsor to collect the van. They made a point to avoid entering the van, although they did eye the interior through the dirty windshield with much curiosity. They then hauled it to Connecticut using a Wethersfield Maintenance Division flatbed trailer truck driven by DeRoehn.

Members of the Connecticut State Police Central District Major Crimes Squad and the Wethersfield Police Department searched the van at the secure sally port of the Wethersfield station. As lead detective in the case, DeRoehn observed the search in progress. Crime Squad Det. Chris Sudock of the Connecticut State Police began by digitally photographing the inside and outside of the van. Sudock and a few others then systematically removed Bill's entire life from the van, item by item, and took an inventory.

Included in the inventory were items of lawn equipment, bins of clothing, work tools, business books and adult videotapes. All had been haphazardly crammed into the van's interior. Knowing not to step foot in the van, DeRoehn approached the open sliding doors and took a good look around. He saw the blue seat back with stains on it visible to the eye.

Sudock also noticed a stain on the blue upholstered seat back. A bright white light test confirmed its presence. A presumptive test using the chemical phenolphthalein was then conducted and the stain showed a positive result for blood. Although the back portion of the bench had not been itemized on the search warrant, "blood" was itemized, and so Sudock had reason to seize the seat back.

When the time came, Sudock removed the van's two non-matching seat cushions in plain view because those items were not specifically listed in the search warrant. Once cleared, the van was dusted for fingerprints and palm prints, hairs and fibers were collected, and front and rear carpet samples were removed and marked as evidence.

It was obvious that the remnants of original seating material on the portion of the metal frame where one sat were the same as the material on the seat back. The cushions, however, were enclosed in a pillowcase made of lighter fabric. They appeared to have come from a sofa from someone's living room. Unlike the seat back, the cushions were not bolted to the bench. They were visually examined with high intensity white light for bloodstains and returned to the interior of the van.

Items in the van that were ultimately seized and held in custody were as follows:

- Item #1 Hairs and fibers from the rearmost portion of the vehicle

- Item #2 Rock containing stains and attached hair/hairlike fibers from the rearmost portion of the van

- Item #3 One blue in color carpet sample from the floor of the rearmost portion of the van

- Item #4 One light-blue-in-color carpet sample from the passenger side vertical wall of the rear cargo area of the van

- Item #5 One light-blue-in-color carpet sample from the driver's side vertical wall of the rear cargo area of the van

- Item #6 Red-in-color bloodlike flakes from the carpet of the driver's side interior rear wheel well of the van

- Item #7 One steak-type knife with a black-in-color plastic handle and with red-in-color blood-like stains on the cutting portion, from the floor behind the driver's side front seat of the van

- Item #8 Hairs and fibers from the middle section (floor and seat) of the van
- Item #9 One pink in color carpet sample from the floor of the middle section of the van
- Item #10 One blue in color fabric covered seat/back portion containing red in color blood-like stains from the rear seating area of the van
- Item #11 Hairs and fibers from the front-most section (floor and seats) of the van
- Item #12 Latent print lifts number LP #1 through LP #7 from the interior surfaces of the van

The search warrant included all of the items worn by Arizmendi on the date she went missing: a tie-dyed T-shirt, jean shorts, black sneakers and a woman's blue "rock" watch with a blue band. The search did not produce any of those items.

The media would subsequently report other items that were found in Bill's van: one pornographic tape titled "Score Fantasy Girls," and five other videos. Police later released grainy images of two of the women on the videotapes in hopes that they would be recognized. To date, neither woman in the tapes has been identified.

The pornographic items in the van pointed to Bill's insatiable sexual hunger and a possible addiction to pornography. He had hired hundreds—approaching 1,000—of prostitutes over the years while pursuing an active sex life with girlfriends on the side. He loved getting his *"ding dong sucked off,"* he once wrote to me. As with his other girlfriends, Dori had no inkling of his habit.

Occasionally, he would pay prostitutes for more than just blow jobs. There was the time in 1994 when he hired a prostitute in Newport News, Va., and *"shacked up with her for 3 days in a motel room."*

The incident followed his father's death, when Bill was uncharacteristically liquid due to a modest inheritance. He purchased $300 of crack cocaine and *"this chick fucked my brains out for 3 days straight."* He states that he *"took a hit or two here and there but the crack was mainly for her. I remember it would make me sick (throwing up) every time I'd smoke it. But it also had me hard as a rock and going and going like the energizer bunny."* Bill went on to tell me that the woman *"stands out so much because she gave me the best 'top sex' (girl on top) that I've ever had in my life. I mean the BEST. We were just grinding and found an unbelievable rhythm, it's like I was trying to break it off inside her and she was doing the exact same.*

"I told her I was trying to put her out of business for a few days. But I think she got the better of me. I know when we parted ways my pelvic bone was sore and bruised for days."

Bill remained in prison on probation of violation charges through June and most of July 2004. DeRoehn, also a phlebotomist, took advantage of the yet-to-be-charged murder suspect's incarceration and retrieved two blood tubes from him. The detective left the tubes in an evidence refrigerator at the Wethersfield Police Department overnight and transported them the following day to the crime lab, making sure that there had been no tampering in terms of broken seals or leakage.

DeRoehn tried to talk to Bill during that time, but Bill continued to maintain his right to remain silent. Indigent but not yet formally declared so by the court, Bill could not afford an attorney and would have to wait until an arrest was made in the murder of Nilsa Arizmendi before he was assigned a public defender, free of charge. Even so, he did make a point of telling DeRoehn, "I don't even know the girl you showed me a picture of."

On June 2, 2004, Bill allegedly told another inmate that authorities could not get a murder conviction without a body. At his subsequent trial in January 2007, it was determined that the statement could not be presented as evidence to the jury, but could be used to impeach him in the event that he chose to take the stand.

Although the investigation may not have been moving at a breakneck pace, it had picked up speed. Connecticut's D.O.C. was recording telephone calls between Bill and Dori. During the calls, Bill frequently reminded Dori that their conversations were being recorded. During a phone call dated July 5, 2004, Dori dropped her guard. The two were arguing and Dori said, "You got in back of the v... drive that van." She abruptly stopped in mid-sentence.

Bill said nothing. When law enforcement later asked Dori Holcomb about that comment, she stated that she was referring to the fact that Bill always got in trouble when driving without a license. The man just needed to stop getting behind the wheel.

On July 14, 2004, DeRoehn met with Ace Sanchez who identified the man he knew to be "Devin" Howell from a photo identification lineup. A few weeks later, three samples were submitted to Mitotyping Technologies in State College, Pa., for analysis. They were: a section of the seat seized from Bill's van, blood sample cards from Valeria Arizmendi and blood sample cards from Bill.

Any forensic examiner will tell you that when it comes to convicting a murderer, it is less about finding the body and more about finding the blood. As fate would have it, there was plenty of blood to be found in Bill's van.

17.

All things considered, everything was going well for Bill in the spring of 2016. Yes, he was depressed and bored, as always, and frequently wrote me long letters in the wee hours of the morning, but he also had a few pleasant distractions. One day, he went outside to the rec area when one of the nearby bars had a live band playing outside. The wind was blowing in just the right direction, so it sounded as if the musicians were set up in the prison parking lot. *"And the guys (in general population, next door) were nice enough not to play basket-ball. So I laid a towel down and took my shirt off and put it over my eyes and just laid out listening to the band and doing my best to pretend I was at a beach. They played a lot of southern rock hits. Lynyrd Skynyrd, Molly Hatchet, Allman Bros, etc. For being in prison, it couldn't have gotten much nicer. It did however make me crave an ice-cold Budweiser (or maybe about 6 of them)."*

A frog would sometimes visit the P.C. inmates. They first saw him sitting on a window ledge and were all impressed that he could climb the four feet of brick wall to get to that spot. Bill picked him up and was *"freaked out a little bit"* because he was expecting toad feet, but the creature had *"sticky feet"* like a tree frog. Freddie the Frog was about the size of a medium-sized toad and colored similarly, but more gray than brown and would blend in perfectly on a big gray rock in the woods.

A mouse also frequented the outdoor rec area. Bill took great interest in the rodent's lineage and even hoped that he could make it his personal pet, as the wrongly accused prisoner did with Mr. Jingles in "The Green Mile." Was it a mole rat, he wondered? *"This critter was too big and had* too short of a tail to be a mouse. He was too small and had too short a tail to be a rat." Since he had eyes and came out in the day to eat bread, Bill figured it wasn't a mole.

"He doesn't really look like a grasshopper mouse and he eats bread and apple cores so he's not solely a carnivore. He's about the size of a small hamster and his tail is about 2 inches long (much longer than a hamsters). His fur is brown (dark) about the color of rust. And his ears are small and don't really stick out like they do in the picture of the grasshopper mouse (that I sent him in a previous letter.) But he's really cute and has become quite used to us.

"The pile of wooden privacy fence sections he lives under is about 6 or 7 feet from the perimeter of our outside rec fence. When I feed the birds I throw the bread on top of this pile and around the perimeter of it. Often, Marvin the Mouse will come out and eat a little bread, and then carry a piece back under the fence with him. I threw out an apple core the other day and within 2 or 3 minutes he came out and was munching on it. He sat there for a good 5 or 10 minutes, while there were 4 or 5 of us just sitting (standing) there watching him.

"I am very curious to know what kind of mouse he is. He is unlike any mouse I've ever seen. His head is more rounded like a hamster than pointed like a mouse. I read in the stuff you sent about a 'vole.' I've never seen a vole. Can you send me a pic of one and also of a 'deer mouse' and a 'house mouse.' I've had the little white mice, gerbals, and hamsters as pets and he looks like none of these. And he's too big with too short of a tail to be a typical field mouse."

After a few weeks, the mouse stopped showing up for visits. Bill sadly realized that it had probably died of dehydration since visiting the prisoners resulted in spending too much time away from a water source. When Marvin first went missing, Bill thought to put out a container of water, but by then it was too late.

"I miss the little guy," he wrote.

The same man who grieved the loss of a pet mouse was simultaneously capable of intense hatred toward human beings. In one visit, he shared with me the grudge he held toward his deceased sister-in-law, Debbie. She was married to his brother Randy, *"the nicest guy in the family."* According to Bill, Debbie was mean to the bone. When Bill was in the seventh grade, he went to stay with Randy and Debbie for a while. He was a chubby kid and she would tell him to go on a diet. When she gave her children snacks, she would make Bill drink water instead. Years later, when Bill's father died, the four brothers all got an equal interest in the family home and had to fix it up and sell it within a year. Bill and Mandy had broken up at the time, so Bill, with nowhere else to go, would sleep on the floor at his father's empty house until the final sale took place.

Debbie came to the window one day, saw Bill sleeping and called the cops. Bill was left to explain to the police that he was not a squatter. He had a quarter-interest in the house and had every right to be there. It reminded him of the time Debbie showed up in court when he was being held on a traffic violation. Debbie went over to the prosecutors and urged them to lock Bill up. Bill's lawyer returned to the defense table and asked, "Who is that Debbie woman?" Bill explained that it was his meddling sister-in-law who had it out for him. "Well, she's telling the prosecutor that you are no good and that you deserve to go to jail." Bill glared at Debbie standing across the courtroom. God, he hated her.

But hate is too mild a word to describe what he felt for Debbie after she *"snuck over"* to the family house when Bill was out one day, unchained Bill's dog from the tree in the back yard and took him to the pound to die. Bill had adopted Poco from a family that was moving. Poco was part Collie/part German shepherd. Bill describes him as a beautiful dog with a pelt of glorious black fur. Poco went everywhere with Bill. When he returned home from work to discover Poco off of his chain, Bill went to the S.P.C.A. to see if the dog had escaped and been found. The worker informed him that Debbie brought in Poco, who she claimed was a stray that she had found and the S.P.C.A. put him to sleep. Bill was devastated. "Aren't you supposed to wait 30 days before doing that?" he demanded.

No answer was provided.

He felt powerless.

His brother Randy subsequently suffered from complications in relation to uncontrolled diabetes. He was on dialysis for kidney problems and one of his legs had been amputated because of extreme neuropathy. Shortly after the second leg was amputated, Randy died. "What happened to Debbie?" I asked during a prison visit.

"She's dead too," Bill said.

"How did she die?"

He sneered. "Misery!"

I laughed.

He didn't.

Honestly, I could not judge him for despising Debbie. If anyone laid a hand on one of my dogs, there would be hell to pay. But Bill's loathing for Debbie goes beyond the dog incident. What bugs him the most about Debbie is that she was right about him. He wrote to me, "*She told me when I was 15 shortly before or after my mom died that, 'You were born a fuck-up and will always be a fuck-up.' And all I've ever done is prove her right.*"

Bill also has a history of hating snitches such as Tommy Rodrigues and Jonathan Mills. Mills served time in prison with Bill at Cheshire C.I. around 2005 through 2007 and was housed with Bill again at Corrigan C.I. in 2014. It eats away at Bill that his former cellmate received the $150,000 in reward money, in whole or in part, offered by the New Britain Serial Murder Task Force, formed in 2014, to any individual who could assist in finding the person who left seven bodies behind the strip mall. Granted, Mills cannot keep that money for himself—Bill claims that the snitch will likely give it to his mother to pay off her house. But the fact that Mills has any claim to it greatly bothers him—especially since he states that so much of what Mills shared with authorities was nothing but a lie.

I can see why Mills getting that reward makes him mad. After all, the crimes committed by Mills are just as deplorable as those committed by Bill. On Oct. 10, 2000, Mills strangled his neighbor—the single mother of a 2-year old girl—and dumped her remains in a wooded section of the fairgrounds in Guilford, Conn. Two months later, armed with two knives, he broke into his aunt's house in search of money for drugs. Katherine Kleinkauf was asleep in bed with her two children, ages 6 and 4. When Kleinkauf awoke and confronted Mills, he stabbed her 45 times. The children awoke during the struggle and he stabbed both of them six times.

Mills then made off with the dead woman's ATM card and got high on heroin and crack. Later that morning, 10-year-old Alyssa Kleinkauf returned from a sleepover at a friend's house to discover the lifeless bodies of her mother and younger siblings. Years later, she would stare down Mills in a courtroom, stating that she still cried herself to sleep at night and woke up in the morning hoping it was all just a nightmare. Mills was convicted of those crimes in 2005, at the age of age 32. The four murder convictions brought with them the possibility of execution, but jurors voted against it after hearing about Mills' physically and mentally abusive childhood at the hands of an alcoholic father who gave his son alcohol and taught the boy to steal.

Criminal informants like Mills are part of a pervasive underground legal system that is practically invisible to the public. Without the assistance of inmates serving time for deeds that are often equally horrendous to the ones that authorities are investigating, unsolved cases would remain just that—unsolved—and victims and their families would be left in the dark. The practice is by no means perfect, however. Snitches are known to lie. Even when they speak the truth, guilty men and women receive special perks from the prosecution—promises to forgo arrest or punishment, or lesser sentences, for example.[25] In the case of Jonathan Mills, a quadruple murderer made off with a large stash of money that could have easily been applied to the cost of his lifetime incarceration—a hefty bill that far exceeds the cost of an Ivy League education. Think about that the next time your pay your taxes.

18.

July 2004–May 2005

Having duly served his sentence on the active probation violations, Bill was released from prison on July 22, 2004. The results of the blood test had yet to be issued and authorities could only hope that Bill would not flee before they had all of the evidence required to make a solid arrest.

It must have greatly troubled DeRoehn, knowing that the man he believed was a killer had been released indefinitely and was free to murder again.

On Aug. 20, 2004, a forensic examiner issued her findings. Bill and his maternal relatives were excluded as contributors to the biological material on the seat fabric. Valeria Arizmendi and her maternal relatives, including Nilsa Arizmendi, were *not* excluded as contributors. Further, 99.63 percent of the population in the forensic database was excluded as having the same mitochondrial profile as developed from the bloodstained seat sample.

It was not looking good for Bill. On Sept. 21, 2004, a DNA analysis of the two cuttings from the bloodstained car seat back confirmed that Valeria Arizmendi was the mother of the source of the DNA profile. The expected frequency of individuals who could be the mother of the source of the DNA profiling was 1 in 7,400 in the Hispanic population.

A second search of the van was performed in January 2005. Police pulled up some stained carpeting soaked through to the underside portion and observed large, reddish stains in the plywood underneath the carpet. Also seized were debris and hair/root consistent with being forcibly removed. Notably, the blood sample taken from the flooring did not carry the DNA of Arizmendi or Bill. It belonged to someone else—another possible victim.

The chief medical examiner examined the van a few months later, but could not determine if the blood was pre-mortem or post-mortem, nor could he render an opinion on the extent of the injury suffered. Bill had purchased the van from a former girlfriend's parents. The previous owners of the van were contacted—along with other family members who had operated the van—and they reported that, to their knowledge, no one had ever bled to excess in any part of the van.

In November 2004, Dorothy Holcomb was called to the station for questioning. She confirmed that Bill was the exclusive driver of her van and he was in possession of both sets of keys. Detectives also interviewed a 61-year-old man, Michael Stein, who claimed to be a good friend to both Bill and Holcomb. He reported that Bill said the photograph of Nilsa did not look like one of the two people that he had picked up on the Berlin Turnpike and he denied knowing the name "Nilsa," admitting that it was an unusual name to forget. Bill also told his older friend that he discarded the bottom portion of the seat cushion in the garbage "a long time ago" because he spilled oil and gas on it from his grass-cutting business equipment.

By early May 2005, with DNA evidence in hand, Connecticut law enforcement was exceedingly close to arresting Bill for the murder of Nilsa Arizmendi, despite not having found the victim's body. There was just one thing left to do: get a written statement from Bill's friend, Ashley Martin.

Martin must have been stunned when about 10 police officers in uniform approached his home in Hampton, Va., on May 13, 2005. Included in the group were Inspector Hankard from Connecticut and local officers from Hampton. Martin invited them inside and talked to them for about two hours. He was informed that surveillance had previously been conducted on the home and officers saw him clean out the van with Bill. This, of course, was a fabrication by the police. Martin bought it.

Martin agreed to go to the local police station for further questioning. After almost six hours at the station, police finally got what they needed. Bill's close friend since age 11 signed a written statement indicating that he assisted Bill with cleaning the van during Bill's Thanksgiving visit and he observed an intact blue seat bench with matching cushions at that time. He described the cushions as being stained and stated that Bill rolled them up into a garbage bag and discarded it on the curb for pickup. He wrote that the van had a bad odor.[26]

As Chef Emeril Lagasse would say: "Bam!" Bill was promptly arrested and charged with murder. He presented in New Britain Superior Court on May 17, 2005, at which time he was assigned a public defender. Bail was ordered at $2.5 million. The case was continued to June 24, 2005, and Bill was sent to Cheshire Correctional Institute (C.I.) to bide his time.

For Bill, castigation was looming on the horizon. For law enforcement officials and members of the prosecution, a joyless legal victory was about to commence.

*

Bill later told me about the circumstances leading up to his arrest for the murder of Nilsa Arizmendi in May 2005. He notes that it occurred on Friday the 13th, what he called "Bad Luck Friday," the day his "Luck Ran Out."

He was living with his friend Harry in North Carolina and worked doing home remodeling and construction. He left the job at 2:30 p.m. that day and made the two-hour drive to Hampton to spend the weekend with Martin. There was no point in sticking around North Carolina, he explained to me, because Harry's home was out in the boondocks where there was no excitement to be had—or women to pick up. Not that he always struck gold at the country bars in Hampton. Sometimes he got lucky, other times he didn't, but he *"enjoyed the chase just the same."*

Bill associated Martin's home with good times. Martin had converted the detached, two-car garage into "a man cave of sorts. There was some furniture, a refrigerator to keep the beer cold, a dart board, pool table, and poker table as well as a T.V. and video console. The garage was designated for the adults, while the house, with no smoking, drinking, or bad language, was designated for the *'kids'* and could be monitored by the adults via *'baby monitor.'*"

Shortly after 4:30 p.m., he had *"just taken a 'Bong-Hit' and cracked open (his) first cold Budweiser and was in the process of racking the balls for a game of pool. Ashley glanced out the garage window and saw 2 men in suits approaching and commented, 'Who the hell are these guys?'"* Bill looked out the window *"and immediately recognized Detective Rob DeRoehn."*

He wrote: *"While Ashley exited the garage to confront the 2 men in suits, I headed out the back door. Once out of view of the detectives, I jumped the back fence and crossed through the back yard of a couple of neighbors. I then crossed the street a few houses down and cut through another yard into an alley way. Had I kept running, I might have gotten away that day. But I took to hiding in a hedge-row of a nearby neighbor.*

"It was not my 'Lucky' day. Shortly after taking to ground in the cover of the hedge-row, the home-owner exited the home and began to mow the lawn. Fearing discovery by the homeowner, I waited for his back to turn and exited the hedge-row and proceeded down the alley. My brief attempt at hiding had given police enough time to set up an immediate peremiter and I was spotted exiting the alley. After a brief foot chase, I was caught and arrested as a Fugitive of

Justice in the Murder of Nilsa Arizmendi. The cops, at the time, had no idea they had just arrested CT's most prolific serial killer. And by coincidence, on the same day former serial killer Michael Ross was Executed in Connectictut's death Chamber."

Bill later found out that the detectives had spent the morning hours of that day visiting people who knew him, including his Aunt Ann and his sister-in-law, Debbie, who told authorities that they had not recently seen or heard from Bill and had no information on his whereabouts. They knew to visit Martin's house for obvious reasons. Bill had been paroled to Martin's residence in October 1999 after serving time for traffic violations and spent Thanksgiving there in 2003. He wonders now if he had not gone to Martin's house on May 13, 2005, would they have located him so quickly? Maybe not, but Det. DeRoehn, with evidence in hand, was clearly on a mission to take Bill down.

By the spring of 2005, Bill did not stand a chance.

19.

In the early summer of 2016, Bill was growing frustrated with some of his fellow inmates at the Protective Custody Unit at Walker:

"The neighbor I used to cook with has now decided to go on a diet. So not only do I not have the sponsorship for the meats we used to cook, but now he's eating the trays that he used to give me that he didn't eat when we cooked. His cellie would also give me a lot of the trays that he didn't like. But now with this new diet my neighbor is on, he now gets the trays his cellie used to give me.

"So not only is he not cooking with me anymore, he's keeping the trays he used to give me when we cooked. And he's taking his cellies unwanted trays which I used to get also.

"And all this happens when I run out of money and need the trays the most. I told my neighbor yesterday 'It's f'd up, you go on a diet and I have to lose weight.' I said it to him jokingly but I was serious.(27)

"The guy has plenty of money and knows I'm broke as beans so I don't really understand why he's collecting and eating trays that 3 weeks ago he wouldn't touch. Anyway, it is what it is I guess. And I'm sorry to write and vent like this. It's just tough in here not really having anyone to talk to or vent to."

By the end of August, Bill was told that he would have recreation time alone, without the other prisoners. His lawyers had phoned the D.O.C. and asked for a separation order between Bill and another inmate, Rico, who was being questioned by law enforcement regarding statements that Bill allegedly made to him at Walker C.I. concerning the crimes. Having the time alone was *"both good and bad."* He was *"missing out on conversation and the unwanted extra trays, but on the good side,"* he *"had the rec yard"* to himself. *"A 20 x 20 foot rec yard can get crowded pretty fast when you have a couple guys walking laps and a couple others trying to play basket ball, all in a little 20 x 20 'dog cage.'"*

Despite the meditative calm of the rec yard, tension was mounting on all sides. The 2016 presidential election filled the airwaves with an unprecedented degree of conflict and melodrama. Like most Americans, Bill was surprised that Trump became the Republican nominee. He wanted a Kasich vs. Bernie stand off, in which case he would have voted for Kasich—if he were allowed to vote. The Olympic games were also in full swing and that made for some good television.

"Well, gotta go. Womens beach volleyball just came on ☺ GO U.S.A!!! (And then...) Just my luck. 10 minutes into the volleyball game and storm rolls in and we loose satellite signal on the T.V. ☺"

Nevertheless, no amount of interesting TV (which Bill referred to as *"the Idiot Box"*) could mask the fact that his depression was again spiraling downward to suicidal levels. Reading Mandy's harsh words about him in police interviews provided to him by his attorneys did not help his state of mind, and despite an increase in his insulin dosage, his blood sugar readings were high. *"I can't seem to be able to get under 200 and am often in the 300s."* His lawyers were stalling on delivering him the stacks of discovery that they had in their possession and he felt out of the loop concerning the legal case against him.

He knew that a transfer was in the works. Either Rico would have to go to another facility or Bill would have to leave Walker C.I. It seemed likely that Rico would be the one to go, since there were only two other P.C. units in Connecticut—Cheshire C.I. and Bridgeport C.C.—and Bill could not go to Cheshire C.I. because his nemesis, Jonathan Mills, resided in that P.C. unit. He desperately hoped that he would not be sent to Bridgeport C.C. He had been there and knew that Walker C.I. was a walk in the park, in comparison.

Brooding over ending it all, on Aug. 16, 2016, Bill wrote a short will and mailed me the original.

To: Whom it may concern.

I William Devin Howell #305917 request that in the event of my death that all of my personal belongings and property be released to Anne K Howard.

The purpose of his leaving his belongings to me was so that I would have three large boxes of legal discovery in his possession to assist me in writing this book. He subsequently gave me all of that material, including hundreds of pages of crime scene photos. Two staff members at Walker C.I. witnessed his signing of the testament. He also signed a living will requesting that I make the final decision on matters regarding artificial life support. Not surprisingly, he did not want to be resuscitated.

The defense lawyers' efforts to keep Bill separate from the problematic inmate backfired and in early September, he was transferred to Bridgeport C.C. Rico got to stay at Walker C.I.

*

The white prison transportation van raced north on Route 8 with Bill caged within a smaller cage in the vehicle's interior—not unlike his purported victims. He could look out the small back window as the van tore past cars and trucks along the highway. At one point, he turned and saw the speedometer up front reading 95 mph. A state police car led the van and two others followed, with lights flashing and sirens blaring. It felt like a presidential motorcade, he later told me. I was reminded of King Kong being shipped via oil tanker from Skull Island to New York City.

Connecticut was in the midst of a heat wave. Temperatures reached the 90s during the day and hovered in the high 70s at night. With no central air conditioning, the P.C. unit at Bridgeport C.C. was little more than a sweltering hot cinderblock housing 15 very smelly men. The cells did not have electrical outlets, so portable fans were not an option—although a small ventilation duct blew a current of warm air across the bunk in Bill's cell and he would frequently readjust his position to get the maximum value of that mild gust.

The food was the same at Bridgeport C.I., since all prison food in Connecticut came from the same distributor, but he had no hot pot to spice things up. The absence of power outlets in individual cells also meant no television and no radio. There was a TV in the recreation room, but with 14 other inmates playing cards and shouting back and forth, it was impossible to hear the shows. Besides, Bill wrote, "*that TV always played sports and I have no interest in sports.*" ("With the exception of women's volleyball," I thought, "and that preference was for obvious reasons.")

His dimly lit cell contained a writing desk, but no chair. When he wrote letters to me, he did so by placing his flip-flops on the cement floor before the desk and kneeling on them so as not to hurt his knees. He complained that the 60-watt light bulb mounted to the ceiling above the sink, along with a desk with no additional light and no chair, posed a threat to his legal case:

"With about 3,000 pages of evidence I have that needs to be read, organized, and analyzed, I feel these conditions are not suitable for trying to defend what is probably one of the highest profile cases in the state."

The only perk was that the prisoners were given ice at lunch and dinner. Ice did not exist at Walker C.I. and he used to crave it. Now he had it, but he "*sure didn't want it like this. I guess it goes to the old adage 'Careful for what we wish for.'*"

He was initially placed on suicide watch at Bridgeport C.C. He was released after a short period of time, even though his mental status did not improve: "*I told them and still tell them that 'I had rather go out in a body bag than be stuck at this facility.' I guess they don't care or think I'm playing games but either way they sent me back to the housing unit.*"

In all of his years as a prisoner, Bill had never been "*four-pointed*" until he went to Bridgeport. Not that he had always been a model prisoner. His D.O.C records indicate that he received six disciplinary reports for numerous violations since 2007. He admits to being in "*two or three*" fights with inmates, and other violations for the possession of contraband, a pornography collection and a sewing needle and cassette tapes that his former defense attorney, Ken Simon, had given him. Notwithstanding those incidents, being four-pointed marked a new low in his life as a prisoner.

Bill explained to me that "four points" is a procedure used by the guards to control unruly inmates. They cuff each of the prisoner's limbs to the corner of a freestanding fiberglass bunk mounted to the center of the floor (thus the expression, four points) and leave the man in that horizontal position for about two hours. "*It usually takes about eight men to get down on one prisoner and carry out the process,*" Bill explained. The prisoner is then "*shot up in the buttocks with Benadryl and Advil, and something else.*"

What brought about Bill's four point at Bridgeport in September of 2016 involved a conflict with a female staff member. He was in a cell that had a little window opening that allowed him to see the television that was on in the main area about 20 feet from his cell. He could not hear it, but just being able to stare at the television all day provided a decent distraction. Bill asked a male guard to change the channel because he did not like what was on the TV that day. The guard obliged and changed the channel, but then the woman at the front desk protested because she was watching the show that was changed. In retaliation, she turned off the TV.

Bill was outraged.

When the woman's shift ended, she told the worker taking over the desk not to turn on the TV. When she returned the next morning, Bill said to her, "If you are going to punish me like that when you are not even on your shift, I am going to get back at you and kick this door." He proceeded to pound his foot against the steel door for two hours.

The guards eventually transferred Bill to a cell down the hallway with a smaller window and the TV now 40 feet from the window, as opposed to 20 feet. Bill resumed kicking the door of that cell in response to the transfer. That was when he was four-pointed. The next morning, the lieutenant promised Bill that he would be transferred back to the cell that was 20 feet from the television, but the female worker went over the lieutenant's head to higher ups and Bill was denied the transfer.

The positive side of being four-pointed, according to Bill, was that in the first two hours when he was cuffed to the post, he could not sleep, so when they finally did allow him to lie down at 4:30 p.m., he experienced the deepest sleep that he had had in years, still heavily drugged. He did not awaken until the next morning, due to a nightmare. He dreamt that his adult daughter, who he had not seen in almost two decades, had died in a breech birth delivery. Mandy was the one to tell him that their daughter was *no longer with us.*

I wondered if Bill subconsciously associated his daughter with his victims in that dream. I also wondered what he would have done to that female prison worker if he were not trapped in his cell? "It's not like I would have killed her, Anne," he later told me. "But if I saw her on the outside, let's just say I might have slashed her tires when she went inside a store."

20.

May 2005

Thomas Rodrigues Jr. had a checkered past. Also known as Mason Marconi, the 35-year-old Massachusetts native had a lengthy record of felony convictions in his home state and also in Connecticut.

When he first met Bill at Cheshire C.I. on May 28, 2005, Rodrigues was being held on a parole violation. He encountered the mild-mannered Southerner in the recreation room on the lower tier of the prison after breakfast. With time to waste, Rodrigues sat beside Bill and the two struck up a conversation.

"Two and a half million dollars," Bill complained. "Can you believe that?"

"Shit, man ..." Rodrigues said. "That's your bond? What the hell they saying you did?"

Bill gave a "damned if I know" shake of head. Eager to learn more, Rodrigues pressed on, "It must have been some bad shit, cause two and a half million dollars ain't for no parole violation. Come on, man, what'd you do?"

"I didn't *do* anything," Bill said, mildly aggravated. "This detective, DeRoehn, he drove all the way to Virginia to extradite me back to Connecticut. I got charged with murdering some prostitute. She had this pimp, a druggie named Angel, and he says that he last saw her with me in my van."

"That all they got against you? Just what her pimp said?" Bill did not answer.

Sensing Bill's rising irritation, Rodrigues knew to stop asking more questions. While some guys liked to boast about their crimes, this one seemed like the quiet type. He would be a hard nut to crack, but hearing about DeRoehn's involvement gave Rodrigues motivation to try again the next day. "Did they find any of her blood?" he asked Bill after breakfast.

"Maybe. I don't know. The cops have my van. I drove it for two years. There was a lot of shit in that van. I used to keep my stash in the back seat. Fuck, I should have gotten rid of the whole part of the back seat where I kept my stash, because that's where the blood was. I only got rid of part of it. I covered the rest with oil and gasoline. I told the detective that if they found any of her blood, it was because she had a fight with her pimp in the back of my van."

"Huh ..."

"I need to get a speedy trial because they got nothing on me. Nothing. Just some drugged-up pimp saying I was the last one he saw with her. You know what? I hope Ace overdoses before they find the whore's body. That would be perfect. No witness, no trial. I'm clear."

"Yeah," Rodrigues agreed.

Deep in thought and obviously wracked with worry, Bill reflected, "I wish DeRoehn didn't show me that picture of her on the way back to Connecticut. It took me by surprise, you know? I was wondering why they drove all the way to Virginia to pick me up and I was thinking maybe it was about something else, so I asked him why did you come all that way to get me, and he takes out this picture and shows it to me. I couldn't believe it. He saw I was shocked, you know?"

Rodrigues shrugged. "Doesn't sound like a big deal. You're like, who's that? Why you showing me this lady's picture?"

"Yeah. Right. I didn't even know her name. I thought it was Maria. That's what she used to call herself. DeRoehn says in the car, 'Do you know this woman Nilsa?' I'm thinking, 'Who the fuck is Nilsa?' I didn't even know her real name."

The next morning, Rodrigues saw Bill in the recreation room. "Food around here sucks," Bill said.

"Don't it? What the fuck was that shit they gave us for breakfast?"

Bill chuckled. "I call it crap with cake. Oatmeal and farina and some kind of fucking bird seed ..."

"I think it's cream of wheat, huh?"

"Yeah, but mixed with some other nasty shit." He gestured toward the concrete wall of the recreation room where a sheet containing the day's menu was posted. "You see how they describe the food. Chicken Stir Fry my ass. That shit last night was nothing but slop. It literally looks like baby puke over rice."

Rodrigues laughed. "Yeah, man!"

"When they bring the trays into the day room, the place stinks like a fucking morgue. I swear, I did not see one person eat that meal last night."

"The cheeseburgers are all right."

"Yeah, those are good," Bill agreed. "Today, we got turkey tetrazzini. I'm gonna be awake all night with indigestion. Bad enough that I can't sleep anyway."

"Bro, you still upset about that DeRoehn guy?"

Bill looked away. "He just won't let up, you know? But he's got nothing on me, like I said. It's all circumstantial. Fact is, I *did* beat the shit out of that whore in the back of my van. Broke her nose and then threw her out. Far as I know, they won't find her body anytime soon. No body, no conviction."

The two talked in the recreation room three mornings in a row. Some of it was small talk. Turned out, they were exactly the same age except for a few weeks. Bill was born on Feb. 11, 1970, and Rodrigues on March 10, 1970. In the course of their conversations, Rodrigues failed to tell Bill that he also knew DeRoehn. Rodrigues met the detective in the 1990s when he worked as a paid informant for one of DeRoehn's colleagues and earned a total of $795 over a five-year period for divulging information about other criminals. Only the year before, Rodrigues worked as an unpaid confidential informant for DeRoehn. Twice in 2004, Rodrigues set up drug buys in and around Wethersfield and called DeRoehn about the arrangements so DeRoehn could send men in for the bust.

When it came to singing like a canary, Rodrigues was well rehearsed. He previously cooperated with Massachusetts authorities on drug cases and served as a witness in two unrelated murder cases: one in Massachusetts and the other in Middletown, Conn. He knew from experience that memory could fail him when it came to the minute details of what other inmates divulged. Therefore, after he and Bill spoke, Rodrigues returned to his cell and immediately wrote everything down. Altogether, he made three separate entries: on May 28, May 29 and May 30, 2005. The entry dated May 29 was particularly damning. Rodrigues wrote that Bill laughed after telling him that the victim's nose had "bled all over the place" after he beat her. He stated, "I did it, but they can't prove it."

On the morning of May 30, 2005, Rodrigues phoned his girlfriend from prison and told her to phone the Wethersfield Police Department while he was on the line. A dispatcher answered. Rodrigues asked to speak with DeRoehn. He said that the call concerned the defendant named Bill or William Howell. That Rodrigues, one of DeRoehn's former informants, was housed in the same prison at the same time with Bill was pure happenstance. DeRoehn had done nothing to arrange for it. Needless to say, he was probably very happy about the stroke of luck.

"What's Howell saying?" DeRoehn asked.

"All tons of shit man. He admitted to doing that."

"Admitted to doing *what*?"

"He said he beat the shit out of her in the back of the van. Broke her nose and threw her out of the van. Ah, he said he has to hurry up and rush the case because it's all circumstantial right now. He doesn't want them to find a body."

"Did he say anything about the body?"

"No. I'm talking to him, talking to him. We talk every day so, um, I'm sure it's going to lead up to that. He talks a lot about prostitutes, you know, how much he hates them."

"How often do you get phone calls, Tommy?"

"Man, not really too, too much. I get one now and then I'll get another one at 3:00. Listen, man. I wrote all this shit down. Maybe you'll see something I don't understand, you know? I have like about three or four pages."

"Where you keeping that shit?"

"In my cell. That's another thing. I got to get that out of there, ASAP."

"Um hum."

"Because I have a bunkmate that's nosey as shit. I can tell he's going through my shit every time I'm not in the cell, man. I'm worried, you know? There's lot of shit there, man, that this guy Howell has already said in two days. It sparked my interest, when he said your name."

"You didn't tell him you knew me, did you?"

"No man. No way. So what do you want me do next?"

"I'll be in touch," DeRoehn promised.

"But what do you want me to *do*?" Rodrigues asked. "Hang tight to that shit?"

"Yeah. I mean, hey, if he's offering shit you know just— " DeRoehn paused; his mind likely racing with potential scenarios that could ruin the end goal of Bill giving away the location of the victim's body. "Just don't press him for now," he warned. "I'll get back to you."

"All right. Later, bro."

"Bye." DeRoehn hung up the receiver. He must have felt cautiously hopeful. Rodrigues snitching on Bill was a huge break in the case. Nevertheless, he knew from experience that it could all blow up into a million pieces if he did not proceed in a manner that dotted every Constitutional "i" and crossed every Constitutional "t" with respect to the defendant's legal rights.

DeRoehn gave Rodrigues a long lecture at the start of their phone call the next day. "You need to remember the legal consequences of your cooperating with us in this investigation, Tommy. Howell has been formally charged with murder and he has an attorney right now. That means that you became an agent of the state in this investigation when you called me yesterday."

"Yeah, I know."

"Listen, Tommy. This is important. You can't ask Howell any questions on the subject of Nilsa Arizmendi. Got it? You can't agree with Howell if he says anything about it or even nod your head if he speaks about her. You can talk at length about anything else, any other murders or crimes, because Howell hasn't been charged with anything except the Arizmendi murder."

"What do you want me to do about the stuff I wrote down? My bunkmate is gonna find it."

"Send all that to the Wethersfield Police Department and disguise it as legal mail. Just write 'legal mail' on the outside of the envelope. Capt. Carlon at C.C.I. will give you the address. OK?"

"Yeah, man."

Rodrigues mailed the information within an hour of ending the call. He couldn't get rid of it soon enough.[28]

*

Frustrated by the way in which I portrayed his dealings with Rodrigues in the initial book manuscript that I mailed to him, Bill asked that I include his interpretation of the events in a letter dated Feb. 16, 2018:

Howell's arrest in the Arizmendi case had been all over the news. After all, it was big news. It's not everyday a murder arrest is made where there is no body. Not only no body, but no murder weapon, and no eyewitness to the crime.

Rodrigues had been following the story closely. Not just for the previously stated facts, but because the arrest was out of Wethersfield, a town he knew well. Rodrigues was familiar with the lead detective on the case, Rob DeRoehn. Rodrigues had worked personally with Detective DeRoehn on several drug cases where Rodrigues acted as a C.I. (confidential informant) where he was paid by DeRoehn to set up drug buys wherein the subsequent drug dealer would be arrested. Rodrigues and DeRoehn seemed to work well together.

Now with Rodrigues in jail with problems of his own he sees this big time circumstantial murder case out of Wethersfield and makes a wish. On May ? 2005 Rodrigues's wish comes true when he sees murder suspect Howell enter into his housing unit. Rordigues can hardly contain himself and feels he just found his way out of jail. Rodrigues knows how to work the system, and more importantly, how the system works. The role of a jail-house snitch is no stranger to him. He has been a jail house snitch. He had two prior murder cases and he was now in need of another "get out of jail free" card.

Later that night he dreams of "sugar plums dancing through his head" as Christmas has certainly come early i.e. the arrival of Howell in the unit. Howell, however, had no clue that he had just stepped into the serpent's den.

In the days to follow, Rodrigues would try to get close to Howell. Making small talk, asking if he needed anything, and just trying to lend support to Howell's adjustment to a new environment. Even going as far as to telling Howell who he would do good to stay away from (he didn't mention himself.)

His plan was working and Howell was begining to drop his guard a little and seemed to be a little more comfortable speaking with Rodrigues.

Rodrigues was elated. He knew he wouldn't need a confession from Howell, just a couple little facts he could build a story around. A few days in, Rodrigues begins to ask subtle little questions while making small talk. In one exchange Rodrigues asks "From what I can tell from the news, I can't believe they even arressted you. Who is the chick anyway?"

Howell thinking nothing really of it replys "I'm not even sure. She kinda looks like a chick I gave a ride to a few times but thats not her name. I gave her and her boyfriend a ride and they got in a fight in the back of my van and he gave her a bloody nose and the next thing I know is that I have a murder charge."

JACKPOT!!! Howell had just given Rodrigues the fuel for the Bon-fire he had planned. He had the few minor details he needed, the rest he could make up himself. It was now time to call his old friend Detective DeRoehn.

21.

As the saying goes, "Denial isn't just a river in Egypt." Human beings possess a remarkable capacity for closing their minds to the most obvious faults about themselves. We often perceive the alternative of facing the truth, which most observers already see despite our defensive protestations, as just too humiliating, disempowering or a combination of both. And so, we demonstrate over the course of our respective lifetimes a vast array of self-sabotaging character flaws that often go with us to the grave.

In our first year of written correspondence, the cumulative effect of Bill's letters left me with the impression that he was in denial regarding his history of violent behavior toward others—particularly women. I asked him about the assault case involving Dori, which ultimately led to his arrest on an outstanding warrant and extradition back to Connecticut. He wrote back:

"All I can say is that Dori was the aggressor. She punched me in the face with her fist and I slapped her back. I didn't punch her and I didn't slap her hard in trying to hurt her but I did slap her upside her noggin to let her know that she can't just punch me in the face and me not do anything. She knew I couldn't call the cops because I had an outstanding warrant for probation violation for driving on suspension. And I knew that if I did nothing at all that the next time she got mad I was going to get hit again. She called the cops and I left before they got there and they took out a warrant for assault on me based on her statements. It got thrown out and she never hit me again. Nor I her."

His take on the matter is corroborated by a police report dated March 24, 2004, noting that the domestic violence incident, which occurred on Jan. 25, 2003 (notably, one week before Bill's first victim went missing) was "14 months old and there has been no violence since." The report states: "The victim would like the matter closed. The victim wants to drop charges. Says it was her fault, she started it."

Apparently Dori's erratic behavior stemming from her untreated bi-polar disorder had provoked Bill to lose his temper. That said, is there ever a valid reason to "slap" a woman "upside her noggin"? The initial police report said she had a black eye. Bill told me that the police lied. There was no black eye.

In a follow-up letter, Bill described himself as a gentleman in his dealings with women:

"Have you noticed there are no xgirlfriends coming out of the woodwork claiming any abuse or violence towards them?? I dated 3 women in CT alone and no one has ever come forward to say 'He used to abuse me... or I always thought he was strange or weird or could be capable of the things they are saying about me.' I was always a happy person and made others happy that were around me. Hell, I was even invited to my first x's (in Connecticut) wedding, and I attended. And her husband got a little jealous because she got a little too drunk at the reception and spent a lot of time talking to me and another guy friend she invited to the wedding as well. He and I attended her wedding together so neither of us would feel awkward. We all smoked weed and the guy I went to her wedding with was her (and mine when I lived in Torrington) weed dealer."

Did Bill really have harmonious relations with all of his past girlfriends? Perhaps there was no physical abuse in his relationships with two women that he went out with when he first came to Connecticut, but what about his first love, Mandy? According to one of Mandy's acquaintances from Virginia, toward the end of the relationship, she confided that if she didn't leave Bill soon, she feared he would kill her. Mandy said, "Devin is crazy." After Bill's arrests on the current murders, Mandy was interviewed by the police and related details of a relationship that included domestic violence.

Bill strongly disagrees with that portrayal. *"I loved her like I loved no other. It really hurt me when I read her statement she made to the cops about me.*

"I definately regret the way I treated her. Not showing her just how much I loved her and taking her love for me for granted. I'd get drunk and pick fights or start arguments with her when she'd done nothing wrong. There were definately times when I was just an asshole towards her. But at the end of the day, she knew she was the boss and I would do anything she says. I don't know why I was the way I was but I learned from it. After I lost her I never treated anyone like that again.

*"But I wasn't a drunk that constantly beat her like she portrayed me to the cops. I slapped her one time and that's because she kicked me in the nads. And we got in a bad flight in FL and I picked her up by the arms and threw her onto the bed. I threw her on the bed because I knew it wouldn't hurt her. But honest truth, that is the extent of me **ever** putting my hands on her."*

He also described the time when he and Mandy were splitting up and Mandy had turned her affections to another man. In the parking lot of a 7-Eleven, Bill and Mandy's new flame, Seth, got into a vicious fight. Bill grabbed a tire iron from his car and raised it to his rival, but Mandy got in the way and he accidentally ended up hitting her with the iron and causing injury. He felt bad about it, he told me, as the swipe was an accident: *"I was trying to knock the shit out of Seth. I was trying to take his fucking head off."* I responded that it must have hurt poor Mandy, getting hit with that tire iron. *"Yeah,"* he replied, *"but it only left her with a little bruise on her leg. That's all she got from it."*

"When I watched a police video of Mandy being interviewed," he once told me. "She looked so sad." The transformation in Mandy's demeanor, from that of a shy and sweet-spirited adolescent, to a melancholy, albeit attractive, middle-aged woman, genuinely baffled him. The fact that the father of her children was now accused of being a serial killer did not strike him as a factor contributing to her apparent personality change.

In 2013, Bill completed an "Alternatives to Violence" program in prison consisting of 24 sessions intended to teach inmates how to cope with violence in their lives. That a government-sponsored program could come close to addressing the depth of Bill's anger is an absurd proposition. Nonetheless, the prison system made the effort to restore the inmate's humanity under the false assumption that just one person suffered at the hands of his savage rage—not seven.

In his defense, Bill's point is well taken when he states that his fights with Mandy and Dori did not demonstrate a violence that was directly linked to the crimes that he was alleged to have committed. There are a lot of men with similar histories involving pushing and shoving and a few punches thrown at their significant others. It is deviant behavior, to be sure, but it does not carry the gravity of killing seven people. Drawing the conclusion that Bill hated all women, including the ones who he was romantically involved with, would be wrong. There is something far more sinister that provoked him to do what he did to those seven people in the back of his van. Eighteen months into our correspondence, I was still baffled by what his motive in killing seven people could have been.

22.

August–September 2006

The wheels of justice move slowly, sometimes so slowly that a defendant unwittingly gets caught in the mechanism and ground finely to bits before a trial even takes place. And it is usually a loose tongue that gets him to that precarious place.

More than a year following his arrest for the murder of Nilsa Arizmendi, Bill's trial was pending, but a date had not been set. He attended a murder-related court appearance in New Britain Superior Court on Aug. 10, 2006. Afterward, he was held in a cell at the Walker Reception area in Suffield to await transportation back to his current place of residence, Cheshire C.I.

In the "Bullpen" at Walker, Bill met another inmate. He asked Jerry Mortimer where he was going. "Bridgeport," Mortimer answered.

"Bridgeport? Do you know a guy named Tom Rodrigues?"

Mortimer nodded. "He's on my tier."

"The guy's a fucking snitch. Do you know that?"

"No," Mortimer honestly replied.

"God, yeah! He's snitched for the Wethersfield and Harford police a lot of times."

"How do you know?"

Bill cast an icy gaze at Mortimer. "'Cause he snitched about my murder case. He's telling lies about me." He walked across the cell to a thick folder of papers, brought it over to Mortimer and sat down. "See this?" he spread the top few pages over the bench. "It's his police record."

Mortimer glanced down. The papers included a black-and-white photocopied photograph with the name "Tom Rodrigues" written underneath along with the inmate's date of birth. Mortimer saw that they were talking about the same Tom Rodrigues. "You probably shouldn't have all this stuff. Where'd you get it?"[29]

"My attorney gave it to me. Now, look, if you're going back to Bridgeport to see Rodrigues, I want you to send him a message. Tell him I got all his personal information from these reports. I know his addresses, all the places where his mother and family live. I'm going to kill all of them, especially his mother."

Like a raven from "Game of Thrones," Mortimer returned to Bridgeport C.C. and relayed Bill's ominous tidings to Rodrigues. In turn, Rodrigues notified D.O.C. staff, who contacted the police and state attorney's office regarding Bill's threat.

Back at Cheshire C.I., Bill allegedly told his cellmate, Jonathan Mills, that when he was at the Bullpen at Walker, he ran into Mortimer and informed him to "tell Tommy that he is a snitch and I am going to kill him."[30]

In response, Mills told Bill that his threatening Rodrigues through Mortimer was "pretty stupid." In January 2007, when state police asked Mills for a written statement about what Bill told him, Mills refused. A convicted quadruple murderer, Mills just wanted to serve out his life sentence and put the memory of sharing a cell with Bill behind him.

Approximately one month following Bill's discussion with Mortimer, on Sept. 15, 2006, members of law enforcement entered Bill's cell pursuant to a search and seizure warrant. In particular, they were interested in finding evidence pertaining to Bill's threat against Rodrigues and his family. They got what they were looking for in the form of photographs of Rodrigues, a criminal history and record checks containing not only his personal information, but also the names, addresses and telephone numbers belonging to his family members.

It seemed Bill was a man with a plan. He had also written the name "Jerry Mortimer," along with Mortimer's inmate number, on at least two of the documents. His attorney, Ken Simon, printed the material at his client's request and provided it to him during a legal visit. Nonetheless, a judge subsequently determined that it was not the product of attorney/client privilege. The prosecution could view it prior to trial.

A court order was later issued for Tommy Rodrigues to remain on site for the entire five days set aside for the Arizmendi murder trial. In preliminary proceedings, Judge Michael Sheldon ruled that the portion of information provided by Rodrigues to DeRoehn once he became a state witness (i.e., the moment when he phoned DeRoehn from prison) could not be allowed into the record. However, statements given by Bill to Rodrigues in the days prior to Rodrigues phoning DeRoehn could come into the record. It would be key evidence for the prosecution, regardless of the fact that Rodrigues was a career criminal on top of being a reputed snitch.

Ultimately, Rodrigues would not be called upon to testify. By day four of Bill's trial, anything Rodrigues had to offer would be an unnecessary nail in the defendant's coffin.

*

Early on, I asked Bill how he felt about what went down between DeRoehn, Rodrigues and Mortimer. Here's what he had to say:

In your recent letter, you asked my opinion of Det Rob DeRoehn. I will say this, once he gets his teeth into something he won't let go. He is a very tenacious detective who will do whatever he needs to make his case. I know that in my case he lied about various things including my reactions to his questions (on the drive back to Connecticut). But that was him doing what he needs to close a case. He lied to Dori about many things in an attempt to turn her against me in hopes that she would say any little thing that he could use against me.

What I learned in my case is that the cops, and prosecutor as well, don't play fair. All they care about is a conviction and have tunnel vision in regard to anything else.

As far as jail house snitches go, they are all scumbags and all have vested interests in their testimonies. In regard to the Arizmendi case, I never confessed anything to anyone. I told Tommy Rodrigues that I had given Arizmendi and her boyfriend a ride a few times and that they had gotten into a fight in the van and her boyfriend had given her a bloody nose and that's how her blood got in my van. He took that and turned it around into all this other shit he claims I said... which was all bullshit.

Then Brian Perleski (the prosecutor) stands in court announcing how he has made no promises or deals with Rodrigues for his testimony. But yet, afterwards Perleski had Rorigues's case transferred from another jurisdiction, to New Britain where Perleski got him released on Special Parole.

Rodrigues was facing up to 20 yrs and for making up lies on me he got to walk. But yet the prosecutor stands in court and claims 'I've made no promises or deals with Rodriguez for his testimony.' What a joke!!!

All these jail house snitches know that they can say whatever lies they want and the prosecutor will use it and give them a deal in the process wether it be a better deal at their own trial, or a recomendation in a sentence reduction or even for favored placement, housing, jobs within the prison itself and last but not least, reward money. Jail house snitches will be crawling out of the wood work against me in the case I'm facing. Every scumbag crackhead I've come *in contact with in the last 10 years is going to be claiming I confessed to them. The shit has already started. There are already 5 C.I.s claiming I said this or that. And how do you prove you didn't say something?? They can say whatever lies they want and the prosecutor will use it and the press will print it as though it is truth.*

As a loosely associated issue, what lawyers would call an ancillary matter, I asked Bill about his musical tastes during a prison phone call:

Me: One more very important question, Bill.

Bill: (long pause) Yeah?

Me: You can only choose one. Led Zeppelin or Pink Floyd?

Bill: Huh. That's hard. (Pause) I guess it depends on the mood you're in, you know? Zeppelin for a party. Floyd when you're mellow. Good question.

Me: Aerosmith or Lynyrd Skynyrd?

Bill: Aerosmith.

Me: Really? That's surprising, you being from the South and all. Okay. One more. Beatles or Stones?

Bill: Stones. Definitely.

Makes sense. The Stones do sing about snitches, after all.

23.

Jan. 24–25, 2007

The trial for the murder of Nilsa Arizmendi began on Jan. 24, 2007, at the Superior Court in New Britain with Judge Michael Sheldon presiding. Wearing a blue-and-white striped Oxford shirt, Bill sat nervously at the defense table beside public defender Ken Simon. Sitting at the prosecution's table was attorney Brian Preleski.

Eight witnesses were called upon to testify over the course of five days. Angel "Ace" Sanchez took the stand on day one. Predictably, the first objection to a portion of Sanchez's testimony came from the defense early on. Simon did not want the jury to learn that Bill allegedly got high with Arizmendi and Sanchez during their first meeting. Judge Sheldon overruled the objection and let the information in for probative value.

Presented with a photo of the back interior of Bill's blue van, Sanchez responded that it was the same van interior that he observed in 2003, except the photograph, taken during processing in May 2005, depicted a back couch with bottom cushions of a different fabric and color. According to Sanchez, three weeks prior to Arizmendi's disappearance, that couch had *matching* seat cushions. Simon challenged the observation, pointing out on cross that there was a lot of equipment in the back of the van, including a lawn mower and a weedwacker. Sanchez maintained that he was still able to eye the bench with matching cushions from his position in the passenger seat.

Sanchez described an easygoing arrangement between himself, Arizmendi and Bill. When the couple needed a ride, Bill was of service in exchange for some gas money. If they wanted to cop drugs, Bill took them to their destination, no questions asked. He admitted that all of the interactions with Bill were "pleasant."

The prosecution objected to the scope of impeachment, (legalese for the breadth of questioning allowed on cross-examination.) How far back could Simon go in delving into Sanchez's unsavory criminal background? The court ruled that a 1984 conviction in Hartford was outside of scope, but three separate convictions ranging from 1997–2003 could be referenced before the jury.

After lunch, Valeria Arizmendi, assisted by a Spanish interpreter, took the stand. Seeing the victim's mother close-up, the jury was finally given a glimpse into the full tragedy of Nilsa's disappearance. Valeria described a warm and loving adult daughter who, trapped in a deadly addiction, still visited the family on Christmas, Easter and Thanksgiving. Valeria also made her daughter a special meal for her birthday every year. That Nilsa abruptly stopped appearing at holiday family gatherings was not only unusual, it was alarming. The youngest of Nilsa's four children, Miguel, was 10 years old at the time of the trial. The mother who had taken him to the park and phoned on a regular basis had not attempted to contact him, or anyone else in the family, for almost four years. Valeria had not moved during that time or changed her phone number. Nilsa knew where to find her.

Every criminal attorney knows that the best defense involves pointing a finger at other possible suspects in an effort to plant seeds of reasonable doubt in the minds of the jury members. On cross, Simon asked Valeria if she suspected Sanchez of having anything to do with Nilsa's disappearance. When DeRoehn first visited Valeria, didn't Valeria say that Sanchez had recently altered his appearance? Whether the Arizmendi family entertained doubts about Ace's involvement in the early days, Valeria didn't take the bait. She replied that she told DeRoehn that she had heard from others that Sanchez had cut his long hair short, but that she in no way suggested to DeRoehn that this was a purposeful attempt by Ace to hide his identity.

Det. DeRoehn testified for the prosecution on the second day of the trial. It was ruled that Bill's look of shock when DeRoehn showed him the photograph of Arizmendi as they drove back from North Carolina could not be entered as evidence. At the time, Bill had invoked his right to remain silent and the exchange between the detective and suspect was therefore classified as custodial interrogation. Moreover, any statements that Bill may have made during that long drive were also suppressed as evidence under the Miranda law. On the other hand, if Bill chose to take the stand during the trial, any statements could be used to impeach him.

Judge Sheldon also determined that the blood that DeRoehn had taken from Bill was inadmissible because Bill had not been charged with the crime at the time; also, he did not have legal representation.

When cross-examining law enforcement, the defense often employs a type of Keystone Kops strategy by questioning the competence of the investigation itself, attempting to make the detectives look like blundering idiots. Simon addressed each and every one of DeRoehn's errors: from depicting Arizmendi in the missing posters as being much heavier and last being seen on the Berlin Turnpike (not New Britain Avenue, as her sister Lauren reported to the police), to playing God and checking off the box on the D.S.S. form wrongly indicating that the purpose of the inquiry was because Holcomb was fleeing to avoid prosecution.

DeRoehn shrewdly conceded his most obvious errors. Though the poster created by his office said Arizmendi was 140 pounds, he knew from Arizmendi's sister that the missing woman was only 90 pounds in July 2003. He also admitted that he failed to put Nilsa's street name of Maria on the poster. Also, he did not do any forensic testing at The Almar Motel in August 2003, even though there was a possibility that blood may have been detected at the scene with the use of Luminal.

In what could be interpreted as a mindless mistake at best, or perjury at worse, DeRoehn stated that he checked the box on the D.S.S. form indicating that his inquiry was for the purpose of preventing a suspect from fleeing prosecution because he took it to mean that he was referencing Bill, not Holcomb. As a veteran investigator familiar with filling out government paperwork, it seemed a stretch for DeRoehn to make that assumption. Nonetheless, DeRoehn's misrepresentation on that D.S.S. form did not seem to faze Judge Sheldon.

Simon asked DeRoehn whether he had lied to Holcomb when telling her that the purpose of his visit to her home in November 2003 was in relation to a connection of lawn care equipment thefts. DeRoehn answered that police lie to suspects from time to time. It is part of their training. If he said he were there on a missing person's report, the opportunity to locate the van would be lost and Bill would flee.

Simon was probably getting frustrated at this juncture. DeRoehn was hardly green when it came to testifying for the prosecution. After decades on the job, he knew just how to choose his courtroom battles: concede the small errors that occur in the course of most investigations and maintain integrity and authority on the stuff that really matters.

When it came to describing the processing of Bill's van in May 2004, DeRoehn depicted his actions as being flawless. There was no way that he would allow Simon to cast him in the light of a corrupt Mark Furman planting a bloody glove at O.J.'s Brentwood estate. DeRoehn stated that he never stepped foot in Bill's van when it sat in the sally port. He stood at a safe distance and simply observed the search. He did peek his head into the van once, but only once. And it was a quick glance. He was also meticulous in his care of the tubes of Bill's blood when transporting them to the lab. No seals were broken and there was no leakage.

It is unknown what Simon was thinking when DeRoehn finished his testimony and stepped down from the stand. It is safe to speculate that after hearing the testimony of Bill's best friend, Joseph Ashley Martin, on the following day, Simon realized that it was time to urge his client to throw in the towel and accept the prosecution's deal for manslaughter 1. After all, the state could pull that offer from the table whenever it wished ... and time was running out.

*

The state's fourth witness, Chris Sudock, a detective for Connecticut's Central District Major Crime Squad, took the jury step by step through his careful search of Bill's van in May 2004. The court ruled that the most important evidence seized from the van, the blood-stained seating material on the bench's frame and back portion, could be entered into evidence. The new replacement cushions, however, were excluded as evidence. It was a small loss for the state, since the replacement cushions contained no blood anyway. Their presence merely implied that Bill had ripped out the original bench upholstery that contained blood.

The second blood sample from an unknown potential victim that was found in the van's carpeting in the search on May 10, 2005, was not entered into evidence. It would, however, take on the utmost importance in future investigations.

The state's fifth witness, an assistant director at a forensic lab in Meriden, Conn., described to the jury the way in which cuttings from the car seat were packaged in microcentrifuge tubes, placed in clear plastic bags that were then heat-sealed and placed into an outer envelope called a convenience envelope that was also sealed, initialed and placed in an overnight mailer. The seals of the items and tubes were not broken and no leakage or indication of contamination or tampering was observed. The items were forwarded to a forensic expert at Mitotyping Technologies in State College, Pa.

It was a cold Friday in late January when the court recessed for the weekend. Judge Sheldon instructed the jury to "have a good weekend and don't freeze and remember, please have no conversations with anybody at all about what you've been learning here and hearing here." Additionally, Judge Sheldon reminded members of the jury to ignore all media coverage about the case and to not undertake any personal investigation, research, site visits or experiments that could result in mistrial.

After the jury was excused, Simon approached the bench with an unusual request on behalf of his client. Bill needed a warmer cell and a writing utensil for future proceedings. Since the start of trial, Bill had been residing in punitive segregation due to being found in possession of a small amount of cigarette tobacco. Though allowed to shave from time to time, there was no hot water or a mirror to look at. He could not receive visitors, use the phone or write and send out letters. The cell's frigid temperature resulted in sleepless nights. Simon asked Judge Sheldon if the court could do anything to "help solve this problem," as it was having an impact on his client's mental acuity. It was difficult for him to stay awake in court and assist counsel with his defense, according to Simon.

Judge Sheldon was not moved by Bill's plight. He found that the imposition of sanctions rested in the domain of the D.O.C., not the court. He only promised that Bill would be given a pencil and paper to write with on the next day of trial.

Bill trudged back to his ice-cold cell that day. Sleepless nights in uncomfortable cells were nothing new to him. To keep busy, he wrote a poem:

An innocent man.
I sit in Jail.
An innocent man.
I can't make bail.

They take my freedom.
Try to make me submit.
But the crime I'm accused
I did not commit.

I try to tell them
And make them see.
That I am innocent
and should be free.

They do not listen.
and turn a blind eye.
So here I sit
as Time Ticks by.

A Jury Trial,
now on my mind.
I pray my innocence
They will find.

24.

When I went to Bridgeport Correctional Center for our monthly visit on Sept. 12, 2016, the heat wave had subsided and an autumnal chill was in the air. I drove along Route 8, a 67.34-mile state highway that runs north to south from Bridgeport, through Waterbury, then Torrington, and all the way to the Massachusetts border, where it continues on as Massachusetts Route 8. The infamous part of Route 8 in Connecticut where a total of six murdered females, many of them drug-addicted prostitutes living in Waterbury, were deposited between 1988 and 2004, stretches for only about eight miles and is not far from my home. Bill was a teenager living in Virginia when most of those murders took place.

The tip of Route 8's triangular burial ground is Harwinton and the lower corners are Litchfield and Thomaston. Granite cliffs dominate that section of the highway. On that day, the trees that topped the cliffs were starting to turn a brownish yellow in anticipation of a lackluster foliage season ahead. Passing through Waterbury, a seagull floated against the clear blue sky announcing the nearness of Connecticut's coast. My mind turned to one of the more recent Route 8 victims, Jessica Muskus. In a televised interview with an investigative reporter for the local news the year before, I mentioned the similarities between the recent findings of skeletal remains behind the shopping mall in New Britain and the unsolved Muskus murder. Two of Bill's alleged victims were Waterbury residents, so he was familiar with picking women up in that area. The 22-year old mother went missing from Waterbury on July 31, 2004. Her skull was found at the foot of a steep embankment alongside Exit 41 on Route 8 in August 2006. It was detached from her other remains in a manner similar to that of the remains found in New Britain.

"I didn't kill Jessica Muskus," Bill told me during one of our visits. He thereafter gifted me a large box of The Whole Shebang potato chips and cheese curls, snacks available only to incarcerated consumers (unless you want to purchase a bag for $20 on Amazon). When I returned to my law office and opened the box, I found a large amount of DNA testing and other documents at the bottom of the box. Rifling through the paperwork, I saw that law enforcement did compare the DNA sampling of Muskus to the bloodstains in Bill's van on two separate occasions, in December 2004 and once more in May 2014. The results were negative.

"Did you see that the DNA testing for Muskus was negative?" Bill asked during our next visit.

I nodded. "But it still doesn't prove anything. The van was seized in April 2004, three months before the Muskus murder. It was still in police custody when Muskus was killed. If you did kill Muskus, it wouldn't have been in your van."

"Well Muskus died at the very end of July. I had already left for Virginia, or Carolina, I forget which one, but I had already left Connecticut by then. If you could find a receipt from Dori's credit card back then, you would see that she had purchased me a bus ticket to go south before Muskus went missing."

The inner city location of Bill's new home, Bridgeport C.C., stood in sharp contrast to the sprawling farmland of Suffield, where Walker C.I. is located. Otherwise, the actual physical structures were similarly drab and unwelcoming. Inside the lobby, a large one-way window stood to the right side of the door. Someone called out "Can I help you?" I had no idea where the individual was located, or where to respond. She knocked on the other side of the window, above a metal slatted opening in the glass. I went to it to announce my visit, only to be told that visiting hours don't start until 1:40 p.m. "Your website says 10 a.m.," I said.

"That's wrong."

"It does say 10 a.m. I checked this morning."

"It's wrong." No apologizes were offered, no promises to correct the site. This was a state prison, after all, and the standards for inmates and visitors alike were just a step above a Third World boarding house.

I considered sitting in my locked car in the prison parking lot for the next several hours and catching up on emails and phone calls. Looking at my surroundings, I thought better of it. I texted my husband and asked for a recommendation on where to go. World traveler that he is, he advised that I drive to the neighboring town of Fairfield, a far nicer community, he said. He was right. Crossing the city line was like the color coming on screen when Dorothy enters Oz.

Unfortunately, I made the mistake of going to a Chips Family Restaurant, which looked like it could be a family-run diner but turned out to be a franchise serving gag-worthy wraps consisting of warm, fatty chicken on white lettuce, tasteless tomatoes and oozing with cheap mayonnaise and margarine. I left my booth and went to the restroom. When I returned, a stranger was sitting in my seat, texting on her phone. "Excuse me, this is my table," I tried to sound pleasant, although I was a little unnerved. What about a coat on a seat back and a half-eaten meal don't you understand?

She kept texting. "Hold on, I'll just be a minute." She continued to text with me standing there, confounded. Evidently, I did not drive deep enough into Fairfield when choosing the venue.

Back at the prison, I could not help but notice that the staff was much friendlier to me than the staff at Walker C.I. Not knowing the purpose of my visit, they viewed me as a lawyer meeting with her client, not a dirt bag writing a book about a serial killer. When I last visited Bill at Walker C.I., the security guard at the front desk picked up the phone and said "Howell has a visitor." Long pause. "Uh huh ..." Longer pause. "I know. It's ridiculous."

Locked inside the visiting room, I had plenty of time to study a mural on the prisoners' side of the Plexiglas, facing visitors. Not even a Starving Artist Sale at a 2-star hotel would dare display that mural for purchase. I figured that it was a project given to bored inmates, something to kill the time instead of making license plates. In the mural's center, a Connecticut flag and an American flag flew atop the Latin motto for the state of Connecticut. There was an emblem in the middle and emerging from the emblem were depictions of historic scenes loosely related to the Nutmeg State. A farmer plowed his land and a battle took place. I could not be sure if it was a scene from the Revolutionary War or the Civil War. The men wore blue uniforms.

A one-dimensional J.F.K. sat to the right. His eyes were so close to his nose that he looked like an emaciated owl. To the left sat Abraham Lincoln. They must have run out of brown paint because his hair was painted jet black, as was his beard, which rested under his chin so it looked like he was a clean-shaven man wearing a costume beard for Halloween. There was also a graduate adorned in cap and gown; beside him stood a yellow-haired woman wearing a mini-skirt that rose close to her crotch. "Kudos to the artists for getting that one past the D.O.C.'s censorship," I thought.

Bill eventually entered the area on the other side of the Plexigas accompanied by three heavily armed guards. At Walker C.I., there was only one guard in the background; seeing Bill shrouded with this level of protection refreshed my memory with respect to his serial killer status. Were he to escape, more innocent people would die.

He wore a white T-shirt and beige pants, not the usual one-piece beige jumpsuit. He had lost weight. He looked younger, almost fragile. Our 30-minute discussion was steeped in death. Several times, he said that he would leave the new facility in a body bag, that he was about to "hang it up," and there was no point in living anymore. Labor Day weekend marked the anniversary of Dori's death. For the first time, he told me exactly how she died. Until then, I did not know that she committed suicide. An autopsy was never performed, he said, because she had no life insurance.

At the time of her death, Bill told me, Dori's boyfriend had left her. She was living in a tent behind her sister's house and going to the bathroom in the woods. Bill was in prison for the murder of Nilsa Arizmendi. I wondered if that fact, along with suspicions that he murdered more women in addition to Nilsa, caused Dori's drinking and depression to escalate and push her over the edge. I held back from asking Bill that question, as he presently seemed on the verge of a nervous breakdown himself.

"Why aren't they putting you in the suicide unit?" I asked.

He cynically smiled. "Last time I told an officer here that they would have to take me out in a body bag cause I was going kill myself, he said, 'Fine. Go ahead. Save us all some money.'"

His goodbye to me that day was one that a man gives on his deathbed. He did not want to be resuscitated. I needed to remind his attorneys to give me all of his personal possessions upon death, including all legal discovery documents in his possession to help me with finishing the book. He deeply appreciated the kindness that I had shown him and would not have lived this long without my presence in his life. When he stood to leave, I placed my hand to the Plexiglas and he placed his hand opposite mine. I felt compassion in that moment and was genuinely worried that this would be the last time that I would see him alive. "Everything will be okay, Bill," I said, not believing my own words.

He nodded in agreement. His eyes said, "Everything will be okay when I die and only when I die."

In prior letters and visits, we had discussed our spiritual beliefs. He said he would like to believe that there was a

God, but he doubted it. He hoped at death that his existence would simply extinguish into a dark, eternal sleep. Christian at my core, I asked him to promise me that he would confess his sins to God and seek forgiveness in the event that he ever tried to take his life again. Surely if Hell is real, Bill's soul would be at the top of the list as fuel to burn.

Bill never got back to me on that request. He later wrote to me concerning his lack of faith:

"I remember you made a comment once about "man made religions." That stuck out in my mind and I remember that as soon as I read it I thought, "Man made religions for man made Gods." You know I'm not religious, so it amazes me when I see stuff on the news like someone praising God for saving them when the tornado destroyed their house and all their belongings. I mean, if God had the power to save them, couldn't he have saved their house too?? And wouldn't it be God that sent the tornado in the first place?? If God does exist, and has the power people say he has, then he's an asshole for letting all the shit happen in the world.

I'm just saying."

From a humanistic perspective, it stands to reason that if Bill is right, that God does not exist, then no blame can be given to an all-knowing God that failed to intervene. The responsibility for the murders of seven individuals and the traumatic residuals that will resonate in the lives of their family members in the years to come rests squarely on Bill's shoulders.

25.

Jan. 29, 2007

Ashley Martin probably would have preferred a root canal without anesthesia to testifying at the New Britain Superior Court on the morning of Jan. 29, 2007. Unfortunately for Martin, as a hostile witness for the prosecution, he had no choice in the matter. Bill's longtime friend was served with an interstate subpoena ordering him to appear and testify in court two weeks earlier. He tried to fight the process in a court in Hampton, but without success. He was provided with a plane ticket, paid for by the state of Connecticut, and transported to Bill's trial.

It's usually not a good thing for a witness's credibility to give a lot of "I do not recalls" in response to the opposition's questions. After state's attorney Brian Preleski got through with Martin, it almost seemed like the witness had a mild case of amnesia.

Preleski: And how long had Mr. Howell been staying with you prior to Thanksgiving in 2003?

Martin: That I can't recall.

Preleski: And did Mr. Howell have Thanksgiving dinner with you that year?

Martin: No, because I believe we went to my parents' house, my wife's parents' house and he stayed at my house. No, I can't—I can't recall.

Preleski: And what kind of vehicle was Mr. Howell driving back then?

Martin: That I don't recall, either.

Preleski stepped forward and offered photos of the interior and exterior of Bill's blue van. His recollection refreshed, Martin stated that it was the vehicle that Bill drove on the week of Thanksgiving of 2003, and the same van that they cleaned out on the driveway. On entering the van, Martin testified that it contained "regular odors" including the smell of grass, oil, gas and some body odor.

He went on to testify that he did not recall there being any seat cushions on the bluish-grey bench in the van, matching or nonmatching. Further, he didn't see Bill remove any cushions or dispose of them in any manner. The answer was in direct contradiction to a portion of the written statement given by Martin to police on May 13, 2005, with initials showing his voluntary approval of the information in the margins of the document:

We emptied out the van together. I remember the van had a light blue rug. I saw the bench seat in the back of the van. I saw the bottom bench cushion and the back bench cushion were present. I saw both red and dark red stains on both the bottom and the back cushions that were very noticeable. Devin said that the cushions were stained, but didn't give any further explanation. Margin, JAM.

While giving this statement, Inspector Hankard showed me a picture of one of the cushions inside the van. I recognize it as being (a) photograph of the same cushion with red and dark red stains. I signed, dated and timed this photograph as the picture of Devin's van I saw during Thanksgiving 2003. Margin, JAM.

While inside the van I smelled a very strong odor. It wasn't gas, oil, or grass. It smelled like body odor. Initials, JAM.

Right around this time I watched Devin take the bottom bench cushion off, roll it up, and put it in a plastic bag. Devin put the plastic bag at the curb for pick up, which occurred sometime later. Margin, JAM.

From an evidentiary perspective, the five-page document, initialed by Martin in 19 locations and signed five times, was Bill's death knell. When Martin took the stand less than two years after writing the statement and testified differently, it made him look like, well … a liar. More precisely, he looked like a loyal friend *and* a liar.

On cross-examination, Simon tried to show police coercion. According to defendant's counsel, the written statement was not reliable because there was a show of force used by the police. First, a large group of them unexpectedly showed up at Martin's home and questioned him for two hours. This was followed by a lengthy interrogation at the police station that lasted upwards of four hours. Martin was "very nervous" and just wanted to give the police what they wanted so he could go home.

Judge Sheldon wasn't buying it. He overruled Simon's objection to the admission of the written statement, finding that Martin was not in police custody when the statement was made, and he was in fact free to leave. Moreover, his nervous state was a given. It did not indicate that he had been threatened in any way. It was not a threat when the police told Martin that the failure to cooperate could lead to a charge of aiding and abetting a fugitive. They were simply doing their job. Finally, 10 or so officers may have initially approached Martin's home in May 2004, some in uniform, but when he was questioned at the station it was only by two detectives.

Judge Sheldon went on to read aloud to the jury marked contents of Martin's written statement, the introduction of which stated that it was given of Martin's own free will, without any threats or promises being made, and that he was not high or under the influence of drugs, alcohol, or medication at the time that the statement was made. Sheldon slipped up at one point and read a portion of the statement was not supposed to be read to the jury. "After Devin got out of jail in Connecticut, he stopped at my house."

Preleski immediately interrupted, "Your Honor," but the damage was done. The jury heard the prejudicial statement that Bill had been in jail and Sheldon's remedial instruction to "strike that statement" could not erase that fact. Simon pounced on the opportunity to request a mistrial.

The jury was excused.

Preleski and Simon approached the bench and gave argument. Preleski said that a mistrial was a "rather drastic step" for "something of this nature." He suggested that a "reasonable curative instruction" as the one that had already been given by the judge was appropriate. Sheldon agreed and denied Simon's request for a mistrial, stating that he did not believe that any prejudice would flow from his accidental reference to Bill's prior incarceration. The jail time mentioned had nothing to do with the case at hand.

Overall, it was a horrible day for the defense. On redirect, Preleski got Martin to admit that he had phoned and written Bill since his arrest, thus implying that the two had spoken about what Martin would say at trial. He may not have understood what all the hoopla was about the bench seat and cushions when police questioned him two years earlier, but he sure knew now. He also admitted to recently giving Bill financial support while in prison, which contributed to the "bromance" issue insinuated by Preleski in his line of questioning.

Preleski: And you described yourselves as best friends; in fact, you love Mr. Howell, don't you?

Martin: I mean I like you know, yea, I've known him a while.

Preleski: You've known each other since you were children, correct?

Martin: Yes, sir.

Preleski: You don't want to see anything bad happen to William Devin Howell, do you?

Martin: Yeah, I guess you can say that.

Preleski: And it would be a bad thing for your friend to be convicted of murder, wouldn't it?

Martin: It would be bad for anybody, but—sorry—yes.

At the end of the second day of trial, the state's offer of manslaughter 1 was still on the table, but it probably would not be there much longer, especially after the victim's DNA evidence was presented the following day. One imagines Simon making a mental pro vs. con list in his head on the drive home that evening. Based on such an overview, he would know how to advise his client the following day.

PRO	CON
There is no body. Victim could be MIA from drug OD or other causes.	Victim always kept in contact with family. She has not done so in almost four years.
	There are no other suspects but Bill.
Although Ace Sanchez stated that Bill was the last person seen with the victim, Sanchez was not exactly a stellar witness. He was a drug addict with a long history of incarceration, so who knew if a jury would believe what he said?	Last person seen with victim was Bill.
First lie detector test on Sanchez showed deception, but the second lie detector test was "inconclusive."	Lie detector tests cannot be entered on the record as evidence.
Bill had a pattern of going South for the winter.	Bill left Connecticut soon after DeRoehn showed up at Holcomb's house in November 2003, perhaps indicating that he had the intent to flee.

	Martin's written statement describes removal of blood-stained cushions by Bill. He testified at hearing that no such cushions were removed. Judge Sheldon finds no police coercion. Martin is caught in an apparent lie.
	Sudock removed a non-matching set of cushions from the van's bench during the first search in 2004. Bill may have removed the original cushion because it was stained with blood.
Only a small amount of victim's blood was found in the van. It could have been from a nosebleed or the result of the victim's alleged fight with Sanchez in the back of the van, per Bill.	*Victim's blood/DNA found in Bill's van.
Rodrigues is a career criminal and snitch. He lacks credibility and is motivated by self-interest (i.e. lenient sentencing from the prosecution and other favors).	*Rodrigues will soon take the stand and tell the jury that Bill confessed to killing Arizmendi.
	*Bill allegedly went on to threaten the lives of Rodrigues and his family.

*Indicates evidence that has yet to come before the jury.

Once the evidence with an asterisk was presented, the trial would end and the state's earlier offer of manslaughter I, with a sentence of 15 years, would be off the table. The jury would then deliberate and, with the cons outweighing the pros, a finding of guilt for murder 1 was entirely possible—some might say probable. That verdict would result in the defendant serving 65 years in prison—basically dying of natural causes in lock-up.

When Simon showed for court the next morning, he advised Bill to take the plea deal for manslaughter 1. Bill agreed to do so under Connecticut's Alford Doctrine, whereby a defendant does not admit to guilt, but concedes that the state has enough evidence to support a conviction. Although he agreed to the plea, he told Simon that he first needed to phone Dori Holcomb and pass it by her. No sooner had the words come out of his mouth when Simon rushed up to the bench with the prosecutor and got the deal on record.

Bill's initial reluctance to enter the plea deal transformed into a stubborn stance of innocence at sentencing but by then, of course, it was too late.

26.

The day after our visit at Bridgeport C.C., Bill wrote that he had informed his attorneys that he was leaving a package for me in the event of his death.

"Needless to say, they seemed to get a little pissed off. They seem to think that after all this is over that you are just going to slam the hell out of me. I told them 'You might be right, and I don't doubt it, but she is going to write what she wants to write anyway, weather I talk to her or not. At least this way I have an oportunity to correct some of the lies and let her know what's true and what isn't. And what she writes after that is on her.'

"They aren't real happy I'm helping you. But I also told them that if it weren't for you that they wouldn't even be sitting there talking to me because I would have suicided out a long time ago... which is true."

The next day he wrote:

9/14/16

Last night I tried to suicide out. I'm writing about it tonight so obviously it didn't work out too well. Another thing I'm a failure at. It seems as though my only success is at failing.

Anyway, I tried wrapping a 'turnoquet' around my neck and tightening it to the point where it would cut off my blood flow and cause me to pass out where I would be left lying on the handle of the turnoquet so it couldn't un-wind.

Harder done than thought. I tried it twice and both times I ended up starting to strangle before passing out. Believe it or not, it's a lot harder to strangle yourself than you think. It left me with a sore neck and a bruise no one noticed or cared about. (31)

If I try suicide again I'll definitely try something different. But I may have a 'saving grace' coming my way.

The "saving grace" to which Bill referred was that a counselor at Bridgeport C.C. recently informed him that there was another warrant out for his arrest for a capital offense in Virginia. Her information ended up being incorrect, but for a time, it lifted Bill's spirits by leading him to believe that he would be transferred to death row in Virginia and *"they kill ya quick down there. They don't put you on death row and then make you die of old age. Down there, they put you on death row and 5 or 6 years later you are done."*

He went on to state that whatever the warrant was for, he did not do the crime. *"But if the death row conditions are right, I'm thinking of copping to it just so they'll kill me. A needle in my arm that puts me to sleep is a lot better than what I had in store for myself."*

He asked me to do some research and find out what kind of chemicals Virginia used in its lethal injections. *"Isn't one of them the same thing they use to put you under for surgery???"* He also wanted to know if death row inmates in that state could have a television in their cell and also if they were allowed to work a job *"or get any kind of monthly stipend."* He wrote that a television and a job and the promise of imminent death by lethal injection *"would be worth copping out to a murder I didn't commit."*

Desperate to get out of Bridgeport C.C., on Sept. 20, 2016, Bill wrote to the *Hartford Courant* to inform the media outlet of his suicidal thoughts. The newspaper published an article about it, which resulted in Bill being sent back to Garner C.I. Once he was locked inside the medical unit at Garner C.I., a prison psychologist determined that Bill was to remain on suicide watch for an indefinite period of time.

Stuck in *"the butt naked cell"* at Garner C.I., Bill sulked over the fact that the personal property removed from Walker C.I. and transferred to Bridgeport C.C. had never been returned. Making matters worse, he heard from a staff member at Garner C.I. that the man in charge of protecting the prisoners' property in storage at Bridgeport C.C. had been previously busted for stealing prisoners' personal property when he worked at Garner C.I. Bill considered filing a lost property claim, but it would take months for officials to investigate and process it.

Bill hated the staff at Garner C.I. They never gave him an extra tray of food and he said that there were times he was so hungry he wanted to eat his foam cup. It was all he could do to contain his rage:

"They try to screw with me so bad it almost seems like they are trying to make me snap. And then if I do they try to put it all on me. I've seen the shit before where they push and push and push and then the guy snaps and knocks a c/o in the head And then they are all like, 'see, we were in a dangerous atmosphere' when they themselves contributed to it and caused it to happen."

The inmates in the mental health unit at Garner C.I. were not much better:

"I learned tonight that 'therapeutic' is when they tie your wrists and ankles to the bunk and shoot you in the ass with a syringe full of Thorazine. They just did that to the guy that was beating and banging. He started again this evening and they called and ordered a 'therapeutic.' They have a screwed up way of 'therapy' around this place."

The next morning, another inmate was four-pointed with some more *"therapy."* The incident entertained Bill. Evidently, one of the inmates was locked in the single shower stall and when it came time for his shower to end, the inmate *"refused to 'cuff-up' and come out of the shower. It took them an hour and a half to get him out. They peper-sprayed him 3 times and all of the cops were coughing and gaging except for the inmate in the shower.*" Finally, what Bill called "*the goon squad*" showed up dressed in SWAT gear. The inmate finally gave up, knowing that the officials "*were about to come in and beat the shit out of him.*"

"Geez, Howell," a corrections officer later said, "I thought *you* were supposed to be the psycho!"

Bored out of his wits, Bill wrote to tell me some West Virginia jokes. This one was called "*The West Virginia Literacy Exam*":

> *M R Ducks*
> *M R NOT*
> *S A R*
> *C M WINGS*
> *M R DUCKS*

Another West Virginia joke: "*What do West Virginians do for Halloween?? Answer: Pump-kin*"

The lunacy contained in Bill's letters during his second stay at Garner C.I. began to mess with my mind. I had a dream one night when my husband was out of town, which I jotted down on the back of a napkin by my bedside so as not to forget it when I awoke the next morning. When Chris returned home, he found the note, scribbled in barely legible penmanship. It prompted him to ask me if I was all right:

Basement in childhood home.

Me hiding Bill—part of a plea agreement with the prosecution.

I keep him in a cage. Shackled hands and feet.

I am the only one giving him food and water.

Fear him breaking out. I delay going to basement. I am afraid.

He sleeps on a hide-a-bed in the cage. No toilet. Soiled mattress.

I am in over my head. (underlined twice)

I steal food from restaurants—bring him seafood salad roll with fries.

Basement has turned into a madhouse. He eats take out pizza with other dangerous men. Guards hose down prisoners with a high power spray to keep them from escaping.

Chaos. Hell.

Was I all right? On some days, the answer was yes. But there were the other days—dark days full of dark thoughts, when the connection that I had fostered with a serial killer "suspect" weighed down on me like a wet blanket. "I *am* a good guy, Anne," he told me in one of our visits. "I'm the guy who holds the door open for you at The Dollar Store."

27.

August 2007–September 2015
The first three bodies are discovered and identified

On Aug. 20, 2007, a man looking for a place to hunt behind a strip mall in New Britain found what appeared to be a human skull. Local police came to search the grounds. Within two weeks, a total of 50 bones belonging to three unidentified women were recovered. Authorities speculated that the bodies were likely left on the surface and not buried, and animals and the weather had gotten at a significant portion of their remains.

The FBI created a computer image of what one of the victims would have looked like. Dental records and DNA culled from the 50 bones were entered into the missing persons database. Months passed and there were no matches. Two years later, the skulls of two of the victims, named Jane Doe 1 and Jane Doe 2, were transported to Quantico, Va., for analysis. In 2009, the brother of a New Britain woman came forward to say that one of the forensic busts looked like his missing sister.

Age 48 when she went missing, Diane Cusack lived on Oak Street in New Britain and was last seen in the late summer/early fall of 2003. The last contact police had with Cusack was over a routine landlord/tenant dispute in July 2003. In December 2010, Cusack was identified as one of the three victims based on DNA comparisons with family members. One month later, police publicly announced Cusack as Jane Doe 2.

Jane Doe 1 would take longer to identify.

Joyvaline Martinez disappeared from her mother's home in East Hartford on Oct. 10, 2003. In the weeks that followed, family members worried because Martinez was not around for her 24th birthday later that month or her mother's birthday on Halloween. The Martinez family reported Joyvaline as missing in March 2004. In either 2006 or 2007 (media reports differ), Martinez's mother submitted her DNA for analysis.

Although Martinez's bones were among the remains found in August 2007 and the forensic laboratory was provided with a sample of her mother's DNA in 2008, she was not identified as one of the three victims until May 2013. A newspaper article from the *New Britain Herald*, dated May 9, 2015, described the delay as "a glitch in the state crime lab" that stalled the identification of Martinez for six years.

According to an article in the *Hartford Courant* dated June 25, 2015, it was more than a mere "glitch" that delayed figuring out that Martinez was one of the victims. In fact, the Connecticut state police crime lab was in a state of disarray. Although the forensic laboratory was given a sample of Martinez's mother's DNA in 2008, it took over a year for personnel to even submit the DNA into the Combined DNA Index System (C.O.D.I.S.) Relatives of Missing Persons database. And then, no match in DNA was made.

Members of the Martinez family were shown the forensic bust of Jane Doe 1, but stated that it did not look like the missing young woman.

In January 2013, lab officials conducted an internal review of the C.O.D.I.S. database and discovered a "misconfiguration of the search algorithm." Evidently, "the C.O.D.I.S. Relatives of Missing Persons Profiles, which included the DNA of Martinez's mother's DNA, was not searched against profiles generated from the unidentified human remains database, which contained Joyvaline Martinez's DNA."

Oops.

By then, the state lab had lost its accreditation and its ability to post DNA profiles of Connecticut's offenders on the FBI's national data bank. Making matters worse, "as the backlog of DNA cases grew, the lab's top two DNA scientists built up large amounts of compensatory time and used it to do consulting work for private clients out of state." The internal error of the C.O.D.I.S. database was uncovered and fixed in May 2013, and a match of DNA samples was made immediately. In August 2013, Martinez was officially identified as Jane Doe 1. That finding was confirmed when a forensic dentist examined Martinez's dental X-rays and concluded that they matched the skeletal remains found at 593 Hartford Road, behind the now infamous strip mall.

Remember, there was a second bloodstain found in Bill's van—not his blood or the blood of Arizmendi, but of a separate, unknown individual. According to the arrest warrant filed by Det. DeRoehn on Sept. 15, 2015, Martinez, known as Victim #2 in the legal paperwork, "cannot be eliminated as a contributor from a bloodstain mixture found on the seatback in Howell's van." Additionally, a sample from a hair/root forcibly removed and found in the front section of Bill's van also contained the DNA belonging to Martinez. But for the mistake of the state crime lab, that information would have been given to law enforcement four years earlier and the Martinez family would have been notified as well.

Like Cusack, Martinez was said to have battled with substance abuse issues and was known to frequent the Main and Lafayette streets of New Britain. Beyond that, the two victims could not have been more different. Born in 1955, Cusack was old enough to be Martinez's mother. She had brittle, light brown hair and the haggard, weathered look of a woman who had spent decades with little money and a lot of stress. In contrast, Martinez was strikingly beautiful, with long, shiny dark hair; full, soft lips; and high cheekbones. Find a photograph of her online and you will agree that the young woman could have gone to Hollywood with those looks. As a teenager, she ran on the high school track team and was popular amongst her peers. She was known as a loving member in a family of six children. She reportedly liked to grab her sister's young sons and roughhouse with the boys as soon as she showed up at their New Britain home. In subsequent court hearings, Martinez's family would show up in large numbers to seek justice for their beloved "Joy."

The remains of the third victim, Jane Doe 3, took the longest to identify. Only the right femur and right tibia were available for forensic analysis. In 2009, the state crime lab's scientists, impaired by systemic dysfunction, told the police that they could not produce a DNA profile of Jane Doe 3 because the remains were not sufficient for the extraction of DNA. That all changed in 2012, when Guy Vallaro was appointed as the lab's new director. In addition to bringing about the computer correction that allowed for the identification of Martinez in 2013, Vallaro pushed for a follow-up analysis of the yet-unknown Jane Doe 3 bones in 2014. Sure enough, the now functional lab was able to produce a DNA match. On Sept. 26, 2014, police announced Mary Jane Menard as Jane Doe 3.

At age 40, Menard had a history of drug addiction. According to investigative reports, she was known to hang around the same New Britain streets as Cusack and Martinez. In an affidavit filed for Bill's arrest warrant, completed by Det. DeRoehn on Sept. 15, 2015, a cooperating witness had been interviewed by the Waterbury Police Department and stated that she saw Mary Jane Menard in the passenger seat of a "dark blue or black van" at a street corner in New Britain. She said that the van had high back seats and was "dirty and beat up."

The witness stated that Menard waved and yelled to her from the passenger window. When the van stopped at a stop sign, the witness walked up to the van and started a conversation with Menard, at which time Menard introduced her to the driver as her friend "Bill." The witness described Bill as a white male, heavyset, with dirty blonde/brownish hair that was wavy in the back "like a mullet." Bill also had an unkempt bushy beard and a big belly. She recognized Bill's photo on the news a few months later, when he was arrested for the murder of Nilsa Arizmendi.

Jonathan Mills told police that Bill also shared information with him concerning the death of Menard, stating that she was the fifth person that he killed. According to Mills, Bill said Menard was "a hooker" and he picked her up in New Britain. He raped her six or seven times with the shock absorber he kept stored in his van. When he couldn't rape her anymore, he strangled her inside his "murder mobile" and delivered her corpse to "his garden" behind the shopping mall.

The affidavit references the use of sticks during the rapes. Mills claimed that Bill was concerned because the shock absorber would have Menard's DNA on it.

If what Mills said was true, there is no saying what sense of horror each victim experienced in the face of Bill's brutal rapes and ultimate strangulations.

28.

By the middle of November 2016, Bill was back at Walker C.I. and his personal property had been returned to his cell. When I visited him following the U.S. presidential election, he was a different man than the one that I met with at Bridgeport C.C. in September. He possessed an alpha male energy now—a very distinct "don't mess with me" boldness. I sensed he felt empowered by the fact that he had defied the advice of his attorneys, written about his suicidal thoughts to the *Hartford Courant* and that proactive decision resulted in his ultimate return to Walker C.I.

He beat the system.

Also, during that visit, more than any other visit up to that date, I knew for certain that I sat face-to-face with the killer of seven individuals. The frightened little boy from Bridgeport C.C. was gone, tucked away in the folds of the Ferguson gown left behind at Garner C.I., no doubt destined to return at a later date when times grew worse and more mayhem arose. I looked into his bulging hazel eyes and imagined him wrapping the body of one of his victims in a blanket and sleeping beside her corpse in the back of his van for two weeks, as was alleged in investigative reports.

We discussed Donald Trump's victory and how the events unfolded on election night. Bill went to bed before the final results and awoke for his insulin injection at 5 a.m. to hear Sarah Palin talking on the television about a Trump administration. Like me and many other Americans, he was shocked by the political upset.

"So what's going on in your life these days?" Bill asked me. By then, we had established a casual rapport. Listening to us talk, one would think we were old friends.

"Just the same old stuff," I said. "Chris is traveling a lot on business. I'm keeping busy with my law practice and writing this book." I did not think to share with Bill a concern that had been weighing me down in recent months. My husband was not feeling good. He had lost some weight and was complaining of fatigue. We assumed it was related to the negative side effects of a new medicine that he had been prescribed to control his diabetes. I did not want to worry Bill with my problems. God knew, he had enough of his own.

By February of 2016, however, I had real reason to worry. Chris had lost more than 60 pounds and, frankly speaking, felt like shit. He experienced night sweats and a rash covered his entire body. Our treating APRN totally dropped the ball, missing the most obvious of diagnoses. Cancer. On Feb. 25, 2016, Chris's spleen ruptured due to an abdominal tumor. PET scans and a bone marrow biopsy confirmed the worst: my husband of almost 30 years had Stage 4 non-Hodgkin lymphoma, of the B-cell variety. The malignancy was located in his lower abdomen, spleen and kidney, and there was a splattering of it in his chest, just for good measure.

I shared the news with Bill at the start of our prison visit in early March. "Now I understand how you felt when your mother had cancer," I told him. "It must have messed with your head."

"Yeah, it did. I'm so sorry, Anne," he said. "You know I don't really believe in God, but I am going to ask the chaplain to pray for you and Chris."

Our eyes met. "Thanks, Bill," I said.

I meant it.

When I picked Chris up from his first outpatient R-CHOP chemotherapy session a few days later, the nurse informed me that he had experienced anaphylactic shock. She told me to keep an eye on him during the night. If he had difficulty breathing, I was to phone 911. "Is that all I can do to help?"

I asked, incredulous. "Is there something you can give me to administer? A bronchodilator or a shot of Benadryl?"

She shook her head. "Just call 911."

I went home and searched the internet to see how long it takes for a person to choke to death. The results informed that in the first four to six minutes that the brain is deprived of oxygen, damage occurs. It takes about 10 minutes before irreversible brain damage takes place. I then researched how long it takes for paramedics to respond to a 911 call. On average, it takes about five to eight minutes, but usually about 10 minutes pass by the time the paramedics enter the house and assist the patient.

I tossed and turned with anxiety that night. Mercifully, Chris slept without incident.

"How long does it take to strangle someone?" I later asked Bill. If anyone would know, I figured it would be him.

"They usually pass out after about one to two minutes," he matter-of-factly replied. "They lose consciousness pretty quick, but it takes four or five minutes to die."

29.

After the first skull and the remains of three women were found behind the strip mall in August 2007, local police returned annually to the swampy 15 acres of land owned by the Department of Transportation. They performed line searches and above-ground observations with a keen eye for anything that resembled a human bone. In April 2015, a cadaver-sniffing dog team on loan from the FBI assisted police in finding the remains of four more victims.

The first was identified as Melanie Ruth Camilini, a mother of two from Seymour, Conn. She would have been 29 years of age when she was reported missing by her mother in January 2003. In an incident report, a friend described Melanie as "looking like Natalie Wood or Catherine Zeta-Jones." She had "chestnut color hair long enough to put into a pony tail and is very attractive, good teeth, light skinned and can 'always get her way.'" Bill later told me that Melanie was beautiful. Her mug shots did not do her justice, he said.

Melanie was last seen in the city of Waterbury, where she may have been living. The Rust Belt city is approximately 20 miles southwest of New Britain. Mills told authorities that Bill said Camilini was the first woman he killed. If true, this chronologically lines up with the killing spree alleged in DeRoehn's warrant for Bill's arrest.

It comes as no surprise that women working the streets in Waterbury are easy prey to predators. Drive through the seedy underbelly of Waterbury and if your vehicle's doors are not locked, you will find yourself locking them within a matter of seconds. The steep roads lined with run-down tenement buildings perched side-by-side at precarious angles rise and descend in waves of despair. Windows are adorned with Confederate flags, broken blinds and bed sheets for drapery—or are simply boarded up with plywood. Drug needles and cigarette butts litter cracked sidewalks and alleyways where feral cats prowl. It is not unusual to spot a drug deal in progress or a grim-faced prostitute negotiating a transaction with a john. Even the postman trudging from home to home appears depressed.

The heroin epidemic in Connecticut has exploded in the last decade and Waterbury is one of its greatest demographic victims. Once known for its large-scale manufacturing of brass at the turn of the 19th century, it attracted a vast assortment of immigrants from every nationality and still maintains a train link to Grand Central Station in New York City. When the industrial boom ended, working-class districts disintegrated into poverty and crime, while only a few street blocks away residents in the top tier continued to maintain their charming homes and send their offspring to the local private schools.

There were 81 heroin related deaths in Waterbury between 2012 and September 2015 and 36 opioid-related deaths.[32] The increase in prostitution in the community is directly related to heroin use. Once caught in the drug's satanic snare, even the most ethical of individuals will sell their bodies just to get a fix.

Bill's purported second victim, Marilyn Gonzalez, was also a resident of Waterbury. Age 26, Gonzalez was the mother of two, ages 11 and 7 at the time she went missing. She was last seen near her home on Hillside Avenue on May 15, 2003, at about 10:25 p.m. The photo from a missing person's poster shows a plump Hispanic woman with dark brown eyes and full pink lips. She had an identifying tattoo on her right shoulder: a heart with the initials "A" and "T" contained within it.

The most informative witness mentioned in DeRoehn's paperwork is, of course, Jonathan Mills. He told police that Bill confessed to picking Gonzalez up in Waterbury and raping her in his van. He strangled her, but she would not die, "so he hit her in the face and head with a hammer." According to the informant, Bill told him "the hammer shattered the girl's jaw." He said, "Hillbilly killed the girl and kept her wrapped in the van for two weeks because it was too cold outside to bury her." He claimed that Bill told him that he slept next to his "baby." He cut off the tips of her fingers and dismantled her bottom jaw.

According to Mills, Hillbilly disposed of his victim's body parts in Virginia. Police subsequently dug up the yard behind Martin's house in Virginia in search of the victim's jaw. No remains were found.

If what Mills told police were correct, then Bill tore apart the corpse of Gonzalez like a butcher would tear off a cow's head. Author Roy Hazelwood, a former FBI officer, notes in his books about profiling that serial killers are sometimes meat cutters or electricians who work with cords and wires. Often, the manner of death and the evidence found at the scene of a crime reflects the skills or items obtained in the killer's profession.[33] I therefore took note when Bill told me in one of his letters that he worked for a time as a meat cutter in the deli department at the Big Y grocery store in Torrington, Conn.[34]

One male was found amongst the bodies behind the mall. Danny Lee Whistnant was a 44-year-old cross-dresser. While Whistnant may have engaged in prostitution, he was not a drug user, according to a police interview with someone who knew him. His last known address was in New Britain. His mother reported him missing on July 4, 2003. Apparently, Bill was embarrassed about the circumstances leading up to his alleged murder of Whistnant; Mills said that Bill was not so willing to speak openly about that particular murder. Bill eventually told Mills that he picked up Whistnant by the Stop & Shop in New Britain thinking he was a woman. As he was getting oral sex from Whistnant in the van, he grabbed the "homo" by the hair and the wig came off. That's when he strangled Whistnant.

Nilsa Arizmendi's remains were also discovered in April 2015. That discovery gave law enforcement the confidence to announce at a press conference one month later that they had a suspect in mind. In the background, an enlarged mug shot of Bill was displayed for the television audience to view. In a matter of minutes, that image went viral online. While it took several years for law enforcement and forensics to identify the three victims found in August 2007—Cusack, Martinez and Menard—the four victims discovered in April 2015—Arizmendi, Gonzalez, Camilini and Whistnant— were identified in a matter of months.

30.

The Connecticut Division of Criminal Justice has partnered with the Connecticut D.O.C. and created a Cold Case playing card deck highlighting unsolved homicides, missing persons and unidentified remains cases that have occurred throughout the state. The cards are distributed to prisons across Connecticut in an effort to stir up information and leads in solving cold cases. The cards depict photos of the victims and general information surrounding their disappearance or murder. The idea, though simple, is effective. Inmates have a lot of free time to play cards and shoot the breeze. For example, a guy playing a game of poker might see a photo of a woman he murdered and start to boast.

According to the arrest warrant for the six remaining murders, the cards worked on Bill. During a discussion in their cell at Corrigan C.I. in 2014, Mills claims that Bill picked a card with a photo of Joyvaline Martinez out of the Cold Case playing deck and showed it to him. He told Mills that Martinez "was a hooker" he had raped and strangled in the back seat of his van.

Bill had no remorse, according to Mills. He supposedly said that all of the women he killed "should have known they were going to die because of the lifestyle they were living." According to Mills, Bill explained that he was unable to get back to his "garden" to bury her. He described himself as a "sick ripper." One night, he told Mills that he was going to retire to his room and dream of all the victims in his garden.[35] The most important information that Bill relayed to Mills in 2014 concerned the number of his victims. At that time, only three bodies had been found behind the strip mall. Bill told Mills that there were four more bodies that had yet to be unearthed, and he described the location of the graves in relation to one another.

What does Bill have to say about what Mills told authorities? He wrote to me:

I will say this—one thing I don't like is how some jail-house snitch out for his own good can say I said something and then it's printed in articles as if I really said it. Like in this article you just sent me it refers to me saying something about a 'Garden' or cutting off fingers or something and how its written like I really said that SHIT. That's fiction made by an inmate that gets reported as fact. Or at least fact that I said it. That's BullShit!! People can, and do, say I said this and that when I never said shit. I've read more than that one article that said 'Howell said this or that' and I'm like 'Where the fuck are they coming up with this shit from?' There are a hundred and fifty thousand reasons and inmate has to lie on me.

Anyway, enough about all that. I have no control over what someone else writes and a boring story doesn't sell as good as juicey one weather it's true or not.

Bill rightly complains about there being misinformation contained in his case—inaccuracies that have been shared by the prosecution and local media outlets, largely based on what Mills had to say, as though 100 percent fact-based. As it turned out, a lot of the information given to cops by Mills was incorrect, although it did point to some general and disturbing truths regarding the crimes that Bill was charged with committing. By way of analogy, if asked about World War II, Mills would say that the global conflict last nine years, not six, and that the Soviet Union was an ally of Germany, not America. Nonetheless, he would also say that Germany lost the war and a ton of people died. So the gist of his story would be correct.

Bill eventually gave me a large box that contained a significant portion of the legal discovery that the prosecution was required to turn over to his defense counsel pending trial. Many interviews that were conducted between former prison inmates teem with fabrications and inconsistencies. Clearly, quite a few of them were looking for favors from the prosecution in their own legal matters in terms of lesser sentences or transfers to different prisons. Some of the witnesses on the outside who spoke to police were drug addicts and it is entirely possible that a few were interested in receiving a piece of the $150,000 reward money offered by the New Britain Serial Killer Task Force to anyone who could lead them to identifying the serial killer.

It initially puzzled me how Bill would get incensed about the inaccuracies in his case when in actuality he probably did kill six women and one man. He would also get frustrated when hearing that outsiders were speculating on a potentially abusive childhood. His main reason for wanting to go to trial was "*to set the record straight.*" I told him that even if he had the opportunity to do that at trial, the media would selectively report the most grisly of details and minor corrections that he thought were important would be overshadowed by the savage crimes themselves.

"Why put the victims' families through the trauma of a trial if that is your sole motive in going to trial?" I asked. "Why not just plead guilty, tell me everything that requires alteration, and I can include it in my book? If you don't agree with what I write, I will at least footnote your response?"

He liked that idea. I think, in the end, it is why he chose the legal route that he chose.[36]

＊

People ask if I see signs in Bill that he is a serial killer. They conjure him as Dr. Hannibal Lector or Charles Manson, shifty-eyed and crazed to the core. In fact, on many levels, he could not be more normal. In our face-to-face interactions, he presents as the kind of guy I would hire to do landscaping or clean my gutters.

I am not alone in that opinion. Soon after Bill was arrested for the remaining six murders, a local reporter spoke to an older resident living in the Belvedere section of New Britain who hired Bill back in 2001 or 2002 to mow her lawn, plant shrubs and do some painting. She told the reporter that "the minute she saw his picture" (a mug shot made public following Bill's arrest) she said to her husband, "That's our Devin."

It wasn't until she saw the mug shot that Mrs. Wallace realized she invited a suspected serial killer into her home on at least six separate occasions. She saw "no red flags," adding that he was "very personable" and also "very polite." He had a Southern drawl and "did diligent work" at reasonable cost. Bill lied and told her he was divorced and sending money home for his children.

"Normally cautious," she told the reporter that when she found out the charges against Bill, she was "absolutely shocked." "I thought I was a good judge of character, so I thought if this could happen to me, it could happen to anyone or a senior citizen who's not as aware as I was. I mean, my goodness, my husband even thought he was great."

She even trusted Bill to the extent that she rode to Home Depot with him in the "murder mobile" in which he killed seven people, to pick out shrubs. She had "no qualms about being in the van."[37]

In the first two years of our author/subject relationship, Bill refused to divulge information concerning the crimes that he had been charged with committing, although I sensed that he wanted to tell me everything: "*I really do wish I could speak more freely with you. But as you may or may not know, they will try to use the smallest little thing against me. And basically, with every word I say or write being monitored, it's like Brian Perleskie is there reading every letter to you and sitting on your lap at every visit with a second phone to his ear."*

During that time, I was faced with a colossal chasm between the man that I had come to know and the deplorable acts he was accused of doing—acts that we never discussed.

"I know that I am genuinely excited to get mail from you and to hear about things in your personal life and I always find myself eagerly awaiting your next letter and visit. And that, for my part, is genuine.

"When you sit in front of me at visits the person you see is me. I'm not trying to be fake, or put on a show, or con you in any way. I do not feel that I have lied to you or tried to deceive you in any way. And I do like to think of you as a friend."

✻

On the morning of May 12, 2015, a local NBC news channel aired the announcement that Bill was the main suspect in the New Britain serial murders. He recalls lying on the bottom section of his prison bunk at Garner C.I. and watching the headline newscast. His heart raced. It felt like someone had just kicked him in the stomach. He knew it was coming, he just had no idea how it would feel when it actually took place. Within minutes of that newscast airing, about 12 correction officers showed up at the door of his cell. They had been informed the day before that the state's prosecutor, Kevin Kane, would make the announcement and were notified in advance to transfer Bill to suicide watch as soon as the show aired.

"Get up, Howell," a correction officer ordered. "We're taking you out."

His cellmate sat up in the top bunk. "What's going on?" he asked, groggy with sleep.

"Watch the news," Bill told him. "You'll find out."

31.

Coming to Connecticut

What brought Bill from Hampton, Va., to Connecticut in the first place? It is disarming to realize that a random interaction in an online chat room could result in the human devastation that ensued.

Bill met Jessica in an online chat room in the spring of 2000. He liked her enough, but she lived in Torrington, Conn., of all places—a full day's drive from Hampton, where he was living with his friend Paul. In a matter of weeks and with the help of Ma Bell, the virtual relationship picked up speed and Jessica went to Virginia in September 2000 to meet Bill. Evidently, she liked what she saw because she proceeded to visit Bill in his home state a few more times and decided to move to Virginia at Bill's invitation.

She was 19. Bill was 30.

In anticipation of the move, Bill left Paul's townhouse and got his own place. Jessica gradually moved her belongings, a little at a time, while battling with the family court in Connecticut to permit her to move her 2-year-old son out of state with her. Bill states that Jessica was *"three fourths"* moved in by early November 2000, when he got *"popped"* for driving without a license. The event, as described by Bill, has a slapstick element to it like something from the reality series "COPS."

"I had gotten pulled over for running a stop sign that I didn't even see and was in a place/intersection where a stop sign shouldn't have even been. Anyway, I knew if I gave the cop my name I was going straight back to jail for another 1 to 5 so I gave him a fake name and social and when he went back to his car to run it I jumped out of my truck (an old

Toyota I paid 150.00 for and put a stolen FL tag on it) and hauled ass. I got away but the cop found mail in my truck with my name and addy on it. So a warrant was now out for my arrest in VA again under suspension as an 'Habitual Offender.'"

After Bill was "*popped*" for driving without a license in Virginia and "*hauled ass*" as the officer ran his plate, he called his buddy Harry who was now living in North Carolina, and asked him if he could stay at his place while he figured out what he was going to do. Harry said that was not a problem. In fact, he had an extra room and he would even talk to his boss to see if the boss would hire his wayward friend. Bill then phoned Jessica and told her that she could either move to North Carolina with him or move her belongings back to Connecticut, but that there was no way he could stay with her in Virginia with a warrant now out for his arrest. Jessica was not pleased. She drove to Virginia in a friend's pick-up truck to retrieve all of her belongings and made no further promises at that point in time.

Ever the pragmatist, Bill then bought another $150 "*hooptie*," stole another Florida tag and drove to Harry's home in North Carolina. Though Harry was a good friend to Bill, more like a brother, Bill was not looking forward to living in the Tar Heel State. He describes Harry's trailer as being "*in the sticks.*" One had to turn off a paved road and drive down a dirt road to get to it. In contrast, Hampton, where the two men grew up and once shared a townhouse, resembled a busy metropolis.

A few months later, Jessica's anger had subsided and she invited Bill to Connecticut to celebrate their respective birthdays—hers on February 7 and his on February 11. At the end of that visit, she had warmed up enough to ask him to move in with her at her parents' house. She reassured him that her parents were "*on board with it.*"

Bill accepted the offer, reasoning that he liked Harry and he was very thankful to him for helping him out and giving him a place to stay, *"But when it came down to waking up alone in a trailer basically in the middle of a corn field or waking up beside a nice warm female 11 years my junior... well, to CT I moved."*

Bill spent the last day of the visit putting in job applications in the surrounding area. It was important to him, however, to briefly return to North Carolina to *"get a little money, collect my stuff and thank (*Harry*) for the help that he had given."*

Bill may have turned out to be a serial killer, but damn, if he is not a courteous friend.

On his second day in Connecticut, sometime in late February 2001, he was hired on the spot as a deli worker at the Big Y grocery store in Torrington. Bill socialized a lot while living in Torrington. He played pool at the Billiard Hall across from the Big Y; drank beer at The Yankee Pedlar, a restaurant on Main Street; and listened to live bands near the Wasteland Head Shop on Water Street. His lifestyle disrupts the myth that most serial killers are dysfunctional loners.[38] Bill is one of the most sociable people that I have ever known. Friendship is extremely important to him; he was always eager to escape solitude and spend time with others. He later confided to me that being alone was the very thing that got him into so much trouble.

Bill worked part time in the evenings at the Big Y *"delly,"* named the "Sam the Butcher" section of the store. Within one week, he found a second job—this one with full-time hours—roofing with Benco, also located in the city of Torrington. Though things were looking up job-wise, his relationship with Jessica floundered. She was pressuring him to get married. Bill resisted and the two broke up after a few months. Little did Jessica know—she had just dodged a major bullet. She went on to marry another man and Bill states that the marriage lasted only one year. The two remained on good terms, however, and Bill even went to Jessica's wedding with his weed dealer and the two got stoned with the bride.

In the early summer of 2001, Bill found an apartment in Torrington. His roommates turned out to be heroin addicts and he was desperate to leave. Officially single once again, he planned to move back South. As he drove through Torrington for what he thought would be the last time, he stopped to fill his gas tank at a station just before exiting to the highway. He flirted with the girl working behind the counter and asked her on a date. She agreed and they went out a few times after that. It boggles the mind to think that if Bill did not ask that girl out he would have left town for good and seven Connecticut residents would be alive today.

32.

Following the short-lived romance with the gas station attendant from Torrington, Bill soon found a new girlfriend, Amy, who he met at The Cadillac Ranch, a Western-style saloon in Southington that offers country line-dancing, pub food and a mechanical bull for patrons who are immune from motion sickness. Amy had just gotten a divorce and was living with her two young daughters in the basement apartment of her parents' house in Wallingford.

Bill was driving to North Carolina for the Fourth of July weekend when he was stopped on the New Jersey Turnpike and charged with giving false information to an officer and driving under suspension. He was released on his own recognizance but his current *"hooptie,"* an old green Volvo, was seized. Bill returned to Connecticut via Greyhound.

Back in Connecticut, Bill spent a few weeks riding around town on a bicycle while saving up enough money to purchase another *"hooptie."* He and Amy parted ways and he went to live with friends. He explains that he liked Amy enough—she was *"a good girl but it was like she was too good."* He felt that she needed a man who could be a stable provider and Bill fully acknowledged that he was not that man in any way, shape or form. *"Stability was never really one of my qualities. I was driving with a suspended liscense and was always just 1 traffic stop or D.U.I/liscense check away from a jail cell."* Bill felt that Amy *"deserved better than that"* and there was also the fact that Amy did not like to smoke weed, whereas Bill loved the stuff. *"I always felt like I was sneaking around behind her back to catch a buzz. SO I had to let her go."*

The break-up had no impact on a prior agreement for Bill to purchase a 1985 Ford Econoline van for $400 from Amy's parents. He states that the van looked to be in good shape but it had a bad motor, so he bought a tan minivan which he describes as "*a rust-bucket,*" switched the engines between the two vehicles and sent the tan minivan to the junk yard. In purchasing the 1985 Ford Econoline, he effectively killed two birds with one stone. He now had a vehicle to drive and a place to live.

By August of 2001, Bill officially took on the social status commonly held by sociopaths: he was a drifter. According to Dr. Scott Bonn, the author of "Why We Love Serial Killers: The Curious Appeal of the World's Most Savage Murderers," "sociopaths are likely to be uneducated and typically live on the fringes of society. They are often unable to hold down a steady job or stay in one place for very long. They are frequently transients and drifters."

Bill embraced the drifter lifestyle with the relish of a schoolboy gone camping for the summer. After a long day of roofing, he would shower off the dirt and sweat in the locker room of the local YMCA and go to his night job at the Big Y. When that shift was over, he usually partied with co-workers for a few hours—often in remote, wooded regions in and around Torrington. He resents that the media has called him a drifter, however, believing that it insinuates that he was a homeless, unemployed bum. He asserts that living in his van and travelling back and forth from Connecticut to states down South was not a sign of weakness or failure, on his part:

"*I didn't live in my van because I had to. I stayed in my van because I chose to. I made enough that I could have rented a room somewhere, but I couldn't see spending all that money to have a place to stay 3 or 4 nights a week...*

"*I've never been one to ask for handouts. I've always earned my way through life. Granted, I've had friends help me out along the way, but even when I was 'couch surfing'*

I always paid 100.00-150.00 a week to couch surf. I would rather have nothing and sleep in the streets than be a 'free loader.' Hell, even when I was dating Dori and sleeping in my van 3 or 4 nights a week I was still paying ½ her rent. Granted she had a sweet ass deal where she was living and was only paying 375.00 a month for a 2 bdrm apt. I was still giving her 200.00 a month to help her with her bills and only stayed with her 3 or 4 nights a week."

Sometimes, Bill and his friends played Frisbee in the parking lot of the Big Y after hours or they went to The Big Slide located at an elementary school playground in Norfolk, the next town over. The large, green colored tube descends a steep embankment and deposits its travelers into the lush meadow below. Bill also speaks fondly of a place called Little Woodstock located at a state park in Torrington. He and his friends would build bonfires and party all night.

He usually parked his van for the night in the Benco parking lot. The living arrangement worked out fine. If he tired of his cramped quarters, he could always crash at the home of his "weed guy" for a night or so. Now locked up for life in the protective custody unit of a high-max prison where he is not even allowed to work a dollar-a-day job, he describes that period of his life with an air of nostalgia:

"I had a nice bench seat to crash on and a little T.V. to watch and I was always out doing shit with friends anyway so it didn't bother me to crash in my van at night. Especially after serving all that time in VA. I had protection from the wind and rain and I could go where I wanted when I wanted and had a place everyday so I was content. I had 2 jobs and money so I was all set.

"I could have probably gotten my own place, but it didn't make sense to me. To come up with all the money necessary just to move into a place and then to buy furniture and then I've got a great big anchor on me should I decide to leave or get laid off."

Bill also points out that living in his van saved him a lot of money, which would permit him to return to the warmer climate of Virginia or North Carolina on a seasonal basis. Needless to say, it was also a convenient getaway vehicle if he got in further trouble with the law or if Virginia authorities caught up with him. Sadly, the van in question would also be the place where six women and one man took their last breaths.

When instantaneous license scanners came into effect, Bill decided to up his game and register his home on wheels in the name of the third woman that he met in Connecticut: Dorothy Holcomb.[39] The couple first connected at a bar named Illusions located in Waterbury. They instantly hit it off. Dori was caring and outgoing. She loved to cook *and* she smoked weed. Unlike Bill's last two girlfriends, Dori had her own place, a house that she rented in New Britain where she lived with her two children in a joint custody arrangement. They tried to live together for six weeks, but Bill states that they got on each other's nerves and so he decided to live in his van instead. He basically tolerated Dori's antics and stayed in the relationship for the sex:

"It's true what they say, 'Crazy in the head, Crazy in the bed.'

"I think that was my turn on to Dori. She was nuts but the sex was never boring."

I once asked Bill if Dori had been molested as a child. "I don't know," he said. "I think she mentioned something about being raped."

Bill and Dori dated until sometime in 2004. It was rarely smooth riding for the pair and neither was faithful to the other. Bill wrote me about a fling with a woman he met at Goodwin Park: *"Lisa had been staying with some old guy but he had kicked her out and she was just hanging out in the park to pass the day and told me she planned to sleep in her car. I told her I was going to get a room on the turnpike and if she wanted she could stay with me. She said okay and it was on from there. We had a thing for a month or so. She knew I had a girlfriend but was okay with being a 'side piece.'*

"Lisa was 40 or 41 (I was 33) and she wasn't real pretty but she had an awesome body. I mean she had the body of a 20 year old. Slim & trim with some little A or B cup boobies and not a spot of cellulite or stretch marks on her anywhere. And she loved sex. She liked it in the front, the back, and her mouth. In fact, she gave me the best 'Free' (not from a prostitute) blowjob I ever had.

"The only problem was that she was a drunk. She'd drink Vodka for breakfeast. If it hadn't been for her drinking, I'd have left for her in a heartbeat."

At the exact same time that Bill was cheating with Lisa, Dori was cheating, too: *"I was supposed to have gone with Dori and her friends on an overnight camping trip to some waterfalls somewhere and at the last moment Dori ditched me and stopped answering her phone. Anyway, for like 3 days she wouldn't answer her phone. When she came back from her trip with her friends, she called me and we met up. When we went to have sex I noticed she had 2 bruises (1 on each thigh on the underside and they happened to be exactly where my thumbs were on her thighs to hold her legs up for sex.) So I knew right then someone had banged the hell out of her on her camping trip and that's why she ditched me and wouldn't answer her phone. I later found out that a guy her friends knew had just gotten out of jail and went on that camping trip with them.*

"I mean what could I do?? I couldn't be mad. The same time she was cheating on me I was cheating on her. I just wonder who had the better 'side piece.' I'd say me because I had mine for about a month and a ½ and Dori just got the 3 day camping trip (As far as I know... for that instance anyway.)

"That's the kind of screwed up relationship we had. I used to talk to Michael Stein about her and how miserable I

felt at times and I remember him asking why I stayed with her and I remember telling him 'I guess I'd rather be miserable than lonely.'"

Bill and Dori were still a couple when Bill went on his killing spree from Feb. 1, 2003, to October of 2003. Did Dori sense that something was amiss during that period of time? Her boyfriend would spend only a few nights a week at her home, so she was not privy to what he did in his van during the other nights of the week. The couple watched the ball drop in Times Square to ring in the start of 2004 and went for drinks at the Jekyll and Hyde Club on Seventh Avenue. They got a kick out of the stools at the bar that would rise and lower as patrons drank, and Bill appreciated the comically macabre atmosphere of the establishment. The experience was especially unique because he and Dori were tripping on L.S.D. He then got locked up in January 2004 and served six months for driving under suspension. Dori would visit him during that time.

Dori eked out a modest living as a hairdresser at a Great Cuts salon in New Britain. She arrived at the initial prison visits wearing sweatpants and looking *"all grubby,"* according to Bill. A few months passed and she presented wearing nice clothing. When Bill was released on a two-week furlough to Dori's house in July 2004, she told him that she had met someone else, a farmer from Litchfield, who she had been dating while Bill was serving the six-month sentence. Not one to linger where he was not wanted, Bill moved back South when his furlough was up.

In 2005, Bill returned to Virginia and Dori drove down to visit him for her birthday on March 20th. He used to call her his Spring Chicken, because she was born on the first day of spring. Later in 2005, Dori was evicted from her house in New Britain for two reasons: her new boyfriend often parked his loud Harley-Davidson on the street, which made neighbors complain, and people knew that she was once involved with Bill, who was suspected of murdering

Nilsa Arizmendi. Also, she had been fired from Great Cuts—partly because of the rumors surrounding Bill, but also because she could never keep a job for long because of her mood disorder. Dori was known to mouth off to customers and supervisors, according to Bill.

Dori then went to live with her farmer boyfriend in Litchfield, where he provided a lifestyle that was better than what Bill could and an income from Great Cuts could offer. The breakup confirmed what Bill already knew. He was *"a bad boyfriend with anyone."* He once wrote me:

"That song that says 'Love is all we need' is bullshit... you need a good job and a liscense... or at least a liscense. Nobody wants to date a guy on his bicycle."

Still, Bill tells me that Dori continued to *"step out"* on her new boyfriend with Bill. Even after their breakup, Dori publicly professed her belief in Bill's innocence regarding the murder of Nilsa Arizmendi. In the years that followed, Dori's mental health problems increased. She was always paranoid that people were breaking into her house or drugging her, Bill said—information that is corroborated by Dori's close friend at the time. I asked Dori's friend if Dori knew, deep down inside, that Bill killed Nilsa Arizmendi.

She replied, "I feel bad to think it about Dorothy, but she did start coming off the chain. Maybe the stress of knowing something ... and the last time she visited me in 2007, I attempted to talk to her about the possibility of his guilt and she shot me right down adamantly! She protested too loudly. I knew there was going to be no discussion about it."

Dori met a tragic end. Bill says that she spent a lot of time in the bars with the farmer from Litchfield. Her drinking escalated and when she and the farmer split up, Dori had nowhere to go. She wound up homeless, living in a tent behind her sister's house, where Bill bitterly claims she was barred from coming inside to use the bathroom.

On Aug. 27, 2012, with her former flame now in prison for the murder of Nilsa Arizmendi, Dori finally came undone. Bill states that she passed away from a drug overdose washed down with a bottle of vodka. At the age of 45, she was pronounced dead at Charlotte Hungerford Hospital in Torrington. Her obituary states that she left behind two children (then teenagers), three sisters, a brother and a "beloved dog named Cane."

*

Dori was my best friend. She came to visit me about 6 months before she died. Even though we broke up about a year before I was charged with the Arizmendi case, we kept in touch. And to me, I think we became even closer after we broke up than we were when we were together. Dori believed in me 100% and in a way I am glad she's not around to see those charges and alligations brought against me. For her to hear the alligations against me would have crushed her. As I said, Dori was my best friend and I miss her every day. After we broke up, alcohol slowly consumed her life and she began a downward spiral she was never able to recover from. It really tore me apart because I knew she was at a bad place in her life and I was unable to help her. I often wonder that if I were out if I could have somehow saved her from herself. I think I could have. She still had a lot of love for me and could talk to me about things she couldn't talk to anyone else about... I miss her greatly.

33.

Only three months into our written correspondence, Bill had indicated that he was interested in telling me the truth, or at least, his version of the truth. *"I am very limited in what I can discuss with you at this time. However, after all of this stuff plays out, I will be able to speak with you more freely. But I'm sure you are aware of all that."*

During one of our earliest prison visits, Bill mentioned the possibility of reaching a *"settlement"* with the prosecution. This gave me hope on several counts. From a purely self-interested point of view, I did not want this project to go on for many years and have to take months off work in order to attend a lengthy trial. When the trial was finished, I would need to plow through a voluminous amount of court transcripts in order to get all the testimony and facts right. It would be an exhausting endeavor and could easily result in a dry legal treatise that publishers would not want or readers would put down due to boredom.

I always felt that a guilty plea was the right thing for Bill to do. If I entertained a shred of reasonable doubt in his case, I would have urged him to go to trial and utilize the legal system to resist a wrongful conviction. But the DNA evidence found in his van was overwhelming and the suffering of the victims' families was great. Why prolong and intensify their pain with a drawn-out legal process that would inevitably lead to the same result: life in prison? If he did commit the crimes, then he needed to fess up. I told him as much, in as gently a way as possible. Verbally berating him would not help the cause.

On the other hand, I walked on treacherous ground by offering any input into Bill's decision-making process. It was not my place to interfere with a complicated legal matter that involved a man's liberty. I was not there to serve as an advocate for the victims' families, nor was I there to aid the prosecution. Nevertheless, I could not deny my desire to see Bill step up to the plate and take responsibility for his egregious crimes. It would show me that he had at least a fraction of human decency buried beneath layers of mental sickness and denial.

Again, I had even hoped that he would someday confess *everything* to me after entering a guilty plea. I never wanted him to divulge the truth before that time, as it could possibly result in me being called to testify at the trial for the remaining six murders.

As time wore on, Bill and I began to reference the elephant in the room in our letters and face-to-face discussions. The elephant's flesh and bones comprised the gruesome crimes that he was *alleged* to have committed at that point in time, but the eyes were what interested me the most, since it was the eyes that contained the hidden motives behind the crimes—the diabolical fantasies that impelled the monster to act.

"When this is all over, I will openly tell you everything that you want to know. We can finally talk about the elephant," he promised. *"You will be the first to know."*

I wondered if I could trust a serial killer suspect to keep his word:

"But I've always tried to be a man of my word," he told me the year before, *"and I've given you my word on some stuff and I'm going to try my best to see it through. But I tell ya Anne, it's really hard sometimes. I'm really miserable in here, and I've never been a miserable type of person. I always had the 'happy go lucky' type of attitude."*

Bill's frustration with his legal counsel increased as time wore on. In April 2016 he wrote, *"I have not seen my lawyer since my last court appearance. And I have yet to receive the first page of evidence against me from him. Everytime I ask for copies of my file he gives me the run around as to why he doesn't have it. He's told me about this or that, but I haven't seen or received actual copies of anything yet. And I gotta say, it is starting to irritate me a little. I have a right to face my accusers and view and/or receive copies of the evidence against me. It's been months now and I have nothing."*

It appeared that the delays were not out of the ordinary, however. A private investigator had to redact details of information contained in that evidence before they could hand it over to Bill. It was a lengthy process, and it did not help that the investigator was also preoccupied with working on the high-profile appeal of Michael Skakel, the Kennedy cousin convicted in the 2002 death of Martha Moxley. Moreover, Bill felt that the delays were insufferably long because, in his state of isolation, the clock ticked in slow motion, whereas his lawyers were busy men with family obligations and many other clients to defend in addition to Bill.

By May of 2017, Bill had received a significant portion of the legal discovery, but not all of it. Nevertheless, he indicated at our prison visit that a guilty plea was in the works and he would probably accept the terms offered by the prosecution. I was relieved, though I kept that feeling to myself. "Do what you need to do," I carefully advised. "If you are innocent, then fight for yourself at trial. Don't feel pressured to take the plea just because the prosecution's case is strong. You do have a right to see all of the legal discovery before making a final decision."

"I know, but I've seen enough, and I'm tired of getting the runaround. I just want it to be done," he said. "I don't want the families of the victims to suffer anymore."

That was the first time that he mentioned the victims' families to me, thereby confirming their existence as human beings whose lives he had shattered into a thousand pieces. I later spoke to the adolescent daughter of one of his victims and her father. They relayed to me the immense pain of their situation over the last 14 years First, according to the father, the victim's daughter had to face questions from peers about why she had no mother around at events growing up. Her mother was a drug addict, but she could not tell them that truth, let alone that she was missing. Her father raised her as a single parent. He suffered greatly—always anxious about his former partner's safety on the streets. Before she disappeared, he saw the bruises on her body when she came to visit their young daughter and the signs that she was still using drugs. He worried about her. She was the mother of his child.

This man described Bill's victim as a "beautiful woman" when they were together, before she turned to drugs. Listening to his story, it was hard for me to keep my emotions in check. Over the years, he was left with the job of trying to raise a little girl on his own. It wasn't easy. It was terrible. To this day, every time he looks at the face of his daughter he thinks about her mother. The woman who Bill killed. "I think about her every day," he told me. Then he had to hang up the phone, because he was sobbing. "I'm sorry. I can't talk about it anymore," he said through the tears.

So when Bill and I talked that day, I said, "That's good. You need to think about the families."

In a follow-up letter, Bill included a copy of legal expenses that his lawyers had provided that indicated a future trial would cost Connecticut taxpayers close to a million dollars. I reviewed the list in the hospital cafeteria as my husband underwent a procedure to drain the excess fluid from the area surrounding his left lung. Just when the doctor thought that all of the blood-tainted liquid was gone, more of it filled the tubes, accumulating to over 3.5 liters.

The doctor phoned my cell to tell me that the procedure was over and I could come upstairs and pay a visit. I found Chris lying in a lab-like setting next to a counter containing large glass bottles the color of strawberry soda with a layer of foam floating on the top. It was a disgusting sight, but also a reminder that our bodies are not within our control. Cancer appears. Strange substances form.

The second of three in-patient stays at Smilow Cancer Center in New Haven was equally memorable. It involved the infusion of Methotrexate, a prophylactic treatment designed to prevent the cancer from jumping into the nervous system and attacking Chris's brain. Nurses at Smilow Cancer Center monitored Chris around the clock to make sure that his organs, especially the kidneys, were tolerating the strong chemical. I slept on the window seat in his private room, nicely sedated with .5 mg of Xanax. I awoke a few times in the night to the sounds of feet shuffling and beepers going off. A few feet away, my husband's 6-foot-4 frame lay on the bed like Victor Frankenstein's prodigious science project, being poked and prodded and objectively assessed. Twice in one night, the intercom announced a Code Blue on that floor. I sat up and looked over at Chris. He was still alive.

In the early summer of 2017, my husband and I were walking on a narrow bridge above Death Valley. Given the type and stage of cancer, Chris had approximately a 50 to 60 percent chance of survival. If the R-CHOP chemotherapy did not fully eradicate the cancer by the end of the summer, a stem-cell transplant would be scheduled for the fall. That would involve a three-week hospital stay. Picture a nuclear storm dissolving all of the forests and cities on Earth. According to the oncologist, that is what a stem-cell transplant endeavors to do to any cancer that remains. It is a high-risk procedure—a Hail Mary Pass if the R-CHOP could not finish the job.

In the best case scenario, whereby the R-CHOP treatment was successful, there was no way of knowing if the cancer would return in the years ahead. The oncologist told us that the rate of recurrence in a five-year period, given Chris's initial blood work, was a disheartening 60 percent. Likewise, the other great unknown in my life during the summer of 2017 was whether Bill would provide me with detailed confessions of murdering seven individuals and placing their bodies behind the strip mall in New Britain.

On June 7, 2017, the prosecution offered a plea deal that was not much of a deal, but more of a willingness to close the case. Bill was offered 360 years in prison, the maximum of 60 years being served for each of the six victims. He would have to admit guilt on all counts. A hearing to accept the plea deal was scheduled in July, although Bill suspected that hearing would be continued, which is exactly what happened.

He was still frustrated that his lawyers had not given him 100 percent of the prosecution's discovery to review before taking the deal, but he was desperate for everything to be over and done. "It is the right thing to do," I said at a prison visit in late July.

He nodded, still silent on the issue of whether he actually committed the crimes. "And once it's done," he said, "we can talk about all of the elephants in the zoo."

I was optimistically hopeful that Bill would finally come clean to me—and to the world. Nevertheless, I worried that what he would end up telling me would be nothing but a pack of excuses and lies. Would he finally take ownership of his atrocities and confess everything?

Like my husband's cancer, Bill was keeping me in suspense.

PART II
CONFESSIONS

Kurtz (voiceover) "The horror… the horror."
Apocalypse Now

34

Bill contacted my law office on the day before his Sept. 8, 2017, hearing to inform me that he would plead guilty on all counts. The news brightened my already euphoric mood. The week before, my husband was informed that blood tests confirmed that the R-CHOP chemotherapy had done its job. He was cancer-free. Results from further testing left no doubt. "No PET/CT evidence for disease recurrence in the neck, chest, abdomen and pelvis." The entire staff at Smilow Cancer Center in Torrington shared our joy. We remain eternally grateful to that wonderful facility, along with Smilow Cancer Center in New Haven, for their excellent care and support.

Although Bill's upcoming guilty plea came as no surprise to me given our earlier conversations, it came as an enormous surprise to many of the victims' family members who sat in the courtroom the following day. A few later told me that they had no idea that Bill would plead guilty; they were simply approaching the matter as if it were another routine procedural event where a continuance would be issued and trial set for a later date. It apparently came as a surprise to several media outlets as well. While cameras were not allowed in the courtroom, there were no cameras rolling footage outside the New Britain Superior Court, either—not even a local news channel.

Bill was led into the courtroom dressed in bright orange prison garb, heavily shackled from the waist down. Two security guards firmly gripped his arms. The distance from the door through which he emerged to the defense table was no more than four feet. We were in the presence of a monster and there could be no room for error. A Ted Bundy-style escape, whereby the prisoner was given the opportunity to jump through an open window when no one was looking, was out of the question. "I don't know why they were so bent on security that day," he told me afterward. "I am so fat and out of shape that I would run a few yards out of the courthouse before I got out of breath and tackled by a ton of officers."

He was right about that. Bill had gained more than 65 pounds since being arrested for the murder of Nilsa Arizmendi years before. Seems all those Rice Krispie squares and hot pot meals that he enjoyed in the privacy of his cell at Walker had taken their toll. Five feet, 9 inches in height, he now tipped the scales at close to 300 pounds. I envisioned him fleeing the courtroom with the theme song to "Shaft" playing in the background, waddling down the courthouse steps and awkwardly dragging himself past security. If guards failed to capture him in the lobby, he would no doubt make a beeline out the door in search of the closest Arby's, where he would order a Beef n' Cheddar Classic.

I sat directly behind him alongside my paralegal, Tammy, who often took Bill's calls at my office and conversed with him in the minutes that it took for me to leave the task at hand and get on the phone. It was hard for me to believe that this was the same man that I met with on a monthly basis at Walker C.I. Without the Plexiglas to separate us, he appeared so large. I studied the broadness of his shoulders. "Those poor women didn't stand a chance," I thought. Even Daniel Whistnant, the only male victim, was wiry and destined to lose the fight for his life.

The prosecutor, Brian Preleski, read a statement that summarized the evidence that the state had on Bill: the location of the remains, the witness testimony of Jonathan Mills and the DNA samplings found in the van, to name just a few items. Bill stared straight ahead and displayed no emotion. His lawyers sat to his left. They seemed uncomfortable and made no attempt to speak to Bill or even make eye contact. The shame factor was heavy.

When asked by Judge Joan Alexander if he agreed with the facts as presented by the prosecution, Bill said that he did not agree "substantially" with the facts, but he did cause the deaths and was guilty of the crimes that he was charged with committing. "I killed them," he said.

At the close of hearing, Bill's defense attorney, William Paetzold, stood up and faced the victims' family members sitting in the courtroom. He stated the he and attorney Jeff Kestenband were honestly baffled by the difference between the client that they had worked with and come to know over the last two years and the acts that he committed. In his words, "We are left shaking our heads." I felt that it took great courage for him to say what he said—as the easy route would have been to say nothing at all—and I completely related to his perplexity. I recall thinking, "Okay, I am not crazy after all. They are just as puzzled as me."

On the drive back home, Tammy told me that she did not know if she could ever speak to Bill again when he phoned the office. "When he said, 'I killed them,' it just made me sick. I don't know. Something about hearing him actually admit it ... I felt like I was going to throw up."

Her response told me that she had partially disconnected herself from the horrors of Bill's crimes until that day, so to hear him say "I killed them" was a shock to her system. In contrast, I felt like it was just another turn of events leading to the culmination of my book project—a project, by the way, that I cannot wait to end. The last three years have absolutely drained me—heart and soul. Never once did I believe that Bill was innocent. At every visit, throughout every phone call, I was 100 percent cognizant of the fact that Bill was a serial rapist and killer. How many times did I look at his large hand, wrapped around the blue phone receiver as we spoke through the Plexiglas, and imagine it strangling his victims? I recall wearing a red silk scarf to our first visit.

As he eyed the scarf, I wondered if he envisioned strangling me. I suppose we all have ways of emotionally processing things. For Tammy, disconnect was necessary to maintain her sanity. For me, facing the horror head on was key.

Bill was given the maximum sentence of 60 years for each of his remaining six victims, resulting in a 360-year sentence without parole. I expected Bill to turn back and acknowledge my presence as he was led out of the courtroom, but he kept his eyes lowered. "That was an awful day," he later told me. "It really messed with my head."

For good reason. As the prosecutor referenced Daniel Whistnant's femur bone found in the burial ground behind the strip mall, a family member loudly wailed and left the courtroom. Bill was the sole source of her pain. He would have to live with that reality for the remainder of his days.

I drove out to Walker C.I. a few days later, on Sept. 11th. The weather was the exact same as the fateful day when the planes crashed into the Twin Towers 16 years before—deceptively clear-skied and warm, with a light breeze carrying a hint of crisp coolness. Bill had recently informed me that he would be transferred from Walker C.I. to Cheshire C.I. in the months ahead. I was sorry to hear that; in the last year or so, I had derived satisfaction from travelling the picturesque route from my home in New Hartford to the prison in Suffield for our monthly visits.

Entering the town of Windsor Locks, the Old Montgomery Building stands to the right, its shattered glass windows harkening back to days long past when customers ordered clothing, kitchen utensils and yes, even entire houses, from the Montgomery Ward catalog. A few blocks away stands an old abandoned train station where the soldiers of two World Wars kissed their family members goodbye. The prison is located just beyond the line that divides Windsor Locks and the town of Suffield, diagonally across from the Hood ice cream factory.

When we sat down to talk at Walker C.I., Bill presented as the same easygoing man that I had come to know. His pleading guilty to killing six people and finally acknowledging that he killed the seventh victim for whom he was currently incarcerated changed nothing between us. This confirmed for me that he never entertained the delusion that I believed in his innocence. All of those times when he would look me in the eye and make weak arguments in his case, he knew full well that I was viewing him with heightened suspicion.[40]

"You really would do anything for a Klondike bar," I said.

He laughed. I was referring to him telling me in our last visit that his attorneys agreed to give him the Klondike bar that he had requested in exchange for the guilty plea. "That could qualify as coercion," I had remarked. "You would have grounds for appeal."

"So how are you feeling?" I asked.

"Relieved," he said.

"I'll bet."

"Are you ready to give me some confessions?" I asked.

He looked down at the counter. "I don't know, Anne. I don't want to upset you before your visit to Hampton. I want you and Chris to have a good time." I planned to travel to Bill's hometown with my husband that weekend to get a feel for where he grew up and perhaps interview people including Martin and Aunt Ann.

"Okay," I said, trying to hide my disappointment. "We'll keep it light." We discussed places that I needed to check out in Hampton: Buckroe Beach, the James River Bridge, the house where Mandy grew up and the modest brick bungalow where Bill was raised.

After that, there was little left to talk about—except his crimes. We looked at each other in silence. Bill gave me a mischievous smirk. "Close your eyes and don't open them until I knock on the window," he instructed.

I closed my eyes and waited for an uncomfortably long time before he knocked on the window. When I finally looked, Bill sat before me wearing an evil clown mask that he had made for Halloween. It comprised a white cap made from the sleeve of a T-shirt, with a wicked toothy smile that stretched from ear to ear. For hair, the clown was given the top of a blue mop head. The eyes had been cut out. Bill stared at me through the holes.

"Oh, my God."

He laughed. "Do you like it?"

"I don't know if *like* is the right word, Bill."

He chortled with delight, removing the mask and returning it to the pocket of his jumpsuit.

"Can I just ask a few questions about the murders?" I hedged.

"Sure."

"Who was the first victim?"

His smile faded and his voice grew sad. "Melanie Camilini."

"Did any of the killings bother you more than others?"

"Yeah. Camilini really bothered me. I had never killed anyone before that. See, Anne, I'd been fantasizing about raping prostitutes for a long time. But I never acted on the fantasies—not until Camilini, and then I crossed a line and the fantasy became real."

"Was there something going on in your life that triggered you to act on the fantasies?"

"I guess things with Dori were getting bad," he answered. "Not that I am blaming Dori for what I did. But we were fighting a lot. Her bipolar was getting worse. She needed meds, but she wouldn't take them. She was getting more unpredictable from one day to the next. I was getting angry at her. We were under a lot of stress."

I thought of the different types of rapists categorized by profilers. The "retaliatory" rapist is angry at the world, and often, at a particular woman in his life.[41] "Did Dori nag you? Did she criticize you?"

"Yeah. Sometimes. But I don't want to blame her. I take full responsibility for what I did."

"Why did Camilini affect you more than the others? Just because she was your first?"

"Yeah. But also, I wasn't sure if she was a crackhead. She almost convinced me that she wasn't. She seemed nice. Like maybe she was okay. I found out afterward that she was on drugs. But at the time, I wasn't sure."

"Did any of them have last words?"

"Just Camilini. She said, 'Please don't kill me. I have children. My children need me.'" Tears streamed down his cheeks. "That messed with me. It really did. I wasn't sure if I could do it, after she said that."

"But you did."

"Yeah, I did."

35.

"I was never what I thought of as a "bad"
guy. So I still don't know how it is that I grew
up to be a freakin 'Serial Killer.'"

Letter from Bill, Nov. 27, 2017

"Why did you kill them, Bill?"

"It wasn't about killing, Anne. It was about raping. The prosecutors don't know this, but I didn't just rape three of them. They based that on what Mills had told them. How could they know that I raped just three? The bodies were nothing but bones when they dug them up. I raped all of them except Danny Whistnant."

"'Cause he was a man?"

"Yeah. I picked him up in New Britain after leaving The Cadillac Ranch in Southington. He was wearing a short miniskirt and high heels and he had long, shiny black hair. I thought he was a woman. I drove to a nearby grocery store parking lot for a $20 blowjob. When I put my hand on his head and pulled off the wig he was wearing, I discovered he was a guy and I killed him right off."

"How did you kill him?"

"I punched him a couple of times and then I strangled him."

"Did you strangle Melanie Camilini, too?"

"Yeah. I first tried to kill Camilini by hitting her in the head with a hammer. She didn't see it coming. That's another thing Mills got wrong when he talked to the cops. He said I tried to strangle Camilini, but she wouldn't die, so I beat her in the head with a hammer. That's backwards. I hit her with the hammer first—pretty hard—and it didn't even knock her out. She said, 'Please don't kill me. Don't hit me with the hammer again.' I didn't have the heart to hit her again, if that makes sense, so I strangled her."

"Were you boasting to Mills about the murders?"

He shook his head. "Mills implied that I thought he was jealous because I had more bodies than him, and that I was boasting. I confessed to Mills, but it wasn't in a sense of bragging or comparing numbers. Mills had gotten me what I thought was a bundle of heroin and it was my intent to O.D. By then, I knew that the investigators were on to me, and that I was going down. My confession to him was to get the crimes off my chest before I died. I told Mills that after I was gone, it was up to him what he did with the info I had given him. I wanted the families to get their closure, but I also wanted to be dead and gone when it happened."

Bill did attempt suicide a week or so after confessing to Mills in 2014. He took the anti-anxiety pills that he had stored up in his cell, but the bag of heroin Mills gave him was not heroin at all. The powdered substance contained some other unknown and dangerous drug. Bill lay in his bunk for two days after ingesting the drugs, unable to move his body or lift his head from the pillow. He felt like he was dying, but he did not have the good fortune of receiving a final exit from this world. Mills eventually told officials that Bill had overdosed and he was taken to the medical unit for treatment. He states that his liver tests are abnormal to this day because of that incident.

"How did you feel when you were killing them? Did it give you pleasure? A sense of power?"

"No. No. Anne, it was never about the killing. I just killed them to conceal the evidence. I knew that once I raped them, they would go to the cops and I'd end up back in jail. So I had to keep that from happening. I definitely didn't enjoy killing them. As I choked them out I was thinking— just *hurry up* and die."

"But you didn't rape Danny Whistnant, so you weren't trying to conceal evidence then. Did you kill him because you were angry when you discovered he was a man?"

"Yeah. Exactly."

"When you sliced off Melanie Camilini's fingertips, was that so cops couldn't ID her fingerprints if they found the body?"

"Yup. And Mills said some shit about me dismantling her jaw. That's not true. I just pulled out a couple of her teeth after she was dead."

"So police wouldn't ID her that way, either?"

"Yeah, but then I gave up and stopped. I realized that if they found her, it would probably have been moot anyway. She was the only one I did that to."

"What did you do with the teeth and fingertips?"

"I put them in a plastic grocery bag and threw them into a trash can outside the Family Dollar store on New Britain Avenue."

Interesting. The same man who would open the door for me if I walked up behind him to enter the Family Dollar store was also capable of disposing of human remains in the trash bin outside the store.

In a follow-up letter containing detailed confessions about all of the rapes and murders, Bill wrote:

There is one thing I've been dishonest with you about. And that is that I did remove Camilini's lower jaw in an attempt to hide her identity. I lied to you about this because I was embarrassed by the sheer gruesomeness of it. Even as I was doing it I couldn't believe I was doing it. I snipped her fingertips off with a pair of hand held pruning sheers and cracked her jaw on each side with a hammer. (I think that's what Mills was talking about when he said I beat her in the face with a hammer. But she had already been dead for over a week when I did this.) I then cut her lower jaw off with an extendable disposable razor knife like the throw-away ones you get from a dollar store. I put her fingertips and her

*jaw in a plastic grocery bag and threw them in a dumpster
beside the dollar store on New Britain Ave in Hartford.*[42]

"Mills said you slept beside Camilini's body in the back of the van and called her your 'baby.'"

He adamantly shook his head. "I slept beside her because I had no choice. But I never called her my baby. I told Mills that I slept beside the *body*."

Regardless of whether Bill called his dead victim his baby or not, I don't believe the postmortem mutilation of her body was an extension of his sadism, as is the case with what FBI profiler John Douglas labels "lust murderers," men who focus on the dead victims breasts, abdomen, rectum or genitals to express their anger and frustration. In Bill's case, it appears that his behavior after strangling Camilini was just a sloppy and frantic attempt at further concealing the evidence.

"Why did you pick the forest behind the strip mall to bury their bodies?"

"I knew about those woods because Dori worked at the Great Cuts in that little mall. One day I met Dori at the salon after I had finished doing a hedge-trimming job. I drove to the back of the mall after we ate lunch and dumped all the trimmings in my van over the embankment. I saw that other people had been dumping stuff back there, too. So I started going back there a lot and dumping branches and bush trimmings when I finished my jobs. "

"So you didn't get the idea to dispose of the bodies behind the strip mall because you heard about Robert Honsch putting his dead daughter there back in 1995?" I was referring to a 63-year-old man who was recently found guilty of killing his wife and is charged with leaving the body of his 17-year-old daughter, Elizabeth Honsch, swaddled like an infant: tightly wrapped in two sleeping bags and a sheet of plastic coating, beside a Dumpster behind the same mall where Bill buried his victims. When police found Elizabeth's body in late September of 1995, her flesh was still warm. Honsch then delivered the body of his dead wife, 53-year-old Marcia Honsch, to the Tolland State Forest in western Massachusetts, 40 miles away. The body of Marcia Honsch was discovered by a hiker eight days later. Honsch had shot both of his victims in the head.

"No," Bill said. "I didn't hear about that guy leaving his daughter behind the mall until a few years ago."

"Did you call the place where you put the bodies your 'garden,' like Mills told the police?"

"No. Those were his words. He said, 'It sounds like you were making some kind of a garden back there.' I never called it my garden. I never called the van the 'murder mobile,' either. There's a lot of shit in Mills' statement that isn't true, and also stuff that Ashley said in his statement to the police was incorrect. The original seat cushions that he said were in the van when we cleaned it out actually were not in the van at that point in time. I cut out the original seat cushions and dumped them in a barrel at Goodwin Park a few weeks before I went down to Virginia for that Thanksgiving visit in 2003."

"Did you throw the cushions away at Goodwin Park to get rid of evidence? Were they all bloody?"

"No. I threw them away because I used to toss the weed wacker that I used for yard work over the back bench and somehow it came unfixed and leaked gasoline all over the cushions. I didn't want anyone to sit on it and get a chemical burn."[43]

Well, that was thoughtful of him.

"I saw a sofa by the roadside and I took the cushions from it and put them on the seat. But, like I told you before, when I cleaned out the van with Ashley that day, it wasn't with the intention of destroying evidence of the crimes. I had to take out my lawnmowers and store them in Ashley's garage for the winter. Then I just removed a scrap of old carpet that I had put down on the floor to protect the original carpet from my lawnmowers. I rolled it up and threw it away, too. It didn't have blood on it."

"What happened to the victims' clothing and personal effects?"

"After they died, I removed all those things. I threw them away in random trash cans at gas stations and other places."

"The victims were completely naked when you buried them?"

"Yeah."

"How deep were the graves that you dug?"

"No more than a couple of feet. I got lazy. Also, the water table in that earth was high. If I went any deeper, the hole started filling up with water."

"Did you take a shovel or a spade out to the woods?"

"Yeah. A spade I kept in the van. I stored it behind the guardrail after I dumped the bodies in the ravine. I didn't want anyone to see me walking into the woods carrying a spade."

"And then you covered the shallow graves with soil and leaves?"

"Yeah. I threw leaves and branches on top to make it look natural."

Bill went on to explain that after he raped and strangled his first victim, Melanie Camilini, he threw all caution to the wind. Aware of Connecticut's death penalty, which was repealed by the state's legislators in 2012 and ultimately deemed unconstitutional by the state's Supreme Court in August 2015, Bill felt that he had nothing left to lose. If caught for the first murder, he would wind up on death row. So why not rape and kill again?

"Did you know that you would eventually get caught?" I asked.

"Consciously, I was trying not to get caught. That's why I hid the bodies."

"Why did you choose to rape prostitutes with drug problems?"

"You have to keep in mind what these people were really like, Anne. The victims' families will depict them as angels because that is what people always do in these situations. But they weren't angels at all. These were street people. These were people that you would not want in your home. They were the types who would take the money out of your wallet if you were standing in line at a grocery store with your back turned, just to get drugs. They were thieves and would do anything for drugs."

As he said this, I thought of Mary Jane Menard. Her daughter, Tiffany, told me that her mother had endured hardships in childhood including sexual abuse. She became an alcoholic, probably to numb the pain. Determined to provide a better life for her two young children, she sobered up and took Tiffany and her brother to her Alcoholics Anonymous meetings, dances and pig roasts sponsored by the group throughout their childhood. She raised them as a single mother, working different jobs while pursuing an undergraduate degree.

Unfortunately, Mary Jane, known to her family and friends as M.J., became addicted to painkillers following back surgery, which led her into the downward spiral of dabbling in street drugs before realizing that she had a full-blown heroin addiction. She went on to experience prolonged periods of remission and worked per diem as a substance abuse counselor at a group home in New Britain—helping others overcome their addictions before she relapsed into her own. She was so much more than a "street person," and she was never a thief.

"Did they ever steal from you?"

He nodded. "I've had a few prostitutes rip me off over the years. I had one or two get me to pay first and then they would jump out and run at the next stop sign. I had one empty my wallet while she was sucking me off. I had a few refuse to finish me off, complaining I was taking too long. I don't know if that created enough disdain to turn me into a serial killer or not, but when I was locked up in Virginia between 1995 and 1999, I began to fantasize about raping them. It's what I'd daydream about at night before falling asleep and those thoughts never really abated after that."

In a subsequent phone call, he told me that Nilsa and Ace stole a $20 bill that was rolled up in the ashtray of his van on the first night they met. He said that when Nilsa refused to "finish him off" in July 2003, it made him mad. First, she had stolen $20 from him, now she was trying to steal more from him by refusing to satisfy their $30 transaction. Bill does not like thieves and he considered drug-addicted prostitutes to be nothing but thieves, whereas he is a good person. He wrote:

"I dis-associate myself with my crimes. This is going to sound insensitive and perhaps it is. But while society see's me as nothing but a monster (and perhaps they're right... at least they're not wrong to have that opinion) I don't see myself as that. I always tried to be a good person. I tried to be a man of my word, I tried to help people if I could. I wasn't a burgler, thief or drug dealer (excluding the brief time I was a teenager and would rob SEARS but a lot of that was because the dumb Asses would leave the gate to the outdoor section un-locked.)

*"The only thing I've ever stolen from an actual **person** is the little dirt bike motorcycle and liscense plates to put on my vehicles."*

He notes that there was just one other time when he stole:

"I did steal a bicycle one time in Buckroe. My car had broken down and I was walking home and saw a bicycle laying out in a front yard. I stole the bike and rode it home. But I returned it to the same yard 3 nights later with a note taped to the seat explaining why I took it and ended the note saying lock-up or put away your bike.

"My point is, I wasn't what I considered a 'Bad' person. I wasn't one that was always plotting or scheming on how to get over on people or rip them off.

"While I am a serial killer and I did fantasize about raping prostitutes my fantasies ended there. I didn't meet a girl at the bar and fantasize about rapping her or anything like that. As much as Dori & I fought, I never once thought about killing her."

After pleading guilty, he asked me in a letter: *"Do you believe that good people can do bad, even evil, things without truly being bad or evil? Or do you believe those acts define them?"*

I had no answer to provide in that moment, but I have since given the question a lot of thought. The age-old teachings of the Catholic church offer some insight by categorizing sins as venial and mortal. Venial sins are slight sins; even if they rise to a level of serious moral gravity, the sinner still maintains a connection with God, partly because the individual may not purposely commit the sin or fully understand its consequences. Mortal sins involve the knowing and willful violation of God's law in a serious matter and murder is the greatest of mortal sins.

"I did knowingly and willfully cause the death of Melanie Camilini," he stated in a recorded phone call to my office. He then went through the list of all of his victims, repeating the fact that he did knowingly and willfully cause their deaths.

He later wrote: *"I wasn't 'consumed' by urges to rape, rather, they were made on a more conscious level. Kind of like how someone might decide to go out for a couple of drinks. I decided I'd go out and rape & kill a prostitute tonight. It wasn't something that consumed me in a way that I felt like I had to go do, or needed to go do, but more of something I wanted and decided to go do. I'd be like 'I'm not seeing Dori tonight and I don't have anything to do in the morning, so I think I'll go rape and kill a prostitute tonight if I can't get lucky at the bar.' It wasn't something I was consumed by or felt I 'had' to do. But more something I 'decided' to do because of the opportunity."*

According to the Catholic church, if one commits a mortal sin and fails to sincerely repent, he will live separately from God for eternity. In Bill's case, he committed a mortal sin seven times over, coupled with the mortal sin of repeated and purposeful sexual assaults. In the deliberate commission of his crimes, he showed absolutely no concern for his victims and he has told me that he would have gone on to rape and murder women if he were not stopped. Moreover, he continues to demonstrate a confounding lack of empathy regarding the anguish that his victims experienced at his hands in their final hours, for example, he stated that Diane Cusack either *"enjoyed it"* when he used the shock absorber to pleasure her, or she *"did a good job at faking it."* Does that mindset define him as an evil man?

How could it not?

And yet, despite his loathsome deeds, I worry about him. When we meet, I see a glimmer of goodness in his eyes. I hear genuine affection in his voice when we converse. When he tells me that he considers me to be his friend, I believe it—because the feeling is mutual. It is an enigma that deeply troubles me and while Christianity sheds little light on the dilemma, "The Teaching of Buddha" provides some enlightenment:

Buddha-nature is not something that comes to an end. Though wicked men should be born beasts or hungry demons, or fall into hell, they never lose their Buddha-nature.

However buried in the defilement of flesh or concealed at the root of worldly desires and forgotten it may be, the human affinity for Buddhahood is never completely extinguished.[44]

"I gave those girls a hard way to go," Bill wrote to me. *"My crimes are monsterous and cowardice. But what's done is done and I can't take it back. I told you you might not like*

me so much when this is over. And I don't think you'll ever look at me the same again. Sometimes ignorance is bliss."

At our visit on Sept. 11, I asked for clarification regarding the order of the murders: "Melanie Camilini was your first and Joyvaline Martinez was your last, right?"

"Right."

"Martinez was so beautiful. She looked like she could have been a model." I said this because I had often wondered how he could murder such a lovely creature. Martinez was the youngest and prettiest of his victims—although Camilini, "a Natalie Wood lookalike," ran a close second. He only nodded in response, his eyes devoid of emotion or remorse. Evidently, he was not moved by the young woman's beauty as I was.

The guard shouted, "Five more minutes!" and we said our goodbyes.

"Don't forget to take lots of pictures when you're in Hampton."

"I will," I promised.

"And spend a whole day at Busch Gardens. I know you don't like amusement parks, but Chris will enjoy the rides. Let the guy have a little fun after all he's been through with the chemo. He deserves it."

I smiled and said okay, although I had no intention of spending a day at Busch Gardens that weekend. Just driving along winding country roads on an empty stomach can make me queasy. The thought of jostling about on amusement park rides was therefore out of the question. Besides, the forecast predicted sunny skies and temperatures in the mid-80s. Any free time would be spent with a book at Buckroe Beach.

I left the prison, went out to my car and turned on my digital recorder to relay the details of Bill's initial confessions while they were still fresh in my memory (not that I would soon forget any of it). "It's September 11, 2017, and I just met with Bill ..." If you listen to that recording, there is a long silent gap of space where I am just breathing into the microphone. It takes a lot to render me speechless, but Bill had effectively done so. I tried to continue, but I could not. It felt like someone had just kicked me in the stomach. The digital recording would just have to wait.

A few days later, Chris and I boarded a plane for Bill's hometown. We visited his favorite haunts: the woods where he would party with his friends as a teenager, The Hampton Coliseum where he attended concerts, fast food franchises along Mercury Boulevard and the house where he grew up. When I approached Ashley Martin's house to see if he was around, my husband held me back. There was a sign in the front yard that said: "No trespassing, we have guns … and shovels."

"I don't feel right about you going there," Chris said.

I am glad that he held me back. I later found out that Ashley's father had died only days before. Knocking on his door could have ended very badly.

I repeatedly knocked on Aunt Ann's front door. I am sure she was inside her house, since there was a sporty little blue car with a handicap tag hanging from the rearview mirror and a bumper sticker that read "PRAY" parked in the driveway. The lights were out inside the house and the curtains were drawn.

Poor Aunt Ann had obviously learned to dodge reporters.

36.

*I know I will always be labeled as the monster that
committed these crimes. But I wasn't that monster
at heart. Those crimes may have been what I did,
but they weren't who I was. That kindhearted
guy is who I really was... I don't know how the
monster that committed those crimes got in.*

Letter from Bill, Nov. 2, 2017

Bill believes that the prosecution had "an ounce of
evidence" against him, but "a pound of it" was inaccurate,
largely backed by fabricated stories told by prison inmates
and the tall tales told by Jonathan Mills, including the claim
that Bill referred to himself as a Sick Ripper. According to
Bill, it was Mills who came up with that name. That said,
he readily admits that the ounce of evidence was enough to
convict him of the remaining six murders. Having reviewed
the mountain of legal discovery in Bill's case, I think his
analysis is in reverse. In fact, law enforcement had a pound
of evidence against him and only an ounce of it was false or
misconstrued—minor details that were not probative to the
case.

Among the errors contained in the prosecution's case is
the statement that Bill hid the van at Harry's house in North
Carolina to keep authorities from finding it. According to
Bill, the van was parked in Harry's driveway merely because
he was there for a visit. The condom in his van may have had
one victim's DNA on it, but it did not have *his* DNA. There
was not blood *all over* the interior of the van, he also claims.
He points out that one report states that a Luminal test done

on the floors, walls and ceiling detected no blood. Maybe so, but there was blood on the backbench of his van and likely in other places—enough to prove through forensic analysis that six of seven people died in the vehicle. At the end of the day, do the discrepancies really matter?

The prosecutor, Brian Preleski, read in his statement of facts at the guilty plea hearing that Mills had drawn a "detailed" map of the burial site behind the mall and it lined up with what law enforcement went on to discover. Bill wrote that this is *"literally"* the *"detailed"* map:

SHOPPING CENTER

___

___2.

___4.

___1.   ___5. ___6.

___3.

___7.

The order of the victims in this diagram:
1. Melanie Camilini, 2. Marilyn Gonzalez,
3. Danny Whistnant, 4. Nilsa Arizmendi,
5. Mary Jane Menard, 6. Diane Cusack,
7. Joyvaline Martinez

Bill buried all of the bodies in shallow graves spread over about three quarters of an acre in the swampy forest behind the mall. He placed six of the seven in sets of two, placed a few feet from one another. He states that he did not dismember them. Animals must have done that. In the box of legal discovery that he gave me, there are hundreds of photos of items found in his van, along with photos of the burial site and bones that were found. One photo is especially disturbing; the skeleton remains intact. It lays face down in the shallow grave. Another photo depicts the cracked skull of Nilsa Arizmendi. There are also a few photos of the heavy wrench that he used to threaten his victims and the shock absorber that he used to rape Diane Cusack.

I was asked in a recent radio interview if Bill's sexual deviancy was evidenced in his romantic relationships. I replied that Bill had a boatload of sex, but it wasn't particularly weird. *"As violent as my crimes were,"* he wrote to me, *"it was never like that outside of the times I was committing my crimes. I was never overly sexually aggressive with any girlfriends or anything like that. I loved sex and could go and go and go, but there were never any violent overtones to it. In fact it could often be just the opposite. I enjoyed a lot of kissing, caressing and foreplay. I've had some girlfriends that let me tie them up but I'd tied their wrists loosly to the bedposts or headboard and blindfold them and then tickle and tease their bodies with feathers or ice-cubes. I never tied them so tightly that they couldn't get themselves undone if they wanted and there were never any violent overtones to it."*

In a letter from February 2018, he indicated that raping his victims for 12-hour time periods left him sexually *"empty"* and therefore resulted in greater stamina when he had sex with Dori. He could *"go for hours"* with Dori *"and she had no idea what motivated it."* During his nine-month killing spree, he and Dori sometimes had sex in the back of his van. He suggested that I write about the situation as follows:

As her orgasm spasamed through her body, she had no idea the number of prostitutes that had turned their tricks on that same seat she was now receiving her orgasm on... some of those prostitutes had even died there. But Howell did, and he thought of them as he watched his girlfriend enjoy her orgasm. But unlike some of the others, she was never in danger. After all, one of Howell's golden rules to being a 'serial killer' was to 'never kill someone you know.'

"I spoke with a clinical psychologist about the motive behind your crimes," I told him in a visit. "He asked about your mother. I said that you did not feel anger towards her. She was not affectionate with you, but she provided you with a stable home and what happened in the back of your van had nothing to do with her. He said that you were lying. He said that the rapes and murders had *everything* to do with your mother."

"I hate all that psychological bullshit," his voice trembled with contempt. "It had nothing to do with her. Nothing."

After accepting the sentence of 360 years in prison, I asked Bill how he felt about never being able to have sex with a woman again. His eyes filled with tears. "I think about that sometimes. It's not just about sex, though. It's the thought that I will never have someone to hold, to hug and sit with on the couch. It is more about the affection, you know? That is what I will miss the most."

*

Following the guilty plea hearing, one of Nilsa Arizmendi's daughters reached out to me and asked for details regarding how her mother died. Was it by blunt force trauma to the head? She saw the crime photo depicting a skull that was almost split in two. It was with a heavy heart that I responded to her via email with the details of her mother's last hours on Earth.

Bill told me that the hit with the wrench should not have caused the amount of injury to the skull that he later saw in police photos. He thinks that the deep crack was the result of heavy equipment being brought to the burial ground to dig up the bones.

Remarkably, Nilsa's daughter, now the same age as Nilsa when she died, thanked me for the information and shared it with her sister. However horrendous the news, it provided some kind of closure in the healing process. Sometimes wondering the worst is more painful than actually knowing it.

In a phone call on Oct. 16, 2017, Bill reflected further on the murder of Nilsa Arizmendi:

"She was the only one you knew," I said. "And Ace saw you drive off with her in the van. If you didn't kill her, you probably would have gotten away with it for another couple of years …"

"Yeah. But do you know what? There is stupid shit that I could have done and not been caught. When the cops came to Dori's looking for the van, I knew then what was going on and I shoulda just destroyed the fricking van, you know what I mean? I had the opportunity and I didn't. I mean, when I went to Carolina, I did go because I already had previous plans and everything. I wasn't running, but I did have the heads up that the cops were looking for the van and I could put two and two together. I knew the story that they told Dori was bullshit, that I had no stolen lawn equipment, and if I woulda went down and gutted the inside of the van, you know what I mean, I would probably have gotten away. And why on Earth did I return to the Stop & Shop parking lot with the van after the murder when I knew that would be where the police would look for it? I had opportunities to do things and not get caught and I didn't do them so I don't know if that is something on a subconscious level or just due to laziness or what?"

"Do you think there was any part of you that wanted to get caught so you would stop doing it?"

"Not that I am aware of, that's why I say something on a subconscious level. I didn't do it on a conscious level."

In his book "Dark Dreams," FBI profiler Roy Hazelwood writes, "I don't believe any aberrant offender wants to be caught, even subconsciously … Some offenders have told me that they were scared by their violent fantasies and behavior, but I have never met an offender who said that he wanted to be caught." Bill has told me that if he were not caught, "there would probably be more victims," so the crimes obviously did not bother him that much. Honestly, I don't think the crimes themselves bother him to this day. Although remorseful about what he has put the victims families through—he states, "I would hear them sobbing in the courtroom and it just tore me apart."—I maintain that he feels completely no distress regarding the pain he brought to his victims in their final hours, or the strangulations. I hear nothing in his tone of voice that indicates otherwise, when we discuss them.

Still perplexed with the question of *why* he felt compelled to repeatedly rape drug-addicted prostitutes and strangle them to conceal the crimes, I asked Bill in late December of 2017 how he felt about the rough draft of Part One of my manuscript, which I had mailed to him for his review. "I feel like you psychoanalyze shit and you come to the wrong conclusions," he said.

"Well, I'm working on it, Bill. I really am. I am trying to understand. I am rewriting and changing things in the book even now. You are right that some of the earlier conclusions that I came to were wrong, but keep in mind, when I wrote that stuff you had not even admitted to the killings. It's a work in progress. I am changing and modifying conclusions as you give me more details. The big problem for me is that I still don't understand why you did those awful things because I don't think *you* understand why."

"Exactly!" he exclaimed. "So how can you understand why when I don't even understand why? I don't even get it myself!"

"True, but what I don't like about that way of thinking is it makes you seem like the victim of some kind of mysterious force beyond your control. You once told me that you were 'a good guy with a bad habit.' Raping and killing other human beings, that's a little more than a bad habit. It diminishes the evil of what took place. It lessens your responsibility in destroying so many people's lives. So I don't want to paint you as a victim at the mercy of a force that you don't understand."

"I am not a victim, Anne. I take full responsibility for what I did. All I can say for sure is this—I crossed the line one night and after that, it was *on.* Once I crossed that line, there was no going back. Use your creative liberties with what you write. I might not agree with it, but it is what it is."

To this day, when people ask me why Bill did what he did, I respond with the obvious answers: power, rage, sexual addiction, and sexual sadism possibly stemming from a brain defect that presented at the moment of conception. But the truth of the matter is that I have no definitive answers. And neither does he.

"When you strangled them," I asked, "did you feel the spirit go out of their bodies? I've read that some killers actually sense when the life force departs."

"No. It's not like how you see it in the movies, Anne. When I strangled them I'd do it quickly. I looked them all in the eye except for Camilini. I couldn't bear to look at what I was doing. The rest of them were different. I guess I felt that if I were man enough to kill them, I should be man enough to look them in the eye while I did it." He described squeezing his victims' necks as hard as he could in order to cut off their air supply and the blood supply to their brains "*thereby making them lose consciousness even quicker.*" He could tell when they lost consciousness because "*their eyes would lose focus. This usually happened pretty quickly, usually in a minute or less. After that, the kicking and struggling would stop and it was just a matter of keeping the pressure on until their heart stopped.*" Bill would put his head on his victims' chests and listen for a heartbeat or "*pinch their nose closed and cover their mouth to make sure that they were not still breathing.*" When he finally stopped choking them, "*they'd take a big breath in,*" but he states that it was "*just post-mortem reflex.*"

After reading the entire manuscript, Bill voiced his deep disappointment in me: "*Another thing that bothers me is that after reading through your manuscript, the feeling of how I am just a 'subject' to you… something to be analized and studied. But on my part, all I sought from you was friendship.*

You are definitely 'TWO Faced.' But you seem to play them both well. Or maybe you are just good at telling naïve people what they want to hear. And I think that 'Naïve' part relates to both me and your readers. You have me thinking you're a friend. And have your readers thinking you're some genius that has me fooled into giving you the goods and little do they know that the shit you're printing is made up fairy tales and regurgitated lies."

Despite his disapproval over the contents of the book, he was, and always is, quick to forgive me: *"Anyway, I guess that's enough venting for now. I still Luv ya and hope we are still friends (if you ever considered me one to begin with.)"*

In a follow-up phone call, I told Bill how I honestly feel about our relationship. In the early days, I did think of it as a ruse. I was trying to get a serial killer suspect to open up and trust me so I could explore the dark recesses of his mind. I was cocky and inexperienced, and I attempted to maintain a position of emotional detachment from him and his crimes. Over time, that changed. I got to know a complicated man— one capable of kindness and love and also possessed by inner demons that rose to the surface during a nine-month raping and killing spree that inflicted widespread destruction on the lives of so many.

The mixed feelings that I now have for him leave me in a state of conflict. I have spoken with some family members of the victims. I have listened to them cry. I have wept myself. Simultaneously, I have experienced sorrow for the man responsible for their pain, coupled with outrage at his despicable acts. There are no easy answers other than to say that I cannot relegate Bill to the role of a monster and only a monster. He is a mentally sick human being who I have come to know, care about and genuinely like. And I feel terribly guilty over feeling that way about him.

37.

"Fantasy: the faculty or activity of imagining things,
especially things that are impossible or improbable."

Dictionary

We all entertain fantasies. Why? Because they bring us
pleasure. The brain of a child gazing at the wrapped presents
under the tree in the weeks leading up to Christmas is fired
up with endorphins. Knowing that the fantasy will become a
reality on Christmas morning is almost too much to bear. That
is why children rarely sleep well on Christmas Eve. Their
eyes are wide open at the crack of dawn as adrenaline surges
through their veins. The more impossible or improbable the
gift, like the dangerous Red Ryder Carbine Action 200-shot
Range Model air rifle that will "shoot out Ralphie's eye" in
the film "A Christmas Story," the better the rush.

That was Bill's mindset before picking up his female
victims. He had been fantasizing about raping prostitutes
for years. One day in early February of 2003, he decided
that mere fantasy was not enough. He went to a hardware
store and walked the aisle, looking for items required in
the commission of the crime: ropes, zip ties, duct tape, a
hammer.

"I liked this sick fantasy I had and I wanted to make
it real. It was more like trying to build up the courage to
actually do it as opposed to trying to fight some urge 'not' to
do it. I had to talk myself 'into it' as opposed to trying to talk
*myself 'out of it.' So I didn't **need** to act on it. More like I had*
*finally talked myself into finally **deciding** to do it. And I knew*
that when I crossed that line, my life would change forever.

My fantasy wasn't to just do one. And I knew that when or if I ever crossed that line, that whoever that first one was would just be the first of many."

"So you knew you were going to finally act out the fantasy and rape a prostitute. But did you realize that you would kill her, too?" I asked.

"Yes," he answered. "I knew that I would have to kill her after the rapes."

"How did you feel when you were buying those things?"

"I was nervous, excited—scared!"

I recently met with detectives to discuss Bill's confessions. They wondered if Bill had an accomplice, reasoning that some of his victims were strong and could have successfully evaded strangulation unless two or more perpetrators were present. I rejected the proposition. Bill's crimes were the result of his rich and twisted fantasies. No one else shared his thoughts. That he managed to physically overcome his victims suggests, to me, that he was empowered, perhaps inhumanly so, by a combination of determination and fear at the time of the attacks. He also tells me that he was in good shape back in 2003, walking about one mile a day in his lawn care job, and he had developed a decent level of upper-body strength from pushing mowers and landscaping. Also, all of his victims were caught off guard. Danny Whistnant, for example, was punched several times before Bill pinned him to the floor of his van to finish him off.

All of the victims were murdered in the back of Bill's van. He states that he picked up his first victim, Melanie Camilini, in the area of Grove Street in Waterbury on the first Saturday night of February 2003 between 1 and 2 a.m., after leaving the Cadillac Ranch in Southington. He offered her $20 for oral sex and she agreed. He drove her to the parking lot of a McDonald's in Waterbury to complete the transaction. When it was over, he grabbed her by the throat with his left hand and forced her down onto the backbench while simultaneously grabbing a hammer out of his tool bucket.

He writes that he *"put her hands together like she was praying"* and held her down with his knee as he duct-taped her hands together and tied a plastic grocery bag over them. He told her, *"If I hear that bag rattling like you're trying to free your hands, I will pull over and beat the shit out of you."* He also duct-taped her ankles together and sealed her mouth shut with the tape. He *"did not feel safe"* in their current location, and so he drove to the parking lot of the Benco roofing company in Torrington with Melanie bound to the bench *"so she would not try to jump out of the van at stop signs."* He knew that the Benco lot would be a good spot where they *"would not be bothered by nosy cops. It was off the street a ways, and they'd be closed with no one around on Sunday."* Of course, the location was also familiar to him because it used to be where he worked and parked his van to sleep for the night.

With Camilini in his van, however, Bill had no intention of laying down to rest. He raped her in that parking lot, off and on, for the duration of the night and did not stop until 2 o'clock the following afternoon. Although I am possession of many letters detailing the gruesome ways in which he raped each of his six female victims—the obscenities that he shouted at them, the lewd acts that he carried out just to reinforce his hateful perception that they had no human worth, I don't see the point of barraging the reader with that information. Suffice it to say that the women that Bill raped suffered unimaginable horrors in their final hours on this Earth, and watching them suffer gave Bill tremendous satisfaction. When he said at his guilty plea and sentencing hearing that he deserves death for the atrocities that he carried out, he was 100 percent correct.

He left the Benco parking lot in the afternoon and drove Camilini out to Little Woodstock, the section of a state forest in Torrington where he used to party around a bonfire with his friends from the Big Y grocery store. He raped the young mother one last time and then strangled her in that location.

"Did you sleep with her corpse because it was so cold out? Mills had said that. Is that true?"

"Yes. Yes. I was gonna bury her out in the woods, but the ground was frozen, I couldn't dig a hole so I kinda was freaking out, you know what I mean? Because I got this dead prostitute in my van and I didn't know what I was gonna do. I went to leave and I got stuck in the snow in Little Woodstock. I was like, freaking out because I got this dead prostitute in the van and I'm stuck in the snow so all I need is a park ranger to come by ... So I'm freaking out. I ended up wrapping her in a tarp and I put her behind the seat, and that's where all the blood came from because I had hit her in the side of the head with the hammer and for a week and a half, maybe a couple of weeks, I was driving around with this dead body in my van not knowing how I was going to dispose of it. She bled out during those two weeks post mortem. That's where the large bloodstain came from. That's also what conflicts with what Preleski had to say because he said that the large bloodstain came from Gonzalez, but that's not true. It came from Camilini."

"If the ground was too frozen to bury Camilini at Little Woodstock, how did you manage to dig a hole in the frozen earth behind the strip mall?" I asked.

Bill explained that he did not bury Camilini that winter. Instead, he rolled her bagged body down the embankment behind the strip mall and hid it inside a barrel that was lying in a pile of discarded waste. There were some wooden palates in that pile and he placed them over the barrel containing Camilini's body. He later wrote to me: "*In the old News 8 footage you can see the barrel in the woods that I originally used to conceal Camilini's body in.*"

Then he left for North Carolina to stay with Harry for the rest of the winter. When the grass started growing in April, he drove back to Connecticut for his lawn care business and returned to the site where he hid Camilini. Her body had not decomposed, he said. It looked exactly the same as when he had left it months earlier.

"If you look back and study the weather reports, you'll see we had the coldest winter on record. We went something like 60 days without it ever getting above freezing temperatures. When I left, there was like, two or three feet of snow on the ground that had been there for two or three months, so it was still pretty cold out for April and the sun couldn't get through the tree branches, so it had been like she was in rigor mortis."

"Huh," I said. "That must have been quite a surprise to you."

"Well, I was kinda glad of it," he laughed. "Know what I mean?"

"Not really," I thought.

The detectives I spoke with also wondered if Bill had more victims before Camilini. That is entirely possible. However, his description of her murder and the events leading up to it and afterward indicates to me that she was, in fact, his first. There is an air of authenticity to his story, although I am the first to admit that I may have been duped. If Bill does have more victims, then I think that the crimes took place within that nine-month killing spree in 2003, when the game "*was on*" and he had nothing left to lose, or in the months that followed his release from prison in late July of 2004 until his arrest for the Arizmendi murder in May 2005. During almost all of that time he was living in North Carolina and frequently visited Martin in Hampton, Va. Additionally, since he told Mills that there were four bodies that had yet to be recovered from "his garden" behind the strip mall, any other victims would likely be buried in different wooded locations.

"What about the used condom that police found in the van?" I asked. "Did that have your DNA on it?"

"I don't know where that condom came from. I used a condom the first couple of times I raped Camilini, but I think I got rid of it. They did an extensive search of the van in 2004 and there is a nine-page inventory of everything in that box of legal discovery I gave you of what they found in the van and there was no used condom back in 2004 when they did the first search. So then they go back and do another search 10 years later and they find a used condom? I don't know where that came from."

I asked Bill if he killed all of his victims by strangulation and whether it ended quickly. His answer was chilling. "Yeah. They were all strangled. I didn't want them to suffer, you know what I mean? I was not out to make them suffer. I tried to calm them. I told them that as long as you do what I want you to do, then you won't get hurt. I tried to keep them calm."

He didn't want them to suffer? Are you kidding me? And so much for the promise not to further harm them if they just did what he instructed. Nonetheless, I see that Bill was trying to clarify that he was not what profilers calls an "erotic aggressive" rapist and killer. The most rare of rapists, accounting for only 10 percent, erotic aggressors employ sadistic ritualism with objects such as broken beer bottles or knives to prolong the victim's suffering. In Bill's case, the rapes—though terribly vicious—were purportedly straightforward, except for that of Diane Cusack, which involved a shock absorber and which, he states, unbelievably, did not seem to bother her. He says that he saw the shock absorber as *"a kind of sex toy."* "It wasn't that big," he said.

Well, it looked pretty big to me when I saw the photograph.

"Though I raped these prostitutes (except for the tranny) I didn't do anything I consider really 'sadistic' (by sadistic standards anyway... I know you're thinking how could what I did not be sadistic. I'm just saying I didn't go to extremes to torture or cause them pain)."

While Bill may not have used knives or broken bottles, he did go to the extreme in terms of the level of physical aggression that he channeled when raping his victims and their torment brought him intense satisfaction.[45] He enjoyed their humiliation. More importantly, in terms of psychic abuse, he did something to all of his female victims that far surpassed physical sadism, in my opinion. He cut into their souls with the violent words that he spoke. Calling them nasty names, he asked how many johns they had been with that day, whether they had ever engaged in sodomy before now and then he asked the unspeakable—if they had ever been sexually molested in their youth. In requesting the details of their childhood traumas, he sought to reenact and thereby reinforce his victims' darkest nightmares in real time. He wanted to pile on the trauma. The greater their emotional pain, the better.

That is the face of pure evil.

And when his victims mentioned their family members, no doubt trying to appeal to his sense of decency as a way of preventing further rapes and the possibility of being killed, he simply told them to "Shut the fuck up." They were not allowed to be human. "Otherwise," he told me, "I would not be able to kill them off when I was finished raping them."

I have no doubt that Bill's brain was fired up with electricity as he carried out his sadistic acts. While little is known about the neural mechanisms underlying sexual sadism, a 2012 study found in the Archives of General Psychiatry, in which sexual sadists and non-sadists viewed social scenes depicting a person in pain, indicates that sexual sadists, relative to non-sadists, showed increased responses in brain regions associated with sexual arousal (amygdala, hypothalamus, ventral striatum).[46]

Marilyn Gonzalez was Bill's second victim. In her obituary, she is described as "Always happy and always smiling." Bill picked her up in the Grove Street area of Waterbury in May of 2003 at 2 o'clock in the morning.

Following the completion of the transaction that he paid for at a nearby McDonald's parking lot, he "snatched her up" in the same way that he did with Camilini, bound her to the back bench and drove her to either the Motel 6 or the Motel 8 parking lot (he forgets the number) off Exit 25. He parked the van in a secluded spot where 18-wheelers would park for the night and raped her for several hours. He left the following morning and drove to a Motel 6 parking lot in Southington where he raped her there throughout the day. At around 3 p.m., he drove to the McDonald's parking beside the strip mall in New Britain and raped her twice before strangling her.

He told me that he could not keep reaching a climax due to the number of rapes in such a short space of time, but he *"would go and go and go without getting his rocks off"* and he would *"just have to stop and take a break for a while before going again."*

A man has to eat. In between raping his victims, Bill drove to the drive thrus of his favorite fast food restaurants and ordered meals: "I'd go through the Micky D's drive thru with a half-naked, tied-up prostitute in the back and told them if they made a sound, it would be their last. None of them did."

He turned up the music on the radio in the event that his captive tried to scream or call for help from the backbench of his van. Approaching the drive thru, he asked each female victim if they wanted anything to eat and ordered what they wanted, as if on some type of macabre date. It would be his victim's last meal.

"How could they possibly eat?" I asked. "Their stomachs must have been in knots."

"I don't know, Anne," he flatly replied, "But they always ate."

"And as they ate, you would talk to them about sex?"

"Yeah, sometimes."

"That must have been a head trip for them to get raped and then have you drive them around for the rest of the day, buying them food and talking dirty to them, knowing that they are going to get raped again. They must have been freaking out through it all. Shaking and crying ..."

"No. They were calm as we drove around."

"How can that be, Bill? They had just been raped and they knew another rape was coming soon. They must have been terrified."

"Anne," he patiently explained, "You need to understand that these women had been on the streets for years. I'm sure it was not their first bad experience getting raped by a john. They were probably used to it."[47]

At this point in the recorded phone call, there is a long pause in which I am silently trying to digest Bill's complete absence of insight. In turn, he has told me many times over that his observations of his victims' emotionless reactions to the rapes is accurate, thus implying that I just don't get the warped mentality, the hardness of character, of the women that he raped.

"What were you feeling as you raped them? Rage? Power? Hate?"

"Yes," he replied. "I called them bad names. Put them down. I wanted to humiliate them."

"Did it have to do with all that rage you felt about Mandy and losing your kids, never having a driver's license—all those wasted years spent in prison?"

"Yeah. You know, I think it did."

Again, this confirmed that Bill was a "retaliatory" rapist: infuriated at a woman from his past who he perceived as bringing about a grave and irreversible injustice in his world.

"Mandy took my kids away from me!" he blurted out during one prison visit. "She had my balls over a barrel. She knew that the fight between me and Seth at the 7-Eleven was going to violate my parole and put me back in jail to finish serving the 4½ years of the six that I was on parole for. If I showed my face at her door, she would have called the cops. Had I filed for visitation, I'd go to jail as soon as I walked in the courthouse. She had me by the balls when she grabbed my kids up and moved out of state. Who knows what she has told them about me over the years? Last time I saw my daughter she was just a baby—maybe around 2 years old. But my son, we were really close, you know? I'd stop by after work and we'd go bike riding, or I'd take him to the playground at McDonald's just up the street. A couple times, I took him horseback riding to a place that rented horses for guided rides. That all lasted for about eight months. My son probably hated me for abandoning him. But I didn't. That's the last thing I would do. "

Perhaps the most disconcerting part of the puzzle is figuring out how a man's hatred for the mother of his children translates into taking it out on drug-addicted prostitutes and finding vindication in the act. Alas, we are talking about the workings of an aberrant mind:

"I think that for me that it was the power and sexual control that invigorated me and caused me to repeat these crimes and I don't think I would have stopped until I was caught. And if it weren't for a couple simple mistakes, I may had never been caught ... at least not for years ..."

"After you killed Marilyn Gonzalez, you buried her behind the mall?"

"Right. What I would do is I would pull up behind the strip mall and slide the van door open and I would throw them over the guardrail and they would kinda like roll down the hill and then I would leave and come back the next day. I would park in the McDonald's parking lot and then I'd walk through the little cut-through that leads you to right behind the shopping center. It comes out where there's a Monroe Muffler Shop, facing the Arthur Miller dance studio. I'd go down into the embankment to get the body and I'd come up and drag them into the woods, about a hundred yards from the parking lot."

"Did you do it in the light of day?"

"Yeah. Either first thing in the morning or later in the evening before the sun went down. I had to see to bury their bodies."

Bill states that during the nine-month killing spree, he behaved normally during the day. No one, including Dori, would have known that anything unusual was going on. But he sensed in advance when he would rape and kill that night. It was largely based on his lawn-mowing schedule. If he had no customers the next day, then he knew that he would have the opportunity to rape all night and drive around the next day, raping some more. During that time period, he continued to solicit prostitutes for blowjobs and he claims that they left his van unharmed, only because he had work to do the next day. In contrast, when Melanie Camilini, Marilyn Gonzalez, Mary Jane Menard, Diane Cusack and Joyvaline Martinez stepped into his van, he knew that he would rape them for the duration of the night and the next day and ultimately strangle them. They were walking into a death chamber.

This helps me to understand the disparity in the respective ages and appearance of Bill's victims. As opposed to a killer like Ted Bundy, Bill's target group had nothing to do with shared traits like age or the length and color of their hair. Rather, it was solely based on their being drug-addicted prostitutes and the fact that Bill did not have to work the next day. In one letter, he enclosed a page from a logbook that he kept to document his lawn care schedule in the month of May 2003. On average, he was mowing about five lawns per day and was paid $15 to $25 dollars for each job. On Saturday, May 17, 2003, he mowed four lawns and his schedule was free on the Sunday that followed. Next to the date he wrote "Funeral." He wrote to me in the letter that accompanied the page from his logbook: "*May 17 is a night I picked up one of my victims. I'm guessing this would have been Gonzalez, as I don't think I came back to CT until mid to late April. If I had copies of my complete log book I could tell you all the dates. I only have copies of May and ½ of July."*

"Did you say to Mills that there was a monster inside of you?"

"Yes," he said. "Because there was a monster inside of me."

38.

He discovers expanded areas and situations where he can practice his domination and control of others. And he learns from his own experience, perfecting his technique to avoid detection or punishment. He learns how to become a success at what he does. The more success and satisfaction he has, the tighter the feedback loop becomes.

"The Anatomy of Motive" by John Douglas and Mark Olshaker

Toward the end of a recent prison visit, Bill stood up and said into the phone, "Looking back on my life, all I did was fail."

"Everything you touched turned to shit?" I asked.

He sadly laughed. "Yeah. I was a success at being a failure."

Not with everything. Managing to kill seven people in nine months and getting away with most of the killings for many years was no small feat. When it came to plotting the rapes and murders in his mind, finding discreet locations where he could act out his sick fantasies in private and timing the discarding of the evidence followed by undetected burials, Bill was a mastermind. Without a doubt, the power and control that he derived from successfully carrying out the rapes and murders bolstered his fragile ego, if only for short periods of time.

But he is right when he states that the life that he led building up to the killing spree was nothing but a series of endless failures. He drank more alcohol before the age of 20 than he did in all the years that followed. He started drinking at age 12. By the time he was 16, he sometimes drank in the mornings with other students before going to school. One time, he drank a half a fifth of Wild Turkey and in first period math class, the teacher took him aside and handed him some mints. "Put these in your mouth," she advised. "Your breath smells like alcohol."

He held a valid driver's license for only 1½ years. He reports drinking a case of beer, which was not unusual for him to do, and taking a sharp corner on Todd's Road in Hampton too fast. The car plowed down a few of the yellow signs with arrows that traced the edge of the curve. When he saw the telephone pole ahead, he took his foot off the brake and *"gunned the gas"* in order to go through the pole. He thought doing so was his best chance at survival. The car sliced the pole in half *"like a pencil stick."* The police came to the scene of the crash and took Bill back to the station. They phoned his father. John Howell was recovering from quadruple bypass surgery and was unable to go pick up his wayward son, so a police officer drove the battered teenager back to the house. Charged with DUI, Bill lost his license—a punishment that would have lifelong repercussions.

"Do you know how many years I've served time just for driving without a license? The combination of heavy drinking and not having a license ruined my life and I am not talking about just the jail time. I had no job prospects. I could have been a machinist like my friend Paul. He has a good life, makes decent money. He has a nice house and all his boy toys—motorcycles and boats …"

When he woke up in the morning after the accident, he felt like he had been *"banged up in a football game."* His father said to him, "You need to stop the drinking. Nothing good can come of it."

Bill shared both of these memories with me in the midst of some gruesome confessions, when my mind was immersed in images of him raping and strangling his victims. Whenever he discussed his father in letters or visits, he affectionately referred to him as "*Pops*." The boy who grieved his dying mother, who self-medicated his way through a painful adolescence and quickly developed a serious drinking problem, had turned into a serial rapist and killer whose voice still quivered with sentiment when talking about his deceased father. Why had no one intervened to help him before things got out of hand? This, of course, begs the question: could anyone have helped Bill and prevented the ultimate creation of a serial killer requiring lockup for 360 years?

"I believe he was born a monster," Nilsa Arizmendi's daughter told me in a phone call. "It has to do with his brain. There's something wrong with it. He was born that way."

I think Nilsa's daughter hit the nail on the head. Ultimately, the savage rapes were about so much more than Mandy, or Bill's history of powerlessness, alcohol abuse and personal failure. Paraphilias are defined as "recurrent and intrusive sexual impulses involving one or more forms of sexually deviant behavior." According to one source, "the etiological mechanisms of paraphilias are not well understood. Case studies have reported associations with brain injury and neurobiological abnormalities."[48] In Bill's case, I, too, believe that those neurological abnormalities presented at a young age, perhaps at birth. His sexual sadism in situations with prostitutes was no doubt fueled by different sociological factors, but they merely fueled the flame. They cannot be associated with the flame itself, which exists in Bill's brain.

Moreover, I think that Bill's psychopathic response to the profound suffering of his victims—that he was not only immune to feeling their pain, he found it sexually arousing—is narrowly isolated to that target group of human beings. Show him images of an animal being abused or a friend being knocked down in a home invasion, and he will experience empathy and distress.

Sitting across from him at a prison visit in January 2018, I stated: "If I showed you a video of a prostitute being brutally raped, it would probably turn you on, and you wouldn't feel any empathy."

"Well the first part is true. But I don't know, I think I might feel empathy. I don't know …"

I shook my head. "No you wouldn't—you can't get sexually aroused by violence and feel empathy at the same time. The two feelings can't coexist."

He rolled his eyes. "You overanalyze shit, Anne. By the way, I read most of the manuscript you sent me. I *hate* your book."

"But you don't hate me."

"No," he smiled. "I'm your pet monster, aren't I?"

"Something like that …"

Though Bill says I "*overanalyze shit,*" he acknowledges that sometimes my relentless probing of his mind results in some personal revelations as to why he did what he did. For example, he wrote to me: "*You are the first person I've ever really talked to about all the shit I've gone through and how it made me feel. I've never talked about my feelings to anyone or how angry, hurt and helpless I felt over things. I just kept all that shit bottled up inside. I hated Mandy for taking my kids from me and I think that somehow manifested itself into these feelings and thoughts I had of raping prostitutes. I just wanted to punish someone for how I was feeling and if I couldn't get the right ones, I'd get someone so why not a prostitute who put herself in harms way anyway? I could rape and punish her for being a prostitute while punishing her for my own feelings. I could let my anger and hate out through the rape of these prostitutes in some sort of way of trying to make myself feel better or get the rage out.*

"*I don't know, I'm no psychiatrist, but I think it is all somehow connected. I never had that anger or hate inside of me until after Mandy stole my kids from me.*

"Anyway, whatever the reasons, it doesn't give me the right to do what I did and I deserve the death penalty for the crimes I've committed. Although justice will probably be better served with these life sentences as unless I suicide out at some point, I will die a slow and painful death—probably one foot or leg at a time."[49]

While Bill expresses little, if any, remorse over killing his victims, he does feel great remorse over making the family members suffer. Again, the inconsistency is part of a distorted worldview. Some people are good and do not deserve punishment; others are objects whose existence has no value. No amount of persuasion on my part can change his mind about it.

After killing Daniel Whistnant in June of 2003, followed by Nilsa Arizmendi in late July, Bill killed his fifth victim, Mary Jane Menard, in late September or early October of 2003. While Bill may have felt in control of his desire to rape and kill, the fact that his last three victims died in the space of 10 weeks indicates that he was losing control. The monster was taking over.

He picked Mary Jane up in Waterbury, drove to the nearby McDonald's to engage in the $30 transaction, and then restrained her and drove to the Super 8 Motel in Waterbury, where he raped her throughout the night beneath the glow of the 52-foot color-changing cross that overlooks the city from the site of the former Holy Land theme park. In the morning, he drove to the Motel 6 in Southington and raped her into the afternoon. Mary Jane took her final breaths in that Motel 6 parking lot.[50]

The life and death of Mary Jane Menard tragically epitomizes the face of the opioid crisis that is ravaging our nation. The photo in her obituary depicts an ebullient woman with a winning smile. She appears as a friendly individual who anyone would want as a mother, daughter, sister or friend. Indeed, she was a great mother, daughter, sister and friend to many. She attended Central Connecticut

State University and Tunxis Community College. According to her obituary notice: "She achieved and overcame many obstacles and was admired for her hard work and dedication. She was very active in the community and loved by all. She was a substance abuse counselor who truly loved and helped others. We will always remember her for her strength, courage and personality. She loved to sing and brightened any room with her smile. MJ was a diehard Patriots and Red Sox fan. She loved her baking, burning candles, singing and her family. She will be remembered in our hearts, in our laughs and in our songs."

Bill has stated that the victims' families will forever portray them as "angels" and such depictions are incorrect, at least with respect to the status of his victims when he picked them up. He is wrong about that. Mary Jane's daughter, Tiffany, now 33 years old, has provided me with a complete picture of the complexity of her mother's character and her struggles over the years. Mary Jane was no angel, according to her daughter, but she most certainly possessed angelic traits. In full remission from alcohol abuse for more than a decade, Mary Jane volunteered at Someplace Special, a facility that helps people with AIDS. When Tiffany was 15 years old, her mother met Sammy, a client at Someplace Special. Always one to reach out to the underdog, Mary Jane fell in love with Sammy. Regrettably, Sammy not only had AIDS—he was also a heroin addict.

At 16, Tiffany entered Job Corps, a no-cost education and career technical training program administered by the U.S. Department of Labor. Being away from the family home and living in a Job Corps residence in New Haven served as a necessary escape for a teenager whose mother had started using drugs. The letter that she wrote to me honestly conveys the way that a mother's substance abuse can devastate her children:

I know when she wasn't using she was a stand up person and would not take anything from anyone. I heard that she was prostituting after that. But I'm sure her heroin addiction caused all of it. Heroin is the devil. I was in Job Corps at 16, got my GED, and joined the army at 17. So I guess I didn't have to deal with the home front. Sammy was the love of her life. My brother and I wanted to kill him because we knew he was an addict and AIDS positive and we didn't approve. He was questioned so much when my mom disappeared. He later committed suicide. And now, all these years later, we feel bad because we blamed him. He hung himself over his sorrow over losing my mom. For 13 years I resented my mother. I hated her so much. I would say that if I ever saw her again I would punch her in the face. Because I thought she chose drugs over life. And our love. I thought she overdosed in an abandoned building and that's what caused her death. Now I feel horrible for hating her so much because she didn't choose this, she was a victim. I hope she thought of her children and everyone she loved as she took her last breath. It pains me to know how much she suffered and all this time I blamed her.

I wrote back, "Your mother is in Heaven wrapping her arms around you every day. There is no resentment in Heaven, only forgiveness and love. She is there now, feeling only love for you and your brother."

Tiffany replied, "I know for sure she is in Heaven and smiling looking down."

Tiffany and her brother share the same sense of guilt that the family of Daniel Whistnant feels about blaming the wrong person as the culprit in their loved one's death. At Bill's sentencing hearing, Whistnant's sister described a soft-spoken, easy going and free-spirited brother who took pride in his appearance. When he went missing, the family hoped it was just another incident where Danny had "fallen off the grid." He had done it once before and was later found by the family living in Plainville, Conn. They held out hope in April 2015, when the state's attorney publicly announced that the remains behind the strip mall belonged to women.

The night before finding out that Danny was included in the newest group of victims, his sister had a suspicion that Danny was included in the group of victims found behind the mall. She phoned her mother on May 12, 2015, to inform her, "They found Danny."

According to Whistnant's sister, her mother was sitting in a recliner, trying to be stoic, adhering to the adage that "God will not put on you more than you can bear." Danny was the fourth son that she would have to bury. Whenever his sister drove by the strip mall after that, she "felt horrible" knowing that for so many years, her brother was "close by, exposed to the elements." Danny's best friend, Larry, had been a suspect for many years based on a false accusation given to the police. "To Larry," Whistnant's sister said at the sentencing hearing, her voice choked with emotion, "please forgive us for suspecting you. Let these words resonate in your soul, linger in your brain, each and every day of your life."

Tiffany Menard later told me, "That broke me when the Whistnant family said that about Larry in court. I felt exactly how she felt and I feel like I should have stated that in my statement. Sammy was another person that Howell killed."

Likewise, the daughter of Nilsa Arizmendi has expressed to me her remorse over thinking that Ace Sanchez was directly involved in her mother's disappearance. The family feels bad about it to this day.

When Mary Jane Menard stepped into Bill's van, she was in a state of relapse after engaging in prior periods of sustained remission. The smart and caring substance abuse counselor would never have made such a reckless decision were it not for the drugs that clouded her judgment. Bill knew that his victims were desperate and vulnerable, and he preyed on that weakness. Again, he still cannot get beyond labeling his victims as drug addicted prostitutes and nothing more. Two weeks after pleading guilty, he wrote:

I did feel like they were 'Bad' people. That they would rob you blind at first glance to get their drugs. I also justified my actions by telling myself that they assumed the risk when they decided to walk the street. Like they knew what could happen to them and chose to do it anyway, and that's what made them 'Not innocent' in my book.

39.

*I had become a true Serial Killer, and had I not been
caught and labeled, no one would have known or guessed
such things about me. I was a good guy with a bad hobby.*

Letter from Bill, October 2017

Pulling up to Cheshire Correctional Institute in early
October of 2017 felt like approaching the movie set of "The
Shawshank Redemption." It was a dank and dreary morning.
The ominous brick structure cast its gloomy presence over
a landscape of age-old trees that have stood the test of harsh
New England winters. Eight gargantuan pillars covered in
decades of soot encased the building's outer narthex as owl
gargoyles peered down from the balcony overhead. Entering
the front hall was like stepping back in time, to 1913,
when the building opened after three years of construction
executed by inmates from the State Prison in Wethersfield.

The front doormat carries the words: Cheshire
Correctional Institute, "The Rock."

If the concrete walls of The Rock could speak, what
stories would they tell? The cells of the north block galleys
were purchased from Sing Sing prison in New York and
transported to Connecticut by barge. Those galleys have
since closed down. Additions were added over the course
of the 20th century, all in different styles, with the one
common factor being the high, chain linked fencing topped
by spiraling razor wire that frames each unit.

The difference in ambiance between Walker C.I. in
Suffield and Cheshire C.I. was palpable. Walker often struck
me as a kind of country club for bad boys. In contrast,

Cheshire C.I. is a *real prison* in every sense of the phrase. I know that Bill can attest to that fact. Since his transfer to the facility a few weeks earlier, he had complained of increasing levels of harassment at the hands of a few corrections officers. His cell was frequently raided and any paperwork was confiscated, apparently for no reason other than to incite his ire. Post sentencing, a corrections officer removed eight double-sided pages of a letter that Bill wrote to me which included every last detail of the seven murders. Alarmed by the letter's contents, the officer refused to give the letter back to Bill. He was told that the letter was being held for "investigative purposes."

I thereafter contacted Bill's attorneys to inform that the guards had confiscated his letter to me containing detailed confessions of the seven murders and that he was complaining of harassment by a select group of guards. His attorney, Jeff Kestenband, wrote to the prison about the matter, informing that a possible First Amendment violation was at issue. That letter resulted in the guards returning the letter to Bill, which he promptly mailed to me. In defense of the prison staff, I can now see why they may have been compelled to keep that letter. In the final paragraph, Bill wrote: "*I know you will speculate for years if I have other victims out there somewhere and I can't say I may not elude to at times that there are. (Maybe there really are 6 more buried under Trudys back patio.) But between you and I, I tell you there are no others. But had I not been caught there probably would have been.*"

In a subsequent phone call, he laughed and admitted that he wrote that final paragraph in hopes that law enforcement would visit Trudy Hackler's house and dig up her yard with bulldozers as they had done to his friend Martin's yard. It would be the perfect revenge against Hackler—who he maintains stole more than $2,000 of his hard-earned prison income.

At Walker C.I., our meetings were virtually private. At most, there were two other visitors in the long room meeting with their ex-cop brother or son doing time on the other side of the Plexiglas. Visitors sat far apart from one another at Walker C.I., and just one guard watched on, showing little interest in the meetings that took place. In contrast, the Cheshire C.I. visiting area swarmed with about 20 inmates and their family members. It was sometimes difficult to focus on what Bill was saying over the phone line due to the conversational chatter in our midst.

The other Cheshire C.I. inmates, dressed in khaki jumpsuits, were allowed to sit across from their visitors at long tables. A sign on the wall said that a "brief embrace and kiss" was permitted at the start and close of visits, but any shenanigans beyond that would not be tolerated.

Needless to say, Bill would not be getting any hugs from me. I was a "no contact" visitor, there to see the infamous serial killer dressed in bright yellow and encased behind Plexiglas.

"Some of the officers here are jerks," Bill said.

"They're not as friendly as the ones at Walker," I observed.

"You should see the shit they're doing behind closed doors. I can see that I'm gonna get in a lot of trouble here, Anne. Possibly even killed by a C.O. Of course, it will be covered up. They'll say I was 'resisting' or 'fell down the steps' or something like that. I just want to do my time without being targeted or harassed."

"It's ironic," I said, "That you are in a protective custody unit so as not to get hurt by other inmates, but it's the officers who are your biggest threat."

He smiled. "Right. I get along fine with all the inmates."

A few weeks later, the officer who was giving Bill the most flack raided his cell and found a plastic butter knife. The item was labeled as "contraband." The *New Britain Herald* published a short article about the development, calling the butter knife a "weapon." Bill was issued a Class A ticket, meaning that he was found guilty of the most serious type of offense. He was sent off to the segregation unit for seven days. The seg unit was disgusting, he told me, with "*dry hockers*" on the walls. He was not allowed shoes and socks, so he placed squares of toilet paper on the floor to walk on because everything was covered in snot and black mold.

He was also given numerous sanctions, including loss of commissary for 45 days, and no television, morning rec time, or phone calls for the month of November. He sneered, describing how the C.O. tossed his television over the railing and it went crashing into the bin on the floor below. "He could have tossed my mattress down first. That would have kept the T.V. from breaking." He responded to the loss of commissary in his next letter: "*So that means no stuff off the Christmas list for me this year and no more commissary until after Christmas. Ho Ho Ho Merry fuckin Christmas. So much for any chance of happiness for me over the holidays.*"

Bill said that the deadly plastic butter knife in question was simply being used "*to slice up pickles that I purchased from the commissary.*" He said that he had stowed away "*little plastic butter knives*" for his hot pot cooking at Walker and if a C.O. found one, he would simply throw it away. Not the case at Cheshire C.I. On the hunt, the guards were intent on punishing Bill for his crimes with dogged determination.

In a subsequent radio interview, I was asked about the incident and explained that the knife was merely used to slice up pickles. "Yeah, that doesn't seem so dangerous," the interviewer said.

"Unless there is a guy in prison named Pickles," the second interviewer remarked.

Bill complained about the way in which he was transferred to seg after the plastic butter knife infraction:

The procedure for transferring an inmate to seg is that they cuff your hands behind your back. One c/o holds your cuffed hand with one hand and your arm with the other. This takes 2 c/o's, one on each arm, followed by a LT (lieutenant), a c/o with a camera, and several additional c/o's.

Every time I'd pass through a doorway and the camera view was blocked by the c/o on my right, he would squeeze my hand and twist my wrist really hard just to cause me pain. I think he was trying to get me to pull away from him so they could throw me on the ground and kick and stomp me while yelling 'Stop resisting.'

You may think that I am exaggerating but I'm not. That's the kind of shit that goes on here. The c/o's lie and cover for each other and any complaints fall on deaf ears and just bring more retaliation."

When I sat down for our first visit at Cheshire C.I., Bill looked like he had just seen a ghost. In a way, he had. He stared over my shoulder in the direction of a table of prisoners and visitors about 10 feet behind me. "Oh, my God, do you see that woman over there?"

I furtively turned around. "Which one?"

"The plump one with the wavy dark hair. She looks exactly like Dori. I am not kidding. When she came walking into the room, I thought it was Dori's ghost!"

I glanced over a second time. "She does look a bit like Dori."

"More than a bit. She looks exactly like Dori!"

For the duration of the visit, Bill's eyes drifted from me to Dori's ghost. In our next phone call, I explained that I would not be able to make our visit on the following Sunday. He was more disappointed than usual. I wondered if it was because he would not be seeing me, or Dori's ghost.

*

Bill's sixth victim was Diane Cusack. "She was really out of keeping with your other victims," I remarked. "The others were attractive, some more so than others, but Diane

Cusack was 48 years old and frankly, she looked much older than that in her mug shots."

"Yeah," he agreed. "When I picked her up at 2 o'clock in the morning behind the New Britain Shopping Plaza, I was extremely drunk. The next morning, I looked at her and told her that it was a good thing she worked the streets at night 'cause she wouldn't be able to do any business during the day."

"I assume you raped her through the night?"

He nodded. "I drove her to the parking lot of a bar down on Allen Street in New Britain. It had a little side lot that was private and secluded. In the morning, I drove her to the McDonald's parking lot, where I raped her until around noon and strangled her. I then bagged her up and threw her down the hill. I came back the next morning and buried her."

"Did you use the shock absorber on any victim other than Cusack?"

"No."

"So it was not used on Menard, as Mills had stated?"

"No. He got the two women confused."

"What about the glass Coke bottle pictured in evidence photos? Was that bottle used in the commission of any rapes?"

"No. Just the shock absorber."

Bill's seventh and final victim, Joyvaline Martinez, was walking along Hillside Avenue toward downtown Hartford in mid-October—he does not recall the exact date. He drove her to the back parking lot of a bowling alley along the Berlin Turnpike and raped her for the duration of the night. In the morning, he left that lot and drove around for the day, continuing to rape her. Like Nilsa Arizmendi, Joyvaline Martinez was initially noncompliant. *"Martinez was a little resistant at first as well but instead of hitting her with a hammer, I punched her in the nose and she gave me no more trouble after that."*

The next morning, he drove her to a shopping center located on New Britain Avenue in Hartford and raped her a few more times. At about 4 p.m., he drove to the McDonald's parking lot in New Britain, where he raped her one final time before strangulation. He "*bagged her up and threw her down the hill and buried her the next day.*" He states that he remembers the time in which he dumped the bodies because Dori often got off work at 5 p.m. and would expect him to visit by 5:30 p.m.

"Did you feel anything other than anger and sexual excitement when you abducted your victims?" I asked. "Anything?"

"No. It was like I was in a movie, Anne. It was a movie in my head. I was the bad guy and the women were not real. I know it was real for them, but at the time, they were just playing a part in a movie. I got off on being the bad guy."

Bill expounded on this observation in a subsequent letter. Reading it, I couldn't help but correlate the role he played in the rapes and killings with the virtual role that he would assume in the video game, "Dragon Quest Monsters," that he played in prison:

When I was committing these crimes, it was kind of like it wasn't "me" that was committing them. It was like I was playing a role in a movie or something (a very bad movie.) It's like was playing the role of a rapist/serial killer... Unfortunately, for my victims, it was all too real for them. But for me it was all just fantasy. That's not who I truely was at heart it was just fantasy, just a part I was playing. I think that's how I seperated myself from what I was actually doing. But for my victims, it wasn't fantasy, it was all too real and their part in my little fantasy cost them their life. I had to kill them... it was part of the script.

I think to me that being a serial killer was no different than an actor going to work pretending to be someone else (acting) and then coming back home from work. When he/she's on set, they are that character. But that's not who they

are in real life. Do you understand what I'm trying to say???
*That serial killer rapist isn't **who** I was. It was just a part I*
*played. But granted a '**real**' part in 'real' life. I think I just*
described it the best way that I can. It is really as simple as
that. I'm sure this is dissapointing to your psycologists who
want to pick and probe every little thing and can't accept
that sometimes things do have simple answers. But I think
that the way I just described my actions is the most accurate
what I can describe it. The only people to see the part I was
playing were my victims. Everybody else saw the real me.

   I'm sure there are those that will say that the 'fantasies'
were the real me. But to that I disagree. I know the argument
can be made that since these crimes were in fact real and
people were actually murdered, that you can't get any more
real than that and so therefore the part of me that committed
these crimes must be the 'real me.' I disagree. I do not see
myself as a Monster that was pretending to be a 'good guy.'
But rather a 'good guy' that did some monsterous things."

"So how do you feel, now that you have told me everything?" I asked.

He shrugged. "Talking about it and writing those confessions to you was a way of getting it off my chest. I'd been holding that stuff in for a long time and it was eating at me like a bad cancer. I guess writing it all out was my way of freeing myself of it. I've never told those things to any other person."

"Except for Jonathan Mills."

"Yeah. But he didn't hear the half of it. You did."

40.

Two weeks before sentencing, I drove out to the strip mall located on Hartford Avenue in New Britain. A few clusters of street people walked along the side streets and I saw them in a whole new light. A Puerto Rican woman and man carried plastic shopping bags that likely held their life's belongings. Although the woman looked to be in her late 30s, I wondered if she were younger. Wearing no makeup and poorly groomed, she appeared hardened and weary, not unlike Diane Cusack at the time of her death. I wondered what kind of memories she had trapped inside her head. Had she been raped or beaten by any johns? Was she ever in prison? And the man walking at her side—was he her pimp, the man assigned to "protect" her, or just a friend?

I told Bill about the experience. "That wasn't a prostitute, Anne," he said. "Crackwhores don't walk around carrying their belongings in bags. That was just a street person." Perhaps, but, hypothetically speaking, if Nilsa Arizmendi and Ace Sanchez were moving from the Almar Motel to another motel, as they frequently did, it stands to reason that they would throw their meager belongings into grocery bags. They certainly would not be rolling a three-piece Samsonite luggage set along the Berlin Turnpike.

I recalled the stories that I read in the scores of investigative reports contained in the large box of legal discovery that Bill had gifted me. Members of the New Britain Serial Killer Task Force had interviewed numerous prostitutes who all had sordid tales to tell regarding the hardships of living on the streets. It is a rotten and hellish existence. The likelihood of an early and unnatural death whether by drug overdose, homicide or suicide, is all too real.

I parked at the edge of the McDonald's parking lot, in what I figured was the exact location where three of Bill's victims were killed. It was the same time of day as when Bill killed most of his victims, about 4 p.m. With daylight savings in effect, dusk was fast approaching. I marveled at the fact that the McDonald's drive thru, busy with a long line of customers waiting in their cars, was only about 100 feet away, in full view. Ironically, the McDonald's in question has a large children's playroom facing the main strip.

The cut-through leading from the McDonald's parking lot to the strip mall's parking lot is nothing more than a dirt path going up a short grass embankment. I walked past the Arthur Miller Dance Studio and the Monroe Muffler Shop and went to the guardrail that separated the edge of the strip mall's parking lot and the 15 acres of state-owned forest. Peering into the steep ravine, I imagined Bill's seven victims lying at the bottom, hidden in black trash bags. I wondered if the large, aqua-colored object down below was the barrel in which Bill stored the body of Melanie Camilini until he returned from Virginia in the Spring of 2004.

Behind me stood several large, rusty Dumpsters. Robert Honsch had bundled his dead daughter in sleeping bags and trash bags and left her beside one of those Dumpsters back in 1995. If a strip mall could have a bad energy, this one surely fit the bill.

I walked over to the break in the fence, approximately 20 feet to the left of the guardrail, and envisioned Bill walking into the meadow-like section of the woods and making a sharp right turn to collect his victims' remains. The brush was high and thick. I couldn't get past it. Plus, the "No Trespassing" sign and a toppled-over New Britain P.D. orange cone were enough to dissuade me from going any farther into the burial ground.

I pictured Bill entering the forest in late July of 2004, just after his release from prison after serving time for a parole violation. He recently told me that he went back to the burial ground before traveling to Virginia to make sure that all of the bodies were safely concealed. He "freaked out" when he saw that the body of his last victim, Joyvaline Martinez, was not there. He searched around for it, but animals must have taken it apart and dragged the remains to other locations. That made him nervous—and rightfully so. The skull of Martinez was the first piece of evidence, found by a hunter in January of 2007. Were it not for that discovery, the remains of Bill's other victims could feasibly remain hidden to this day, and Bill would have had the opportunity to kill again after his release for the murder conviction of Nilsa Arizmendi. "Looking back on it," he told me, "I wish I stayed in that woods longer and looked harder for her body. I'm sure I could have found it and buried it again. Then that hunter would have never discovered her skull, and those bodies could still be buried there today."

"Wow," I remarked, thinking about the implications. "I wonder if you would go on to rape and kill again?"

"Who knows?"

"Or maybe you would put it all behind you. It would be your dark secret for the rest of your life. You could go back to Virginia and live a quiet existence, maybe hook up with a woman and have a kid, and no one would ever know about that graveyard behind the mall but you."

"Maybe," he said.

On the drive home, I mentally revisited the possibility that Bill has more victims. I still cannot get the July 2004 unsolved murder of Jessica Muskus out of my head. "How can it be that you suddenly stopped raping and killing when you got out of jail in July of 2004?" I once asked him. "By then, you had gotten into the habit. It makes no sense to me that you could practice self-control and just stop the pattern of behavior."

He told me that living in his van, usually parking it for the night at the Stop & Shop parking lot in Wethersfield, gave him a free pass to commit the crimes, whereas moving back to Virginia in late July of 2004 and thereafter living with friends prevented him from continuing to rape and murder. He explained that having people to go home to, people who cared about him, who were expecting him to return at night, was enough to restrain him from raping and killing. "If I lived with Dori in 2003, I don't think any of it would have happened," he said. "Living in my van made it all possible. I was accountable to no one. Also, I had a lot of leisure time on my hands. Idle hands are the devil's workshop," he said.

While I am not closed to the possibility that there are more victims, I am also not closed to the possibility that Bill did stop raping and killing when he left Connecticut in late July of 2004. While his activities in Virginia were not always upstanding, there appears to be a significant rift between the man who lived in the back of his van in Connecticut and the good ole boy from Hampton. Many of Bill's former friends in Virginia have reached out to me through social media to express their utter shock over Bill's crimes. More than a few have described a genuinely good guy, willing to do just about anything for anyone. One woman said that she lost her purse in high school. "Devin" found it and returned it without touching the money inside. Another woman wrote that he was the "nicest guy" she knew in high school.

At a recent prison visit, I asked him about the grainy photos of two unknown women found in a search of his van. "I'm willing to talk to the detective about those two women," he told me. "I know their identities. I am sure they are still alive today. They definitely weren't my victims. In fact, I am willing to take a polygraph about whether or not I have any other victims. I don't. So I am ready to answer any questions that the detective has about it."

"Be careful, Bill. Sometimes lie detectors don't work. What if you tell the truth and the test indicates deceit?"

"What's the worst that can happen to me? I get more years added to the 360 I already got?"

The following week, Bill contacted authorities to indicate a willingness to undergo polygraph examination and answer any questions that they had about other potential victims. Prosecutor Brian Preleski recently phoned him in prison and indicated interest in doing just that.

Bill is by no means a "typical" serial killer—if there is even such a thing. According to the FBI, a serial killer is someone who commits at least two murders over more than a month with an emotional cooling off period in between. The motive is psychological, often with sadistic sexual overtones. In Bill's case, he was psychologically motivated to rape out of pent-up rage, and it appears that the sole motive behind all but one of the killings was to conceal the evidence of the rape.

A serial killer expert recently asked me if Bill possesses the Macdonald Triad, a set of three behavioral traits that FBI profiler John Douglas believes are common to serial killers and other types of sociopaths: bed wetting as a child, cruelty to animals and arson.[51] While there is no way of knowing if Bill was a bed-wetter (he tells me that he was not), I personally don't see traits indicating that he enjoyed injuring animals. Remember his fondness for Poco, the dog, Marvin the Mouse and Freddie the Frog? On the other hand, one prison inmate stated in an interview with detectives that he told Bill that he killed animals and Bill stated that he, too, "killed animals as a youngster, but laughingly added that you graduate to humans pretty quickly."

Bill adamantly denies saying that to the inmate. He writes: "*I didn't kill animals as a child and nor did I have a sadistic sex life. I was never into bondage, whips, chains or any of that stuff. 90% of what Mills said is true. I did confess to Jon Mills. But he is the only inmate that I ever confessed anything to. All those other inmates that claim I confessed this or that to are all lying and just made shit up or used other shit (gossip) because they either didn't like me or wanted to parlay favor for themselves in either lighter sentences in their own case or parole considerations."*

With respect to setting fires, an acquaintance from Virginia told me that she had heard through the grapevine that Bill once set fire to the apartment that he lived in with Mandy. I asked him about it. He clarified that he was incarcerated at the time of that fire. His son was playing with matches and accidentally lit the drapes on fire, he said.

Serial killers are also known to collect souvenirs to remind them of their murders. The items not only assist them in re-living the events, but also serve as a kind of trophy that reminds them of their gruesome accomplishment. An unusual array of items was found in Bill's van during police searches: a sea turtle figurine made of glass, a tarnished ring, a woman's imitation gold bracelet and—strangest of all—the marriage certificate belonging to the mother of Nilsa Arizmendi. To date, only two of the items have been linked to Bill's victims: the marriage certificate (Bill says he has no idea why it was in the van) and the tarnished ring containing a dark stone.

The tarnished ring belonged to his first victim, Melanie Camilini. He tells me that he kept it *"because she was my first. I didn't keep it so much as a 'trophy' to be proud of, but to remind me of the moment I went from being a man to a monster. I kept it to remember because she deserved that. That ring signified the day I became a serial killer. A murderer. A monster. That ring did not give me happy thoughts or memories, it symbolized the day I fucked my life up beyond repair. The day I took an innocent life for my own selfish desires. It is not a token of triumph. It is a token of shame."*

Before entering the courtroom at sentencing, he instructed his attorneys to turn the ring over to the mother of Melanie Camilini.

I asked him about a woman's green sweater and children's hairbands pictured in evidence photographs. He stated that they did not belong to any of the victims. The hairbands may have belonged to the daughters of the girlfriend whose parents sold the van to Bill. Cigarette butts in the pictures may have belonged to Bill and the victims, and there may have been DNA on those items.

When I asked him why he had written down the name of an online serial killer art gallery, darkvomit.com, in a notebook found during a search of his cell, he answered that he was curious to see what was on that website and what price Petit home invasion murderer Joshua Komisarjevski's sketches were fetching from memorabilia junkies. Nevertheless, there is indication that Bill did wish to keep a log of his murders and not forget committing them: the cell phone bill dated July 26, 2003, found in his cell, with the handwritten notation, "This just shows the day after I killed," and the "Funeral" notation from his lawn care service log book.

"I never even dream of the murders, Anne," he once told me. "Never."

Well, that makes one of us.

41.

"For the mind set on the flesh is death, but the
mind set on the Spirit is life and peace."
Romans 8.6

The purpose of the sentencing hearing that took place on Nov. 17, 2017, was to give a voice to the voiceless. Family members of the victims finally had the opportunity to stand up in a court of law and confront Bill with the insufferable pain that his actions had caused. It is a pain that will never, ever go away.

In his statement of facts, Prosecutor Brian Preleski emphasized that the defendant was not a celebrity; he was nothing more than a prison number: 305917. In so doing, Preleski sought to dehumanize Bill just as Bill had dehumanized his victims. It was the ultimate expression of "an eye for an eye and a tooth for a tooth."

The first victim's family member to speak was Tiffany Menard, daughter of Mary Jane Menard. Tiffany is an attractive woman bearing a striking resemblance to her mother. She was serving overseas at the time of her mother's murder. In the years that followed, she drank heavily to cope with her mother's disappearance, along with the post-traumatic stress disorder that resulted from serving on the frontline in Iraq. Following an honorable discharge, she made two suicide attempts and described herself as "living aimlessly and carelessly," which resulted in two DUIs. It was a time of limbo that lasted for years, until the state lab fixed its egregious errors and informed her and her brother, Brian, that her mother had been murdered. Prior to that, she held out hope that she would see her mother on the streets.

I sat directly behind Bill and watched as he intently listened to Tiffany speak. How ironic, I thought, that this young woman is conveying to the court the greatest loss in her life—the loss of her mother—and that Bill may somehow be relating to her pain. He lost a mother. It shook his world. So the boy who lost his mother at the age of 15 went on to steal a mother away from someone else.

After describing her mother to the court, she said of Bill, "Who named him God?"

Good question. In a recent phone call with Bill, I asked if he was capable of getting beyond seeing his victims as merely drug-addicted prostitutes and understanding that they were good people caught in dangerous addictions. "Is there any way that you can think of them as you think of yourself, as good people with a dark side?"

He replied: "They probably were, Anne, and I don't know what their future could have held for them because I snuffed that out for them. Maybe they coulda gotten straight, maybe they coulda cleaned up their life. Or maybe they coulda went on to do worse things. Maybe in a way I saved a lot of people a lot of harm. I saved a lot of thefts, petty crimes, from happening. I don't know."

To this day, Bill is unwilling to see his victims as human beings at the time he murdered them. Taking that leap into the land of empathy is just too big a threat to his cognitive schemata. He expresses profound regret for what he has put the families through, and he openly wept when he apologized to them at sentencing. He broke down, in fact, but to see his victims as worthwhile human beings during the commission of his crimes would throw the binary moral code that he fights to maintain asunder. He told me that he still does not understand his evil side: "I know I have compassion. I have feelings for human beings in general but I just didn't associate it toward these prostitutes that I killed. There were just like objects. I don't know. I got past that somehow. I killed them and justified it by saying the streets are cleaner.

I know that they were all good people at one time. I couldn't think about that and I put it out of my mind. I couldn't humanize them. If they tried to talk about their families and shit like that I told them to shut the fuck up cause I didn't want to humanize them because once I attacked them I had to kill them."

Listening to his twisted reasoning, I recalled a book I had read as an adolescent, "A Day No Pigs Would Die." The farm boy in that story gets attached to a baby sow and gives her a name. He enters manhood on the day that the pig is slaughtered. It was a mistake for him to name and love her. You don't do that with animals that you have to kill. You keep a distance and see them as future meat on the table. And that is what Bill did with his female victims. The pleasure that he derived in seeing them as objects of his rage-filled fantasies would not have existed if he gave them worth, if he thought, "Hey, this is someone's mother, or daughter, or sister. This could be *my* daughter, *my* sister."

Oddly, he did have a friendship of sorts with one drug-addicted prostitute that he hired. He first picked her up in the Plaza of New Britain and she asked if he could rent a motel room where they would have sex. Bill stayed with that woman for the entire night. Thereafter, when he saw her in the Plaza of New Britain, she would flag him down and ask if she could give him free sex in exchange for having a few hours of respite in the back of his van. According to Bill, she wanted to "rest and relax and feel safe for a while and she'd shoot her dope and we'd just chill out and we'd sit there and talk for a couple of hours." I asked him if, after getting to know that woman, he would be capable of "flipping the switch" if he had no lawns to mow the following day, and raping and murdering her.

"Nah, nah!" he said with conviction. "'Cause I knew her."

I was about to mention the fact that he knew Nilsa Arizmendi, as well, and had no trouble raping and killing her, but he beat me to it. "On the other hand," he acknowledged, "I knew Arizmendi."

"You did," I agreed.

In a strange twist of fate, the person who is presently challenging Bill regarding his perception of his victims is a former prostitute and heroin addict. Maria began writing to Bill in prison after he was sentenced for the six remaining murders. She told him that she worked the streets in Hartford and New Britain during his killing spree and believes that she may have even transacted with him during that time. According to Bill, Maria told him that she "found religion," kicked the drugs and got her life straight. She is now married with children. "How weird," he reflects, "that this nice woman who is showing me kindness in prison could have been someone that I would have raped and killed ..."

After I mailed Bill my book manuscript, I told him that I would consider any revisions that he suggested, for the sake of accuracy. Right off the bat, he didn't like the title. "Is that because it's the name Mills gave the burial ground, not you?" I asked.

"No. I just don't think people are going to want to buy a book called 'His Garden.' With a name like that, it could end up beside a bin of tomatoes at the grocery store."

"People won't think it's a gardening book, Bill. There's also that modifier, 'Conversations with a Serial Killer.'"

"I just think you could come up with a better title, like 'Seven Deadly Sins.'"

"Do you know how many books with that title have been published over the years, Bill? It's a cliché. Besides, I like that 'His Garden' has biblical connotations with the Garden of Good and Evil. Maybe I'm getting too academic. What do you think?"

He sighed. "I don't care, Anne. Call it what you want."

Among some of the problems that he had with what I wrote, is the first paragraph. "You make it sound like I had no control over this monster inside of me. That's not true. I could always control it. I planned all of the murders based on whether or not I had to work the next day. So I could hold out for long periods of time and hire prostitutes for blowjobs and nothing bad would happen to them. I was always in control, Anne, which makes it sort of worse than if I wasn't in control, because it was premeditated on my part."

"But you didn't plan to rape and kill Nilsa Arizmendi," I said. "You got mad at her and then it was as though the monster surfaced against your will."

"Well, yeah, that's true. But I kinda did plan on raping and killing her. I struggled with it in my head when she refused to finish me off. 'Should I do it, or shouldn't I?' Then I made the deliberate choice to go ahead and do it."

"Well it was a pretty quick choice, that's all I'm saying, Bill. And you didn't plan to do it when she first walked into the van, either. Also, you didn't plan to kill Danny Whistnant in advance. Your anger got the best of you."

"Yeah, yeah. That's true."

I believe that Bill is in denial about the lack of control that he had over his impulse to rape and kill. Yes, the majority of the crimes were premeditated and he could refrain from committing them for months at a time. However, if you look at the dates of the murders during that nine-month killing spree, they were happening closer together as time went on. The murder of Melanie Camilini took place on Feb. 2, 2003, followed by a four-month gap until the murder of Marilyn Gonzalez in May 2003. The murder of Danny Whistnant one month later was an anomaly. After the murder of Arizmendi on July 25, 2003, the monster was stirring inside of Bill at a rapidly increasing rate. His last three victims—Menard, Cusack and Martinez—were killed within a 10-week window of time. Clearly, the monster was gaining ground and Bill was losing control.

Most times he could tame it. Keep it hidden. Silence its screams. But with greater frequency, the beast demanded release.

Make no mistake about it—Bill is furious with me over the contents of this book. He feels wounded by my narrative voice—double-crossed because, when we meet, my speaking voice is gentle and kind and contains no judgment. In turn, I am somewhat baffled by his rage. I have tried to add footnotes to clarify his side of things, but let's get real here—he took the lives of seven human beings. How did he think I would portray the situation, or the extent to which his actions in the back of his van disturbed and disgusted me over the course of the last three years? I think what bothers him most is that I did not convey any of those emotions in my letters, or during our phone calls or visits. He sees me now as "fake" and "two-faced." So be it. I think he knows, deep down, that I do care about him. I just can't get beyond the reality of his horrific deeds, nor should I. As for the fact that I concealed my true feelings on more than one occasion, I have no easy answer other than to say that putting all my cards on the table whenever we met seemed like a foolish approach. In that regard, Bill is right. I am a duplicitous woman.

There. Now I have confessed.

I am not sure if Bill will ever forgive me for turning out to be someone he did not expect. He recently wrote:

One thing that really bothers me and gets me upset while reading your manuscript is how you come to visit and I get a sense of 'genuine' friendship & kindness from you and then you go and write shit like 'I sat before a true beast' or how you describe how our visits scare you and/or affect you. But yet you sit and smile to my face and act like a friend.

I understand you are writing a book and playing shit up for your readers, but it still hurts and upsets me when I read it. I consider you a friend and it hurts me to read some of the shit you wrote. I feel hurt, I feel exploited.

I think it is also a little ironic. You talk about how I say I'm a good guy while you sit in front of what you see as a beast. But yet you sit in front of me with a smiling friendly face while you slide the knife into my back.

But the truth is that I haven't tried to deceive you in any way. And I wonder if you can honestly say the same?? Either you've exploited some of our visits for the purpose of playing up your book, or I have a serious misconception of our visits. I feel like me, a self proclaimed serial killer, capable of rape and murder, exhibits better integrity than the person telling me what a piece of shit I am. It reminds me of some old saying I can't really put together. Something about when you point you've got 3 fingers pointing back... or stones & glass houses. Granted I committed terrible heinous crimes. But in many ways, I have more integrity than those that critisize me.

In response to his feelings of betrayal, I have at least tried to clear the air between us about my true thoughts during our discussions throughout the three-year ordeal of writing this book. Here's a clip of a phone call between us in early March 2018:

"When you visit, Anne, I feel like you're a friend and you feel comfortable with me."

"I do."

"But then I read what you write—'Oh, I couldn't stop thinking that he did this and that he did that.' And that's not the feeling I get when you're sitting there in front of me. Then you write that shit in your book. It hurts my heart."

"I know."

"It's like if your best friend went behind your back and was talking bad shit about you, shit behind your back. The same way you would feel about that situation is the way I feel when you write some of the things you write. You seem so genuine when you see me, and we just shoot the shit and you seem comfortable, and then you go and write those things ..."

"Yeah ... I'm trying to tone that all down in the book. On the other hand—"

"I mean, I never knew that's how you felt. Maybe that really is how you feel when you're sitting in front of me behind the glass. But I never picked up on it and got that feeling from it. I never knew that I made you feel so uncomfortable, and that I gave you nightmares and shit like that, and that hurts my heart to know that I make you feel like that."

"Well, in the early stages I was nervous, in our first two or three visits. Not in any way that was personal. I mean, first I knew—what are you going to do? I did know in my gut that you had a target group and that 99 percent of all women out there aren't part of your target group. So, I wasn't anxious for any of those reasons (my own safety) because you're behind the Plexiglas in high max anyway, but it was more about thinking about what you did. What you were accused of doing. And you know, sometimes what you don't know makes it worse. Like the shadow under the bed that the kid sees when the lights go out. I didn't know what the particulars of what you did were. I didn't know why you did it. It wasn't until September when you finally opened up to me, everything changed in my way of thinking when you opened up to me. I get that you of course couldn't have told me until then, but it all changed when I could finally understand. Before that, I was like, what's going on in this guy's head? I didn't know if you found pleasure in killing them. I didn't know if you prolonged their deaths. The finger slicing thing. I didn't know if you enjoyed doing that. The dismantling of the jaw. I didn't know if that was all part of some kind of a sick game for you. There were a lot of big mysteries that made me afraid."

Here, his voice lowers with sadness. "I never knew that that all was going through your head. I thought you were just saying that stuff to cater to your readers."

"Well, now that I know your motive, I can compartmentalize it. But early on, I couldn't help but think that what you did was the totality of who you are. Does that make sense?"

"Yeah, I guess."

"I still struggle with it, Bill, the fact that I like you more as time goes on, but I know what you did ..."

"Yeah, it's not an easy situation."

"No. It's a big deal. You killed seven people. That defines you as a human being. I understand that it's one part of who you are, and there are all these other parts of you. I get that. I don't know if the reader will get it ..."

He dejectedly laughs. "No. I don't think they will ever get it. They don't know me and anyone that doesn't know me is always going to see me as a monster, and I've got to learn to accept that that is what I am. You've had trouble seeing me as a person, and I've had trouble seeing me as the monster that I am portrayed as. I think it's a little of both."

*

As I write this final chapter, Bill is caged like a predatory animal in a human zoo called Cheshire Correctional Institute. Like all wild animals held captive and confined with no hope of release, he is miserable and alone. He is not free to roam the forest and hunt. He is at the mercy of his captors and some of those corrections officers resemble bullies in the schoolyard. They take pleasure in tormenting him. They see it as his rightful due. Perhaps that makes some people happy to hear. For me, it is a sad reflection of the depraved world in which we live.

It has been a disturbing and exhausting venture for me to get to know a serial rapist and killer and hear his confessions firsthand. When all is said and done, however, I still believe that good triumphs over evil. At Bill's sentencing hearing, Tiffany Menard stated that she turned a corner in her grieving process and realized that she "would not live in pity and sorrow anymore." Though still irate at the man who stole her mother's life, she stated, "I want to hate him, but I pray that God will forgive him for what he has done." She later told me that she felt like a sucker for actually feeling pity for the man who killed her mother. On the contrary, I believe her sentiment of pity is the ultimate human virtue.

Likewise, in acknowledging that a man who succumbed to evil stole the life of their mother, the daughters of Nilsa Arizmendi choose to move forward and focus their thoughts and emotions on the love that Nilsa showed others during her brief stay on this Earth. She gave those she cared for special nicknames. In a victims' statement read following Bill's murder conviction in January 2007, the Arizmendi family wrote, "As she approached each one of us, she sang a jingle. She did this as a demonstration of her love and affection. It automatically brought a smile to our faces." That memory brings warmth to their hearts, even to this day. It is something that no one, not even a serial killer, can ever take away from them. And because that memory lives on, Nilsa has the victory.

Photos

Author entering the burial ground behind the strip mall in New Britain, CT, in August 2015. Crime scene tape and a cone from the New Britain PD still marked the parameters.

William Devin Howell on Santa's lap, circa 1973. Howell describes a relatively stable early childhood.

The modest brick bungalow in Hampton, VA, where Howell was raised.

School pic of Howell. He began to put on weight by the age of 8, circa 1978.

School pic of Howell wearing light blue turtleneck, circa 1975.
Howell's mother was actively involved in his school activities.

Howell's school photo wearing orange striped shirt, circa 1976.

Howell and his girlfriend Dori Holcomb in 2003, at the time of his killing spree. His eyebrows are white from working long hours in the sun in his lawncare business. Holcomb committed suicide in 2014, when Howell was imprisoned for the murder of Nilsa Arizmendi. She believed in his innocence.

Quadruple murderer Jonathan Mills. Mills heard Howell's partial confessions regarding the seven murders while they were cellmates back in 2014. He went on to give that information to authorities.

Appendix:

Impact Statement written by Tiffany Menard, daughter of Mary Jane Menard

My name is Tiffany Jane Menard and my mother was murdered by William Devin Howell.

I am reminded daily of the loss and ache and absence of the one person who is supposed to be the most important person in my life, my mother. A mother is supposed to be there when things get tough and for all of the milestones in life but Howell has ripped that away from me, my family and the rest of the victims.

My mom went missing in October of 2003. I was in Iraq since March of 03 so I hadn't had a chance to see her much or say goodbye for that matter. I learned to numb the pain of losing her when I returned from Iraq. Stationed in Germany at 19 years old I started drinking more heavily. I couldn't numb the pain anymore so I attempted suicide once in Germany, then again when I was stationed in Washington State. I was honorably discharged almost 4 years later due to the attempts and returned home. The attempts were prompted by my drinking to the point where I blacked out. I lived my life aimlessly and carelessly, not caring about the consequences of my actions or who I hurt in the process. I remember mom always telling me when I got grounded that I had to pay the consequences. Two DUI's later and a few other alcohol related arrests I finally realized I am not going to live my life with pity and sorrow over the past. If my mother would have been here for me I am sure none of the prior would have happened and my aunt wouldn't have had the stresses of bailing her niece out of jail on a few occasions. You not only changed the outcome of my life but the outcome of everyone she knew. You stripped the youth from us and forced 2 children to be orphaned. Without a father for our entire life, and because of you, we are now without a mother. Since then my family and I had to endure countless years of not knowing. Thinking she was somehow missing and not mentally able to reach out to us. I would see her on the street at least a thousand times only to realize it wasn't her. I always hoped she could still be alive. It wasn't until 14 years later when the DNA results were retested and confirmed that our worst fear was realized. Now I paint a more brutal picture in my mind on the pain and suffering that she endured. I have to think of it every time I go to the highway ramp where you so thoughtlessly laid them.

My mother would have been the one to push our whole family into getting an education. She worked so hard her whole life to get to where she was at. She overcame so many obstacles; an abusive childhood, alcoholism, raising two kids as a single mother and all the while going to school for her degree. She could have done so much in this world if you didn't rip that life from her. You have taken so much from our lives; a mother, daughter, grandma, sister, aunt and a good friend to so many. She was the tough one that we needed in our lives to keep it together. We will continue to miss her at every holiday, birthday party and every special moment in our lives she should have been there for. I know she is looking down on us from heaven. I will always miss the just thinking of you cards she used to give. She always made a point to let us know while she was here how each of us was so important to her and so loved while she was here on earth.

Words cannot express all of the pain and anguish so many of us had to endure since their murders. How can someone make the decision to take not one, but seven lives? It is sickening. Although he feels they were all worthless they were not. Who named him GOD or even made him worthy enough to determine that? Apart from their lives you also affected countless other lives. With every ounce of blood that run through my veins I want to hate you, but all I can do is pray that GOD can forgive you for all that you have done, and I pray that he will give us the peace to continue living our lives.

I also wanted to thank Randy Watts and all of the task force and agencies that worked so hard for all of these years. Never giving up until justice was served. Without you we would still have a monster walking our streets.

For More News About Anne K. Howard,
Signup For Our Newsletter:

http://wbp.bz/newsletter

Word-of-mouth is critical to an author's long-
term success. If you appreciated this book please
leave a review on the Amazon sales page:

http://wbp.bz/hisgardena

Endnotes

1 "Winsted Wildman craze of 1895 made things a little hairy." July 13, 2002. http://www.bigfootencounters.com/articles/ wildmancraze.htm

2 Howell states that the notation on the phone Bill was made to prepare his defense in the murder trial of Nilsa Arizmendi. He wanted to remind his attorneys that he had made phone calls to his friend in Virginia, Paul, that day. His argument was that he would not be making phone calls to a friend on a day when he should have been preoccupied with burying a victim's body. He also contests the exact wording of what he wrote, which was included in a subsequent police affidavit. I have requested the actual phone bill from his attorneys, and they are currently trying to locate it for me to get to the bottom of the matter.

3 Although Ross had eight victims, two of them were killed in New York. In Howell's case, all seven victims were Connecticut residents, murdered in Connecticut. For more information about Ross and his three-year killing spree, see Elliott, Martha. "The Man in the Monster." New York, New York. Penguin Books, 2015. In a letter dated Aug. 14, 2016, Bill wrote to me, "But isn't it ironic that the day they kill one convicted Serial Killer, they arrest someone that later becomes another '*Alleged*' serial killer?? I'm surprised none of the reports picked up on that."

4 Nestel, M.I., Briquelet. "Serial Killer Suspect Was Kindhearted Boyfriend." *The Daily Beast.* May 13, 2015. https:// www.thedailybeast.com/serial-killer-suspect-was-kindhearted-boyfriend

5 When Howell read the first draft of the book manuscript, he responded to my characterizing that initial written contact as "something of a ruse," writing: "It comes accross as you somehow 'tricked' me into talking to you. And maybe you think you did. But I'm telling you, that's not the case. I picked

you to give my story to for many different reasons. But I was always aware you believed I was guilty and would try to be nice to me to get me to talk to you. And for you to think I thought different or wasn't aware you were just playing nice to get me to talk to you is just wrong. I was well aware of your tactics from the begining. But I liked you best out of the other leaches that contacted me and you helped me when I needed it. I think now, 2½ years later, you see me in a whole new light. I feel like you have come to know me as a person and not just a "title" and subject for a book… I feel that we have truely become friends to an extent. I know that I enjoy seeing and talking with you and I value you as a friend and I think you truley see me as a friend as well. Surely you have shared things about your personal life that you would never have shared had you not felt comfortable with me… And I think it surprises you a little bit. I guess you can say we've come a long way." He makes a valid point. At the risk of offending readers, I have come to see Howell as a true friend, however despicable the crimes that he committed.

6   Describing the burial of his victims, Howell writes: "The woods seemed deathly quiet. Like every time I sank the shovel into the earth it could be heard from miles away, sounding alarm and alerting the world to my miss deeds. I just wanted to get the task at hand done and get the hell out of there. To hide the body, to hide my crime, to hide what I had done. To hide my reality. To bury it all in the woods was to bury it all in my mind. To hide the ugly truth of what I had become. To make me human again. To make me live with myself."

7   Howell writes: "I literally remember times watching Forensic Files with my head in Dori's lap and her running her hand through my hair (she used to love running her fingers through my long hair) and watching Forensic Files and wondering what I might have missed and what might get found were my van to ever be seized. And hoping that I wouldn't one day find myself laying in a cell watching my own episode of Forensic Files. But I was always careful and convinced that if the bodies in the woods were ever found that there would be nothing to lead them to me."

8   Howell has given no indication to me that he is racist. When he made this comment, he was recalling the beliefs of many of the white people living in the community of Hampton, Va., during that time period.

9   Backus, Lisa. "Nephew, brother, killer: Aunt, sibling recall a young William Devin Howell" *New Britain Herald.* Sept. 24, 2015.

10   Bill writes: "Little 'Opi' turned into a serial killer because he grew up in a home where sexual situations were never exhibited or discussed and when 'little Opi' got laid, that shit went to his head and overwhelmed him and one fantasy led to another, to another, to another…" In the article, "Persistent Myths about Serial Killers," Katherine Ramsland, Ph.D., cites a 2008 report by behavioral analysts in the FBI's National Center for the Analysis of Violent Crime, "Serial Murder: Multidisciplinary Perspectives for Investigators," that dispels myths that persist about serial killers. One stereotype is that "all serial killers have been abused, come from violent homes, and escalate their violence" over time. In Bill's case, although he came from a dysfunctional home (arguably, like the vast majority of Americans) his upbringing does not appear to directly relate to his crimes. The myths set forth in the 2008 report were reiterated in a 2014 report, "Serial Murder: Pathways for Investigations." Ramsland, Katherine, Ph.D., "Persistent Myths about Serial Killers," *Psychology Today*, Feb. 12, 2018. https://www. psychologytoday.com/us/blog/shadow-boxing/201802/persistent-myths-about-serial-killers

11   Rivas, Anthony. "Serial Killers are more Likely to Have Autism, Head Trauma, or Psychosocial Issues—But not all who suffer are killers." *Medical Daily*, May 21, 2014. http://www. medicaldaily.com/serial-killers-more-likely-have-autism-head-trauma-or-psychosocial-issues-not-all-who-suffer-are

12   Hazelwood, Roy, Michaud, Stephen G. "Dark Dreams." New York, N.Y. St. Martin's Paperbacks, 2001.

13   The sentiments of Robert Howell were found in the comment section of an online article from the *New Britain*

Herald dated Sept. 18, 2015. That article is no longer available online. I am in possession of a printout of that comment section.

14   Bechard, Raymond. "The Berlin Turnpike: A True Story of Human Trafficking in America." New York, N.Y. Sons of Liberty Press, 2011.

15   If Ace Sanchez were the culprit, the murder of Nilsa Arizmendi would probably have been much easier to solve. In his book "Mind Hunter," FBI Special Agent John Douglas writes that the solution rate to homicide in America was more than 90 percent as recently as 1960. Since then, despite great advances in forensics and technology, including big-brother style surveillance in even the most "private" of places, and increased police power, the murder rate has been going up and the solution rate has been going down. Strangers are murdering strangers at a steadily increasing rate, and such crimes are extremely difficult to solve. While Howell was an acquaintance of Arizmendi, he was a stranger to his other six victims. Thus, in finding the serial killer, members of the New Britain Serial Killer Task Force were looking for the proverbial needle in a haystack.

16   Hazelwood, Roy, Michaud, Stephen G. "Dark Dreams."

17   Bill believes that detectives routinely administer lie detector tests that render "deceptive" findings when the person of interest is a serious suspect in a case. When detectives redirect their suspicions to another individual, the results of the lie detector test on the first person magically transform from "deceptive" to "inconclusive" so that investigators can focus their efforts on the second suspect in line. He claims that this also happened when investigators initially determined that the lie detector showed deception on the part of Mary Jane Menard's boyfriend, who was considered as possibly culpable in the early stages of that investigation. When they realized that Bill was the likely perpetrator, subsequent testing of Menard's boyfriend changed to "inconclusive." I am prone to believe his argument. Lie detector tests are not admissible in a court of law for a reason. They are frequently unreliable and can be easily manipulated by the ones administering the tests.

18   See "Serial Murders in Connecticut," "Alleged New Britain Serial Killer Loses Case in Small Claims Court," Dec. 29, 2015. Anne K. Howard. www.rte8murders.blogspot.com

19   Bill states that the police report was false. He had discarded the original bench cushion prior to visiting Martin in Virginia in November 2003. Martin subsequently corroborated that story, telling the press that he was pressured by authorities to later state that he saw stained, replacement seat cushions in the van when they cleaned it that day. "I said numerous times I never seen the seat cushion ... and they wasn't believing it. I told them what they wanted to hear because I thought I was going to be arrested or could be arrested, I was pretty scared." Munoz, Hilda. "Witness Disowns Original Story." *Hartford Courant*, Jan. 30, 2001.

20   See "Serial Murders in Connecticut's" four articles about the author's interviews with Steven Hayes dated Feb. 25, 2015; Jan. 30, 2017; Feb. 4, 2017; Feb. 20, 2017. Anne K. Howard. https://rte8murders.blogspot.com/

21   Bill writes: "Why do you have to talk about my teeth? I know I'm a snaggle tooth but I lost the two front lower teeth as a result of a fight, not because of poor hygene. I brush my teeth at least twice a day and usually 3 times a day."

22   Okier, Susan. "Profiles in Murder." *The Washington Post.* June 16, 1961. https://www.washingtonpost.com/archive/opinions/1991/06/16/profiles-in-murder/8735b36a-7b84-4044-9f85-7f96324df1fb/?utm_term=.efc8a47d5fc2

23   See Ramsland, Katherine, Ph.D., "Persistent Myths about Serial Killers," stating that "most serial killers have very defined geographic areas of operation."

24   In response to my depiction of our first prison visit, Bill writes: "It just isn't how shit went during our visit."

25   For more information on the role of prison snitches in the legal system, see Narapoff, Alexandra, "Secret Justice: Criminal Informants and America's Underground Legal System." Prison Legal News. June 15, 2010. https://www.prisonlegalnews.

org/news/2010/jun/15/secret-justice-criminal-informants-and-americas-underground-legal-system/

26   Howell states that the van did not have a foul odor. He also states that the original seat cushion had already been replaced with different cushions when they cleaned his van that day.

27   In reviewing this section of the manuscript, Bill wrote: "Drop section about me bitching about cooking." I did not because I don't think it will result in retaliation from another prisoner.

28   Bill is extremely unhappy with how I portrayed his interactions with Rodrigues. He states that Rodrigues was excessively friendly and Bill knew that he had to stay close-mouthed when conversing with the snitch. He wrote: "You assume that Rodrigues was telling the truth when he said I confessed. For some reason, YOU and the media, and the public, can't get it out of your head that Rodrigues was telling the truth. It's like you can't even grasp that Rodrigues is full of shit." He also points out that detectives put a wire on Rodrigues for hours at a time after Rodrigues first contacted DeRoehn and there is no recorded information other than meaningless small talk between him and Rodrigues on those recordings.

29   In response to this paragraph, Bill writes: "Mortimer replies, 'You probably shouldn't have this stuff. Where'd you get it?' This is more made up shit by you. It doesn't even make sense that he would say that. And why shouldn't I have it?? Don't I have a right to face my accuser and know their history??? I thought you said you scored well on the Defense Attorney part of your bar exam. (Yeah I know that was a cheap shot, but some of this is bullshit in your book pisses me off.) Reading this shit makes me want to write a book of my own to straighten out the bullshit in your book." In fact, the line "You probably shouldn't have this stuff. Where'd you get it?" was taken from a legal affidavit filed in the matter, so if the comment is false as Bill claims, then the error is connected to the detective filing the affidavit, not me. Likewise, all of the statements made by Rodrigues to DeRoehn conveyed in an earlier chapter were taken

from a legal affidavit filed by DeRoehn in which he documents the exact wording of their conversations.

30   Howell writes: "If you're going to print this shit in quotes as if they were my actual conversations you should include footnotes. In this case you should put in a footnote that your account of this conversation was according to Mortimer and that I deny ever saying anything about the Rodrigues family. If you are going to print someone elses lie about what I said, and print it in a way that it appears that it was actually something I said, you should at least let me defend myself in a footnote. Otherwise you are just printing lies. Because someone said that I said something doesn't mean I actually did." In fairness, I have included his reaction in a footnote.

31   Bill is correct in stating that it is difficult for an inmate to accomplish suicide in prison. According to a May 2006 article, "Suicide Methods in Prison," suicide is the leading cause of death in American jails, and the third leading cause of death in American prisons. However, "without easy or legal access to drugs, weapons, or willing assistants, inmates often use painful, even tortuous, methods of ending their lives." Strangulation and hanging are the most common methods whereby ligature points for strangulation are window bars and bed fittings. Wires, ropes (taken from a workplace), shoelaces, socks or belts are also commonly used. http://www.insideprison.com/suicide-methods-in-prison.asp

32   "Heroin and Opioid Overdoses on Rise in Connecticut Towns" Jan. 6, 2016. http://Trendct.org. See also "Connecticut Heroin Epidemic: Interactive Map of Deaths by Town." http://patch.com

33   "Dark Dreams."

34   Bill writes: "It wasn't a 'meat cutter' I used an electric slicer. I wasn't a butcher or anything like that. But I understand this just makes a better fairy tale for your readers."

35   Although I described this scene as it was conveyed in a police affidavit, Bill writes: "My confession to Mills did not happen as you depict. I never said that 'those women should

have known they were going to die.' I've talked to you about this and how my confession to Mills came about. You have it as though I just casually walked into the cell and was flipping through the cards and came across Martinez's card and just said 'yeah, I raped and murdered her.' I don't know what fantasy you have in your head about how these confessions came about but I'd wish you'd ask instead of taking your little made up fantasies about events and putting it on paper as if it were fact and correction renditions of events." Once again, I feel that Bill is splitting hairs. He did pull the card and show it to Mills and indicated that he was responsible for the murder. Moreover, he has told me many times over that all of his victims should have known better than to put their lives at risk by working the streets and getting into his van, so it is not implausible that he said as much to Mills, as well.

36   In a letter dated March 5, 2018, Bill listed the "lies" that he anticipated the prosecution would present to the jury in the event that his case went to trial. According to Bill, a victim's mother was prepared to testify that a turtle charm key chain that was found at Martin's house in Virginia belonged to her daughter. Bill says that is a lie. He has no idea where that charm came from. Another witness would testify that she saw Menard riding in the van with Bill back in 2003, shortly before she disappeared. The witness was interviewed in January 2015, and Bill suspects she saw his photo as a person of interest on television and fabricated the event based on seeing his photo because he never drove in New Britain with Menard in his van. A prostitute would testify that Bill had attacked her. He states that he never attacked any prostitutes except for the ones he killed. He continues to believe that the DNA found in his van was not as significant as I have led readers to believe. He wrote, "As far as the D.N.A. you know my stand on that. It places them in the van and proves that 2 of them bled in the van. But it was also found by the CME that the amount of blood couldn't constitute a death had occurred or the extent of injury." He does concede, however, that the testimony of Mills, which he states contained some lies and inaccuracies, would still be enough to result in a finding of guilt. "But there was no getting around Mill's knowledge of the shock absorber

or that there were 4 unrecovered bodies still in the woods," he wrote.

37   Naples, Kaitlyn. Konopka, Jill. "New Britain neighbors hired suspected serial killer before arrest." Sept. 22, 2015, WFSB (Meredith Corporation).

38   Ramsland, Katherine, Ph.D., "Persistent Myths about Serial Killers." Ramsland writes, "The majority of serial killers are not reclusive, social misfits who live alone. They are not monsters and may not appear strange. Many serial killers hide in plain sight within their communities."

39   Bill states: "Instantaneous license scanners didn't make me up my game and ask Dori to register the van. Dori insisted I register the van in her name, that way if it got towed or I got caught driving, she could get the van back for me. I later realized she wanted it registered in her name to have power over me. If we'd fight or I'd try to leave, she'd threaten to report the van stolen. She threatened this twice. I told her if she ever made this threat again that neither one of us would have a vehicle to drive. She threatened again to report the van stolen and I rammed the van into the rear quarter panel of her truck. That's how the van got wrecked. It tore the front of my van up and only put a dent in her rear quarter panel. That's when the I got the Criminal Mischief Charge in New Britain… She never made that threat again."

40   Bill writes: "Did I tell you I was innocent or did I tell you 'at this time I'm maintaining my innocence'?? That was not a lie when I told you that. I had not changed my 'Not Guilty' plea so I was in fact still 'maintaining my innocence.' The only lie I've told you was about Camilini's jaw and I corrected that. I've thought about the things I've said to you very carefully and made sure I said things to you in a way that they were not a lie. What about you?? Are you a liar?? It seems obvious that you've lied to me. I can say with clear conscience that I have not lied to you. I wonder if I should be surprised that a lawyer lies more than a serial killer. You said yourself, you had me guilty from the start and you are why innocent people end up behind bars. I hope you are never on a jury, because 'impartial' you are not." In

response, all I can say is that, from the start of our relationship in July 2015, forensic reports documented 6 out of 7 DNA samplings from victims in Bill's van. While I value impartiality, I am not stupid. I feel that Bill is once again splitting hairs here. Yes, he never explicitly professed his innocence to me in our earliest interactions, but he never admitted guilt, either, and he often made arguments in his defense before coming clean and exclusively confessing his crimes to me. Also, there is that poem that he wrote during the Arizmendi murder trial. On some level, he was trying to convince himself that he was innocent or project himself as innocent to others on the day that he wrote that poem.

41   Haddock, Vicki. "Four types of serial rapists—what makes them tick." *SFGate*, The Examiner Staff. Jan. 16, 1996. http://www.sfgate.com/news/article/Four-types-of-serial-rapists-what-makes-them-3159973.php

42   Bill writes: "Removal of Jaw and Fingertips. While this is true, do you really have to tell it??" Since it has already been reported by other media sources, I don't see why not.

43   Bill writes: "You say that I didn't want anyone to sit on the cushions after gas spilled on them. But I didn't want to *sleep* on the cushion because I was worried about 'chemical burn' from gas." I maintain that, during that prison visit, he told me that he removed the cushions because he did not want anyone else to get a chemical burn.

44   "The Teaching of Buddha." 1966 by Bukkyo Dendo Kyokai,

45   Bill writes: "I didn't enjoy making them suffer. I enjoyed humiliating them." I fail to see the difference. Moreover, his sexual arousal during the brutal rapes confirms that he *did* enjoy making them suffer.

46   Harenski, Carla L, Thornton, David M., Harenski, Keith A, Decety, Jean, and Kiel, Kent A. "Increased fronto-temporal activation during pain observation in sexual sadism: Preliminary Findings." *Arch Gen Psychiatry*, March 2012.

47   Here, I believe Bill is exhibiting characteristics of what I consider to be a "selective psychopath." He is capable of feeling

empathy toward others, just not his victims. In the article "How Psychopaths See the World," Ed Yong writes that "Psychopaths, by definition, have problems understanding the emotions of other people, which partly explains why they are so selfish, why they so callously disregard the welfare of others, and why they commit violent crimes at up to three times the rate of other people. ... Here are people who can understand what their victims are thinking but just don't care. Hence their actions." Yong, Ed, *The Atlantic*, May 12, 2018. https://www.theatlantic. com/science/archive/2018/03/a-hidden-problem-at-the-heart-of-psychopathy/555335/?utm_source=atlfb

48   "Paraphilias." *Psychology Today*. https://www. psychologytoday.com/conditions/paraphilias

49   Here he references his poorly controlled Type 2 diabetes. One of Bill's brothers also had Type 2 diabetes and died of kidney failure, but not before losing both legs to amputation due to diabetic neuropathy.

50   Police interviewed one witness who claimed that she saw Mary Jane Menard in the passenger seat of Bill's van at an intersection in New Britain at the time when she went missing. It appears that her statement may be false. Details regarding the location of a stop sign and the direction that the van would be headed in were conflicting. Bill states that everything that occurred with Menard took place in Waterbury.

51   Many FBI authors discount The MacDonald Triad as an outdated theory that is unsupported by research, according to Katherine Ramsland, Ph.D., a professor of forensic psychology and author of more than 60 nonfiction books.

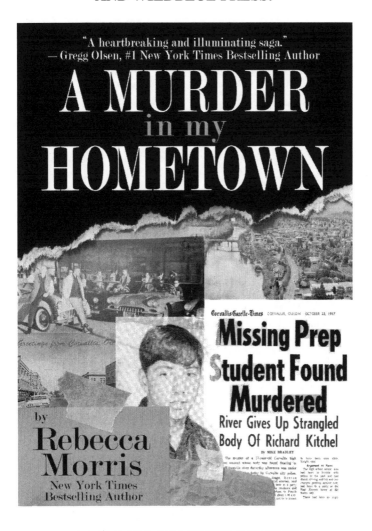

The Mayor of Seaton's

Ten days in one of America's most polluted rivers had not been kind to the body. The cold water had slowed decomposition, but the nibbling of fish had made inroads. The body was bloated, filthy, and foul smelling, as contaminated as the water, sewage, and tree limbs that kept it hidden and submerged until it moved free of a branch or the body's gases caused it to float to the surface. On the afternoon of Saturday, October 21, 1967, thirteen-year-old Dan Eckles and his fourteen-year-old cousin, Jim Crawford, were fishing on the dock of Riverview Marina, the business Dan's dad had bought when he moved his family up from California. Dan and his three older sisters and parents lived in an apartment in the marina, which sat on the west bank of the Willamette River as it wound through Corvallis, Oregon. The longest river in North America traveling south to north – essentially uphill – was Dan's front yard. Some locals grumble and are quick to point out that no rivers *really* flow "uphill." But the river winds 200 miles through forest, farmland, and cities, growing from a mountain stream to a big river before joining the mighty Columbia. Dan and Jim fished mostly to waste time. The boys caught white fish and carp off the dock, but knew better then to keep what they caught. Just once Dan's family had fried up some fish from the river. They all got sick.

As they fished, Dan spotted something in the water. "It's not unusual to see something float by," he said later. But this was a body. "It was face down. It was about a foot and a half from me. I remember I started to reach out to it." He began to grab one of the body's arms but an irrational thought stopped him. What if it came off? He ran for his father, a former Los Angeles sheriff's detective. It would be awhile before Dan fished again.

Detective Sergeant Jim Montgomery was at the river when the body was pulled ashore and photographed. "It was ugly, black, there was green moss on him, there was a chain around his mouth," he said. The police had a long-standing joke about bodies found in the river. "Tow him over there," they'd say, pointing to the east side of the river. Then it would be the purview of Linn County.

But this one was theirs. The body was taken by hearse to McHenry Funeral Home on NW 5th. By the time it arrived, police suspected it could be that of a teenager who had been missing for ten days, seventeen-year-old Dick Kitchel. His father and stepmother had initially shrugged off his disappearance. They weren't worried. Maybe he was off at the coast with friends. They had finally gone to the police after Dick didn't show up for school one Monday. The police department considered him a runaway.

Ralph and Sylvia Kitchel met Montgomery, Captain Bill Hockema, and Assistant Police Chief Ken Burright at the funeral home. District Attorney Frank Knight; the coroner, Dr. Peter Rozendal; and the state medical examiner, Dr. Russell Henry, were also in attendance. Autopsies were routinely conducted at funeral homes. At McHenry, they shared space with a room on the main floor where embalming was performed. It was efficient. Showing little emotion, Ralph identified the body. It was Dick, a sweet boy as a child. He'd outgrown Cub Scouts and had become one of the tough guys, a teenager known for his beer drinking, a drunken car crash and arrest just weeks before his disappearance, and fist fights. Lots of fights, including ones with his dad. One of the first officers called to the river, Lieutenant Roger Schmeltz, had been to the Kitchel home to break up fights between father and son. But Dick was well-liked and had friends in every stratum of high school life. Although one friend described him as "always striving to be better than where he came from," at some point he seemed to have given up on the goal. His childhood had not been easy. He was an only child and his mother, Joan, had moved back to Washington state after her divorce. Both of his parents had remarried; his father for the third time just a few months before Dick's disappearance. Dick bounced between living and attending school in Olympia and being sent back to Corvallis. He lived to get out of the house, according to a friend.

The body had no identification or wallet. But it was Dick. He was dressed in jeans and a gray Oregon State University t-shirt. He also wore a JC Penney undershirt, JC Penney briefs, and a pair of white crew socks with black and olive stripes. The only items in his pockets were two nickels, two pennies, a brass key, and a white handkerchief. Dick had died with his beloved Acme cowboy boots on. Ralph had his own shoe repair business but his first shop in Corvallis was in the back of an Acme store. In a murder case, clothing is held onto indefinitely. But they asked Dick's father if he would eventually want the clothes and boots returned. He said no.

Dick owned two other items that meant the world to him. One was his baby blue '55 Chevy. The other was his Pacific Trail tan suede jacket. He never went anywhere without the car and the coat. The car was history – at least until Dick found the money for repairs. He had cracked it up over Labor Day weekend in a spectacular accident, taking out a row of mailboxes and trees and 150 feet of cedar fence. He was arrested for drinking while driving, attempting to leave the scene, and resisting arrest. Where was his jacket? one of his parents asked. It was the kind of jacket that looked better the more it was worn, and Dick wore it a lot. Not on the hottest Indian summer days in the fall, but there weren't a lot of those in Oregon.

After Ralph Kitchel looked at the body and said, "Yes, that's my son," he and Sylvia quickly left the room. The coroner and the medical examiner undressed Dick. He was small, only five feet two inches tall, 125 pounds. It hadn't mattered when he played on the town's Parks & Recreation summer baseball team known as The Crocs, short for Crocodiles, in grade school. Everyone was small then. His light brown hair fell forward and swept to the right of his hazel eyes. They were shut now. While his friends had grown in height, Dick's persistent small size caused some teasing and helped him form a hard shell. But despite his recent journey into fights and drinking, he was popular and his many friends still called him by his childhood name, Dickie. He was dating at least two girls, one a cheerleader. Now his life was over. No more speeding in his car, spending time with girls, or drinking at private parties. No more evenings at Seaton's, the most popular hamburger hangout for Corvallis teenagers who wanted to see and be seen. He was known as "the Mayor of Seaton's" because of his frequent visits, notoriety, and reputation for both starting fights and breaking up fights between others.

According to his father, he was left-handed. There'd been a pretty good fight, presumably leading to his death. The knuckles on both hands were bruised and he may have struck someone in the mouth as he fought for his life. He had been hit in both eyes, which were bruised. He had also been hit in the nose and he had bled from his ears and his mouth. There was a three-inch wide bruise on his throat. His larynx had been crushed, causing him to suffocate. Rozendal and Henry concluded Dick had been strangled, but not with bare hands. Someone had used an arm or the sleeve of a coat. There was no water in his lungs or stomach, so he was dead before he entered the river. Even his blood, an essential part of its seventeen-year-old host, was ruined and couldn't tell investigators much. The body had been contaminated through and through by the river and any blood samples were putrid. The coroner may have tried to draw blood from Dick's heart. It can be a source of last resort, unless it, too, is decomposed.

At the funeral home, Montgomery and Hockema learned Dick had been to a party the night he disappeared. With information from Ralph and Sylvia Kitchel, they began to compile a list of names of Dick's friends. One of them, or a family member, had most likely murdered the mayor of Seaton's.

The Town

This is a story about a hometown. Mine. It is a murder mystery and a mystery about memory.

Everyone who settled in the West came from somewhere else. My grandparents came to Oregon from Illinois and Iowa in the late 19th century, but family on both sides had been in America for hundreds of years. Corvallis was my mother's hometown for more than 90 years. One day when she was 97, living in Seattle near my brother and me and beginning to fade, she said, "I think I'll move back to Corvallis." I said I would go too. I knew she was daydreaming. She was homesick for a town that may not have really existed. Corvallis was our Brigadoon, a village unaffected by time, too good to be true and a gift to only the few. It didn't appear out of the mist to everyone.

While working on this story, I discovered that *my* Corvallis wasn't necessarily the Corvallis that my high school classmates grew up in. More than a few told me they couldn't wait to leave town. I knew I remembered it as more idyllic than it could possibly have been. Perhaps in response to my own life troubles, I saw the life my parents had and gave to my brother and me as the happiest time in my life and the only years that have been carefree.

My memories start in the 1950s. Each decade has its fears, and when I was a child, we were at war in Korea, worried about communist influences in America, and fearful of the Cold War and the arms race. In my third grade class at Roosevelt School, and in third grade classrooms all over Corvallis, we were taught cursive writing, Oregon history, and how to "duck and cover." We thought the danger was outside our town, maybe in Russia. But Corvallis had its secrets.

Third grade, and the study of Oregon history, came in 1959 for me. It was a huge year because it was the centennial of Oregon's statehood. There were parades and beard growing contests. It was a great year to be immersed in our state's history, but in our studies we never learned about the state's dirty secret, what a historian calls our "schizophrenic relationship with race." To this day, Oregon is home to the whitest city in the US, Portland, according to the 2010 census. It all began on the Oregon Trail.

Many pioneers came West to escape the conflict between the North and South. Settlers from the South and states bordering the South brought more than family antiques in their covered wagons. They brought their prejudices with them. Some brought slaves. Oregon, essentially, was "a Southern state transplanted to the North." During the Civil War, there was an underground movement to support the South and establish slavery in Oregon.

The draw for the pioneers who didn't veer off to the California goldfields or the ones east of the Cascades was the river and the rich farmland on both sides of it. It was a Garden of Eden. The Willamette Valley is 150 miles straight up and down the state of Oregon. The river named for it runs the entire length and then some. The river's basin forms the Willamette Valley, with the mountains of the Coast Range to the west and the Cascades to the east. Corvallis grew slowly, but by the time we were in high school, the population was about 35,000.

If the Oregon Territory, which included parts of what is now Washington, Idaho, Wyoming, and Montana, was going to truly be Southern in character, it needed laws. As early as 1844, the territory passed a series of measures designed to ban Negroes from settling in the area. When Oregon earned statehood, it prohibited slavery but also banned Negroes from living in in the state.

Some of the slaves who gained their freedom remained in Corvallis with the families who had owned them, and were even buried alongside their owners. People of color were prohibited from owning property, yet a few did, including a mother and daughter, former slaves, who bought up land in what became downtown Corvallis. When Eliza Gorman died in 1869, her obituary said she had "won the respect and confidence of the entire community," and a "large number of citizens" attended her funeral.

The first wave of the Ku Klux Klan came and went just after the Civil War, then died out. But by the 1920s, the KKK was flourishing again, including in Portland and Oregon's small towns. The KKK actively recruited members and had a presence on the University of Oregon campus in Eugene, and at what was then Oregon Agricultural College in Corvallis.

On September 30, 1922, some Kleagles, officers of the KKK charged with recruiting new members, hosted a dance in the Foster Building downtown on 2nd Street, later the Montgomery Ward building. On October 18, 1923, a story on the front page of *The Gazette-Times* reported that 300 Klansmen were expected to parade Corvallis streets. Because Corvallis was centrally located, it had been chosen as the site for a Klonvocation. Special trains brought Klansmen from all over the Willamette Valley to town. The next day, the newspaper reported that 500 Klansmen had assembled to take part in a Klonklave at a farm a mile north of Korvallis. Obviously the KKK liked to play with spelling and alliteration.

Led by a marching band, the Klansmen paraded through town in their "uniforms," a full-length white robe with a pointed hat and a piece of cloth covering the face except for the eyes. They made their way to a field "near Abe King's place" north of town, where there was an initiation complete with a flaming cross and speeches. Then they served sandwiches and coffee.

With no editorial comment, the *Gazette-Times* quoted a local KKK leader as stating, "The Klan stands for good in every form, for America, the perpetuation of American ideals, for 100 percent Americanism, and the finest men in the community are enrolled in its ranks." He went on to add: "The American woman has had as much to do with shaping the destiny of America as the American man. The Klan is attempting in every way to elevate the standard of women."

Like other towns across the West, racism was insidious. Corvallis' most exclusive place to bury the dead was Oaklawn Cemetery on Whiteside Drive. When it was laid out in 1935, the cemetery excluded people of color. The rules weren't changed until 1971.

By the 1950s and '60s, despite being a university community, our schools were still astonishingly white. The university didn't have an international faculty until decades later. There was less than a handful of black and Asian students in our high school. There was an uneasy racial, religious, and economic divide in Corvallis. Our parents were educated and we seemed to accept what minorities there were. But we were overwhelmingly white and Protestant. Just as slavery was left out of the curriculum, we may not have known that Corvallis had a history of being prejudiced against the "Oriental," Catholics, and Jews. Rocks were thrown through the windows of Catholic families in town. My classmate, Mark Goheen, whose family was just the fourth Jewish family to settle in Corvallis, remembers a seventh grade social studies teacher at Highland View Junior High locking eyes with him and telling the class that the Jews killed Jesus because he wasn't the messiah they were looking for. "I recall challenging him on that, and classmates congratulating me later for standing up to him," Mark said. "When I told my parents that he had also said 'I have nothing against Jews, some of my best friends are Jews,' they started laughing, which bewildered me because I had no context that this was a common anti-Semitic claim."

His parents, Harry and Molly Goheen, and their three children moved to Corvallis in the mid-1950s. Harry did not convert to Judaism, but the family followed Molly's faith and lived as a Jewish family. There was no temple in town, so they and other Jewish families met at the Unitarian Church. Goheen shook up things as much as anyone in Corvallis ever did. As a mathematician at the University of Chicago, and part of the Office of Naval Research, he had worked on the Manhattan Project, the research that led to development of the first nuclear weapons. But he became too progressive even for universities, refused to continue to work on germ warfare, and lost his teaching jobs at Syracuse, Iowa State, and University of Pennsylvania when he refused to sign loyalty oaths during McCarthyism. The FBI had a file on him, and tried to tell OSC it couldn't hire him, but the college did and he received tenure in 1959. As a professor of mathematics and computer science, Goheen was so dismayed by the lack of diversity in Corvallis that he started local branches of the NAACP and the ACLU. He led vigils and protests, spending his lunch hour often alone, standing in the rain, holding a sign protesting the Vietnam War.

The apple did not fall far from the tree. In the spring of 1966, the theme of the junior-senior prom was "Moonlight and Magnolias." The yearbook said the cafeteria, decorated as the entrance to an old Southern mansion, would long be remembered for its "beauty and splendor." When George Wallace, the pro-segregation governor of Alabama, heard of the prom, he wrote a letter to CHS student body president Rich Johnson saying how pleased he was that "you think of us and our Southern way of life." He recounted his own visit to Oregon to speak at the University of Oregon in 1964 and invited the people of Corvallis to visit Alabama. Rich gave the letter to the *Gazette-Times*, which printed it with a note from Rich that the letter had arrived during final exams and he hadn't had a chance to share it earlier. He asked readers to draw their own conclusions. Sixteen-year-old Mark Goheen replied to Wallace's letter with one of his own, also printed in the *G-T*: "As a student at Corvallis High School, I would like to extend my gratitude to the generous governor of Alabama, who wrote such a kind letter to us on behalf of the friendly people of his state. I am also pleased the governor wants me to come see him. I am glad I am the right color."

There had always been an uneasy racial and economic divide in Corvallis. Yet my classmates and I weren't racist – or was there a quiet racism? Maybe we hadn't been tested. The Pacific Northwest *was* tested after Pearl Harbor was bombed. As tens of thousands of Japanese Americans in Oregon and Washington were housed in internment camps, universities turned their back on their Japanese American students. At Willamette University in Salem, Oregon's capital, ten Japanese American students were forced to leave the school. At the University of Washington in Seattle, many "Jap Students," as they were called in a newspaper headline, were sent to colleges in Michigan, Minnesota, and Chicago that agreed to accept them. The government paid their way if they couldn't afford to leave. Teachers could be fired if they were married to a Japanese American. The prejudice at OSU was unfair, but less dramatic than some other schools: Japanese Americans were forbidden to use the university library after 8 p.m. It was open until 10 p.m.

To borrow Tolstoy's explanation about happy and unhappy families, towns are unhappy in their own way. Corvallis – with a classic town and gown environment if there ever was one – smothered some people and set enormously high expectations for others. It made others feel excluded. My parents had friends from all walks of life. The father of my first boyfriend was a small business owner and was bitter about college people.

But from the beginning, the college was important to the town. It *was* the town. It began as Corvallis College in 1848, was renamed Oregon Agricultural College in 1897, became Oregon State College in 1937, and renamed Oregon State University in 1961.

The town needed businesses like the one Dick's father ran, but there wasn't much intermingling socially except through us, their children. Ralph and Sylvia Kitchel drank and bowled at the Moose Lodge south of town. My parents would never have judged them, but their lives were different. At the dinner table, we talked about life, school, my father's work in radio, and church. Mark Goheen remembers that his family discussed politics, history, war, and racial injustice over meals.

I'm betting Dick's family didn't.

The Partygoers

It was late, a minute before midnight, but the element of surprise is important in a murder investigation. Detectives Montgomery and Hockema, with Assistant Chief Ken Burright, knocked on the door, and when it was answered, invited themselves in. Christmas had come early. Not only were Paul and Juddi Everts home, but Melvin "Mel"

Plemmons and Doug Hamblin were visiting, exactly the young men they wanted to see. Their names had quickly made it to the top of a list of Dick's acquaintances — not necessarily friends, but people he partied with. This was the house and these were the people who may have been the last to see Dick. Like the last night of his life, the occupants of the house were engaged in a drinking game.

It had been a long day for the detectives. Montgomery was at the river when the body was pulled ashore. He, Hockema, and Burright had attended the autopsy and talked to Ralph and Sylvia Kitchel. Then they went to see Judy Appelman, who Ralph Kitchel identified as one of Dick's girlfriends. She lived at 1170 N. 17th Street, just a block north of the high school's football field. Montgomery and Hockema talked to Judy with her father, Duane Appelman, present. Judy was a junior in high school, one year younger than Dick. She had short hair, sometimes worn with a headband or a ribbon. She looked like the all-American teenage girl she was. She was a cheerleader all three years of high school, and an active member of the rally dance committee, the fire squad, and student council.

The detectives told her Dick's body had been found. But she already knew. It had been nearly twelve hours since he was spotted floating in the river and news traveled very fast in Corvallis, faster than the Willamette River. She first heard that Dick was missing, and later heard he had been found dead, from her older sister Molly, who was part of Dick's crowd at Seaton's.

"I didn't know what to say to the detectives," she said later, so she simply told them about her brief relationship with Dick. She had never had a boyfriend and her parents wouldn't allow her to date, but Dick was permitted to come to her house. Starting in the summer of 1967, they would sit on the dark pink velvet couch in the formal living room and talk while her parents sat in the family room and sipped cocktails. She was very shy. "We never held hands, we never kissed," she said. "I think he was impressed that I was a cheerleader." She was petite, and so was Dick, and she thought that was another reason he liked her. Since they were a year apart, she didn't have classes with Dick, but saw him at football and basketball games. She didn't remember him ever attending a rally dance.

Judy's parents were strict, so Judy and Molly snuck out to spend time at Seaton's. Custer's In-N-Out had rectangle-shaped burgers. A&W had root beer. Wagner's had cherry Cokes. The Big O had roller skating carhops. But only Seaton's Barbecue Pit had Gooey Burgers with a special sauce for 19 cents, as well as easy access to beer if you were looking for it. It was the place to be seen. "There was no indoor seating so you would get out of your car and get into the cars of others and smoke," Judy said. "The food didn't matter. You were there to 'tool the pit'" — in other words, to drive around aimlessly. Dick sometimes sat with her in Molly's car. She never saw Dick angry or drinking, and didn't think he had any enemies, but she knew he was a member of a "macho crowd that liked to fight."

On October 10, the night before Dick disappeared, Judy drove some girlfriends to Newport, due west on the Oregon coast, in the family's '54 Ford. It was Judy's sixteenth birthday and she had passed her driver's exam that day. The group attended a performance of The Patriots, a band made up of local Corvallis kids, including Dick's neighbor Bob Wadlow on guitar. Afterward, Judy sped back over US 20, a breathtakingly twisting, narrow road across the top of the Oregon Coast Range that dropped suddenly down into the Willamette Valley. She could usually tell before she entered the house if her father was asleep or not. Her parents enjoyed their cocktails every night, and her father's snoring could be heard from the driveway. Her parents often didn't know if their daughters were home or not.

Judy told the detectives what she knew about October 11, the day Dick disappeared. During the school day, she saw Dick in the parking lot behind the high school. Like Seaton's, it was a place to see and be seen, so much so that even if kids had skipped school, they would show up to check in with friends. It was the last time she saw Dick. She had heard Dick had gone to a card party, that there had been a fight, and that someone gave him a ride home. After the police talked to Judy, she phoned some friends and they came over. One of them suggested they go to Seaton's, so they did. Within a day or two, she heard the ominous announcement on the high school's public address system, news she already knew. Dick had been murdered. She read the details in the *Gazette-Times*.

It was 11:10 p.m. when the police officers left the Appelman home. They drove by the home of seventeen-year-old Mel Plemmons, at 717 W. Lewisburg Road. They believed Mel had been at the party the last night of Dick's life. No one was home. They sat in the car and took a moment to decide where to go next. At 11:59 p.m., they arrived at the home of Paul and Juddi Everts. The rental house at 521 N. 14th Street was a bungalow, two stories with three pillars framing a broad front porch. (Coincidentally, it was around the corner from the boarding house my grandmother ran forty years earlier.) There was a small backyard and a narrow driveway on one side of the home with a small detached garage all the way in the rear shared with the house next door. 521 N. 14th was smack in the middle of a neighborhood filled with college students in other rentals. Montgomery, Hockema, and Burright interrupted the party underway to break the news to the Everts, Doug Hamblin, and Mel Plemmons. The body of their friend, Dick Kitchel, last seen ten days before at that very house, had been found in the Willamette River. There was no reaction. No one gasped or cried out in surprise. It may not have been news to the people assembled. Like Judy, it seemed that they already knew Dick was dead. Had they heard gossip, or did they have first-hand knowledge?

Paul Everts was the son of an OSU chemistry professor. His brothers were an MD and a PhD, but his life was turning out differently. Paul, who had graduated from CHS in 1964, had married Juddi — born Judy Seavy, class of 1965 — in the spring of her senior year. Their daughter was born the same year. Paul worked as a surveyor's helper at Corvallis Sand and Gravel where Juddi worked in the office. The other semi-permanent member of the household was nineteen-year-old Pat Hockett, who also went by the name Pat Taylor, who was a live-in babysitter for the couple.

Dick knew the Everts because he was good friends with Juddi's younger sister, Dawn —born Donieta Seavy, CHS class of 1968. "His home life was not pleasant, neither was mine," Dawn said later. Their friendship was based on a shared angst and not romantic. "His dad drank a lot. My parents fought all the time. He didn't like going home." Dick could be outgoing and friendly but that night he was moody and spoiling for a fight. No one knew why. "He could get obnoxious, mouthy," she said.

Paul told the police that on October 11, Dick arrived drunk.

The guests at Everts' liked to play a game they called "pass out," which was exactly what it sounded like: how much could they drink before they passed out? There had been more than a dozen teenagers along with a few men in their twenties at the Everts' house the night of October 11. Most chipped in a few dollars to be able to drink. Why the Everts – with a young child and jobs – would host regular parties wasn't clear. Maybe the beer money added up and helped them make ends meet. Paul told the detectives there had been a disagreement and Dick had told Juddi to "get fucked." According to the detective's notes, Paul said he told Dick "that was just about enough of that kind of talk, and took him out onto the front porch of the residence and pushed him up against the banister of the porch and talked to him." Paul said he talked with Dick about "various problems which Kitchel was having and what he should do on two charges which were pending against him" in municipal court for drunk driving and resisting arrest. It sounded pretty fatherly, and not entirely true, to the detectives. Paul explained he had offered Dick an olive branch: if Dick would go back into the house and apologize to Juddi, all would be forgiven. Dick and Paul returned to the house and Dick apologized. Later, Paul would change his story and say the fight was between Doug and Dick. Others at the party said Dick never reentered the house.

Doug Hamblin told the police he was twenty-one, but he was twenty-three years old, divorced, and the father of a two-year-old girl. He had attended CHS off and on, but may or may not have graduated. Doug had a troubled history. He was close to his mother, Flo, who was married a total of eight times in her life – two men she married twice. As one family member said, she didn't smoke or drink – she married. Just like Flo looked at marriage as a new beginning, Doug bounced from odd job to odd job: selling car parts to drag racers, buying and selling airplane engines, and driving trucks cross-country. Sometimes he worked as a hunting and fishing guide with a brother. He had been angry his entire life, ever since a piece of a broken beer glass pierced his face and cost him the sight in his right eye when he was a child. According to one of his several wives, he lied and was mean and abusive, even after he quit drinking.

The detectives would learn that Doug had been at the Everts' house twice the night of October 11. Exactly why he was there so often, including when the detectives visited on October 21 and other times, is unclear. He told his part of the story to the detectives. On the night of October 11, some of the teenagers at the party wanted to leave and he offered to drive them home. It was just before midnight because Juddi remembered the television was on and *The Tonight Show Starring Johnny Carson* was underway. Marty, Mel, and Dick piled into Doug's fifteen-year-old, two-toned

DeSoto four-door sedan. Because Marty had a midnight curfew, Doug first drove west to the Tucker house - 2055 Kings Road. Then he turned east on Circle Drive and north on Highland Way and headed to the Plemmons home at 717 W. Lewisburg Road.

Doug said that when he returned to town, Dick, who had been in the backseat, was sitting in the right front seat. But Dick refused to tell Doug where he lived. He told him to keep driving, that he didn't want to go home. Finally, Doug pulled over at 4th and B Street, near the state employment office, and helped Dick out of the car. The right front door, on the passenger side, was broken, and Doug told the detectives he stepped out of the car and stood in the street to have Dick exit the driver's side of the vehicle. Dick didn't want to get out and Doug said he pulled him out of the car. The last time he saw Dick, he was walking south. He then drove back to the Everts' house, arriving at 1:30 a.m., about 90 minutes after leaving. The detectives didn't ask why it had taken so long to drive a few miles, dropping two boys at their homes and one downtown. They asked to look at his hands. They checked his knuckles first; there were no recent bruises or scratches visible, and there were no marks around his face or mouth. But it had been ten days since Dick fought off *someone,* and Doug used his hands in his job as a sheet metal worker. The grease and grit imbedded in his hands could have masked any bruises or cuts. Doug was asked if he would take a lie detector test and he said he would, as long as he didn't have to miss work. He earned $400 a month at Finstad Heating and Sheet Metal; $50 a month went to his ex-wife, Teresa, mother of their two-year-old daughter. He said he lived at 240 S. Third, not far from the river, and not far from where he let Dick out of his car. They took a written statement from him. Then they remembered to ask him – did Doug know anything about Dick's coat? It was missing. He admitted that on October 12 he had found a coat in his car. It looked too small to belong to anyone he knew so he gave it to a nine-year-old neighbor boy. He said he would get it back for the detectives. No one asked why Doug had returned to the Everts' house after dropping Dick off downtown. Almost as an afterthought, the detectives asked about Pat Hockett. Juddi said Pat wasn't home, and had not been home the night of the party. District Attorney Frank Knight arrived at the house, and he and Montgomery questioned Mel. His story matched the others. If they asked him what had happened between Doug and Dick in the car, or where Dick was sitting when Mel climbed out and left the two alone, it wasn't noted.

At 1:40 a.m. on what was now October 22, the detectives went to the home of Marty Tucker. His parents were home and they got Marty out of bed and they all sat and talked in the living room. Marty knew his ride home only by his first name — Doug. Marty was in the right front seat during his ride home and had slid out through the driver's side door to get out. He said that at the time he was dropped off, Dick was sitting in the rear of the car, but he didn't remember which side. Mel was also in the back seat. Marty thought he arrived home a few minutes before his midnight curfew.

Marty's memory of the disturbance at the house was different than his hosts'. He said Paul had taken Dick out to the porch, there had been a scuffle, and Dick had not apologized and not reentered the house. He called it "not a real fight" but told detectives that Paul "had Kitchel by the front of the shirt and had just backed him up to the porch rail and no blows were exchanged." His parents said they had no objection to Marty taking a lie detector test.

Exactly what happened at the party? Who was angry enough to start or continue a fight with Dick on a dead quiet downtown street? The detectives would learn that some of the attendees were more than casual acquaintances. Juddi had had some kind of relationship with Doug. Maybe Paul knew, maybe he didn't. Maybe Dick knew and threw it in Paul's face. There was more than a casual argument on the front porch. Someone had left the party with a grudge against Dick. Did they follow Doug's car? Maybe Dick hitchhiked after he was left off and been murdered by an unknown person. Had he arrived home and had one last fight with his father? Why was Dick's jacket in Doug's car?

The stories about what happened at the party would change over the coming days. Dick's friends called him friendly, likeable, and, sadly, "unfinished." But more than one adult – friends or neighbors of his father – said sarcastically, "it couldn't happen to a better person" and "good riddance." One thing for sure: Dick *did* have an enemy.

http://wbp.bz/hometowna

CHAPTER 1

"Hey bitch, you're a ho!" Later, different people would attribute this shouted challenge to thirteen-year-old Allie Trace.

The focus of Allie's outburst, Sherokee Harriman, stood staring at Allie and the three teens with her. They approached Sherokee at a street corner under a stop sign across the street from Mankin Park, the teen's gathering spot. If a teen was not old enough to drive, there were few other places to go in the small town of LaVergne, Tennessee.

Sherokee, at 14, was not prone to physical fighting. At 5-foot, 3-inches tall and 120 pounds, with a soft complexion and baby face, she did not look exactly intimidating. She tried to keep her lower lip from trembling, shifting her weight from side to side. In a nervous gesture, she pushed a lock of her short, dark hair away from her young face.

"You bitch!" Allie shouted. Pretty in an earthy sense, now Allie's face was pinched in anger. "I'm tired of you saying shit about me!"

The two boys and one girl who accompanied Allie could only stare, eyes wide. Just a few minutes ago when Allie had told them that she wanted to walk over and talk to Sherokee, they had no idea it would lead to this.

"Who are you? You don't even know me!" Sherokee found her voice. "You don't know who I am!"

The boys could not believe it. Girl fights usually made for a cool show, but this was crazy. One moment they were hanging at the park's pavilion, the next they were witnessing an ugly verbal attack. Allie's best friend Debi Hornsby was usually smiling, but now she nervously crossed her skinny arms.

Alec Seether crossed his arms, too, looking from his current girlfriend, Allie, to his ex-girlfriend, Sherokee. One of the kids who stood next to him, Donny Duroy, wondered briefly what Alec was thinking, watching a little girl being attacked, a girl with whom Alec once shared secrets.

"I don't even know you," Sherokee replied. "I've never said anything about you."

"Yeah, you talk about me behind my back!" Allie was not letting up. "But when you can say it to my face, what happens, fucking bitch!"

"I never said anything about you!" Sherokee voice was louder. "I don't even know who you are!"

"Bitch!"

"You better watch it or I'll kick your ass!" Sherokee bravely challenged.

Their voices rose with bravado and the angry exchanges.

A few of the teens would later report to authorities and confide in friends that Debi, the other teen witness, added to the fray by calling Sherokee names. Later, when it was far too late, Debi would deny it.

"He doesn't want you!" Allie was shouting now. "And you better stop talking about me, you ho!"

Debi would later say she tried to get Allie to stop. "Allie! Let's go. Let's just go!"

"You just better watch it, bitch!" Allie shouted at Sherokee.

"You need to shut your fucking mouth!" Sherokee had enough of this bitch with the attitude. She could only be pushed so far.

Alec could not find his voice. He had no idea what to say or do. He knew Allie was mad; she had probably heard the rumor that he was planning to break up with her, maybe return to Sherokee. Earlier, he had told Allie to not start anything when they saw Sherokee approach the park. Now

Allie was verbally attacking Sherokee, and it looked like it may go further.

Both Allie and Sherokee were balling up their fists to physically fight, then at the same time, they seemed to abandon the plan. Their fingers uncurled.

Two younger people watched the exchange from a distance: Alec's sister Angelique and Angelique's friend Micky. The younger Micky took off running away from the park. Angelique soon followed. "Where you going, Micky?" one of the boys shouted at her retreating figure.

Now Sherokee was turning on one heel to head away from the group. Her family lived nearby, less than three blocks away. Sherokee often walked to the park, usually to be alone with her thoughts. But today was different.

"Yeah, get out of here, ho!" Allie called after her. "Bitch!"

The teens turned to walk back across the street to Mankin Park. As they settled in the bench seats to sit under the pavilion, someone turned up their cell phone volume to listen to music. Debi checked her own phone for what must have been the hundredth time that day, sometimes lifting it over her head; still, she could not get a signal. She could never get cell phone service in this park, which annoyed her.

She was unaware of how, in just a few minutes, reception would be a matter of life or death.

CHAPTER 2

A furious Sherokee Harriman walked alone down Mankin Street and took a right turn at the corner toward home. She headed for the neat, square, one-story brick home where she lived with her family: her mother, stepfather, an older sister, and her maternal grandmother. As she walked, she decided she would return to the park. She would teach them a good lesson.

She would show them how much they were hurting her, what their words did to her, and then—then—she might only hurt for a little time, but they would be forever harmed.

Sherokee punched numbers into her cell phone to call a friend, Abraham Ringgold, who was her age. Abe and Sherokee had "dated" in elementary school, which consisted of calling themselves "boyfriend and girlfriend" and passing notes in the hallway. Now they attended the same school and rode the same bus, but they had drifted apart in separate lives, only chatting on occasion.

"Can you come to the park?" Sherokee asked Abe.

"I can't ride my bike," he told her ruefully. "I broke my arm. It's too far to walk."

Sherokee told him there were some people in the park, and they were making fun of her.

Then a text message came across her cell phone from her mother, Heather Edwards. Earlier, from work, Heather had given Sherokee permission to leave the house and go to the park, but only if Sherokee would text her every five minutes to let her mom know she was safe. So at 12:09 p.m., not having received a note, a text message appeared:

(Social media posts are written as they originally appeared, without correcting spelling or grammar)

Hey, its been way longer than 5 minutes, are you alright?

Sherokee put Abe on hold to text back. She punched the keyboard of her cell phone:

Yea sorry

Heather responded:

It's OK. I just don't want anything to happen to you is all.

Sherokee often shared the ups and downs of her life with her mom, and now she confided in her:

I hate this

Heather was busy, but she paused long enough to text back and see what was wrong with her youngest child:

You hate what

It was several minutes before Sherokee's response appeared:

My life

And in a few minutes she added:

I hate being the one to get called a hoe

Heather was sighing and shaking her head. In her eyes, it seemed someone was always calling Sherokee names, making fun of her. Heather was tired of these mean kids, tired of a school that she felt turned a blind eye to her complaints and problems with bullies. She texted:

Who's called you a hoe?

Sherokee did not know Allie. They did not attend the same high school nor socialize in the same circles. So, she replied:

Some girl that doesn't even know me

Seconds later, at 12:44 p.m., she texted Heather to let Heather know she was safe:

I'm home

Sherokee was still on the phone with Abe, and they talked about the bullying kids.

Shyloe Harriman looked up from her perch on the couch when her younger sister came into their home, cell phone clamped to one ear as always. Sherokee seemed upset. She stopped to ask Shyloe, "Is granny in the kitchen?"

"No," Shyloe told her, standing up to follow her.

"Good!" She was mad, Shyloe could tell by her tone. But then, Sherokee—her little "Sissy"—always seemed to be mad. Shyloe sat back down. Best to leave her alone.

Sherokee took the few steps into the kitchen, shedding the white down-jacket she wore over her blouse, clothing she had carefully selected only an hour before. She was wrapping the arms of her jacket around her waist, tying the sleeves together at her waistband as she entered the small kitchen.

Shyloe heard her sister rummaging through kitchen drawers.

Four minutes after she had received Sherokee's text about being home, Heather texted Sherokee, asking:

When did she call you that?

Shyloe walked outside to lounge on the front steps as her sister left the house. "I'm going to the park," Sherokee told Shyloe, storming out the front door.

Shyloe did not reply. She had no idea what was going on, but it was not difficult to see Sherokee was, once again, mad about something.

Abe listened to the silence on the phone after Sherokee told him, "Hold on, my mom's texting me again."

As she worked, Heather Edwards picked up her cell phone to see another text from her daughter at 12:48 p.m.:

I'm going back to the park hopefully they r not there

Heather texted Sherokee the same thing she always said when girls bullied her pretty daughter:

So it was said to you today. Baby girl, that girl is just jealous, cause you are prettier than her

But this time she has no idea if Sherokee read it.

Sherokee was back on the phone with Abe. "Okay, I'm here."

Abe made a few comments, but there was no reply.

Sherokee was walking back to Mankin Park, casually, her heart pounding. She touched the item hidden in her jacket. It felt surreal, but it also seemed to be so natural. Like breathing, or walking, maybe. She was going to show them. She was going to scare them and scare them good, let them see what mean words and names can do to a person.

And maybe, after they learned their lesson, she could be their friend.

If not, they would hurt forever. And at least maybe her pain would not last, not squeeze her heart in pangs of sadness.

The next thing she said to Abe was, "I have a knife."

CHAPTER 3

Abe could not speak for a moment, then he found his voice. "What are you going to do?" he demanded. "Sherokee, whatever you're going to do, don't do it, okay?" He waited. "Please!"

"I'm going back to the park."

"Please!" Abe felt hot tears in his eyes. He could envision Sherokee waving the knife at her tormenters, or maybe she would actually walk up to them with a knife. What if she stabbed one of the bullies? What if she stabbed herself? At the same time, he told himself, *No. That is so not her. It just is not in her to even* hold *a knife!*

Abe was still shouting into the phone. "Sherokee! Sherokee! Whatever you're going to do, don't do it, okay?" Panic was riding in his throat now. *She is going to get into big trouble. Why does she have a knife? She's not going to hurt anybody ... oh God, what if she hurts somebody?* "Please—no—Sherokee!"

Crossing Mankin Street to the park, Sherokee saw Allie sitting at the table under the pavilion with Alec, the other boy, and the girl. Without knowing who they were, Sherokee saw Angelique and Micky had returned, sitting with the group of older kids. Two bicycles rested casually against the benches. They were all laughing and talking, the girls flipping their hair over their shoulders. When someone pointed out Sherokee's return, Allie turned in her seat. She watched her target approach them along the paved path.

Sherokee stopped just past the park entrance. There was a slight smile, a Mona Lisa-type expression on her face. Her hand slipped into the folds of her jacket, fishing for something. She brought it out to clasp in both hands.

The kids just stared at her.

Sherokee looked them over. "So you think it's funny to call me a ho and a bitch?" she shouted.

She raised her fists, clamped together, over her head. Then she swung them, hard, back over her head to punch herself in the gut.

Debi would later say that she witnessed it all. She also reports that she, Alec, and Donny were talking over the music when they heard Allie scream, "You guys! I need your help!"

"I turned and saw Allie beside Sherokee, who was lying on the ground," Debi explains. "And we ran over to her."

Alec would later report he was the first one to Sherokee as she collapsed into the grass.

Abraham Ringgold says now, "It got quiet, then I started hearing people screaming, 'Call 911! Call 911!' Then the phone shut off."

There are conflicting reports about what took place in Mankin Park that day, but one detail remains the same: Sherokee Harriman was now lying on her back, moaning, a kitchen knife plunged into her stomach.

http://wbp.bz/btda

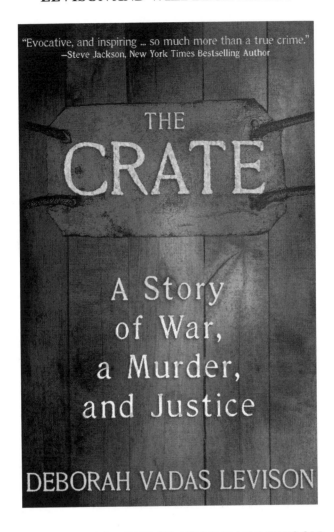

Chapter One

NATURALIZATION

Even in my darkest nightmares, I'd never imagined the words my brother would whisper in my ear.

My family and I had arrived at the hotel minutes earlier. Already the suite lay in a state of chaos, so that when my cell phone rang it took me a few moments to trace the sound and find the device, buried under boarding passes, sunglasses, and baseball hats on the kitchenette counter. I answered with one hand and loaded bottles of Gatorade into the refrigerator with the other.

The kids were arguing, staking their claims for pullout couches and cots in the spacious living area surrounding the kitchen, jostling for the best view of the TV.

"Hang on, I can't hear," I yelled into the phone, slamming the refrigerator door. "For God's sake, can someone turn the air conditioner down? It's like the Arctic in here." I turned around to see the boys poised for a pillow fight, and braced for the inevitable howls. Fourteen-year-old Jake would never allow himself to be bested by his eight-year-old brother, Coby.

Jordyn, our oldest, was seventeen. Coolly, she snatched the cushion out of Jake's hand before he could strike.

I turned my attention back to the phone. A familiar number shone on the screen. "Hey, Pete."

My brother Peter's voice came through muffled by the racket in the room. Still, he sounded strained, and a wisp of apprehension fluttered over me.

"Are Mum and Dad okay?" I shouted over the noise. My parents were eighty and eighty-four, increasingly frail, and with mounting health concerns. They lived in Toronto, hundreds of miles away, and I constantly imagined the worst.

"They're fine, Deb," my brother said, somber, with no hint of his usual chipper tone. I drew back a heavy curtain and unlatched the glass door, seeking the quiet of a balcony. In front of me lay a gorgeous screened lanai furnished with a large wooden dining table and chairs. Another world shimmered outside here on the deck in Florida: bright, mild, calm.

"Now I can hear you better," I said into the phone. "What's going on?"

"Everyone's okay," Peter repeated. He paused. "How about you guys? When do you leave for Florida?"

I glanced around. Beyond the table stood a row of recliners on an open-air balcony that wrapped around the lanai. I pulled a second door closed behind me and walked barefoot to the iron railing, gazing out on a magnificent, unobstructed view of blue Gulf waters.

"We're here! Just checked into the hotel. I'm looking at the ocean now, actually. Are you at work?" That might explain the tension in his voice, I thought; my brother's medical practice involved harried hours of examinations followed by long evenings of dictation, often leaving him stressed and exhausted. He still had a block of patients to see, he confirmed.

I continued, "I know you hate the heat, but it would be nice for you to get away from the hospital for a few days and relax. You sound like you're on edge. When did you last swim in the ocean?" I chattered on, my unease dissolving as I basked in the sunshine and told my brother about our trip.

My husband, Craig, our kids, and I had arrived in Fort Myers that afternoon with Jake's travel team, Xplosion, for an elite baseball tournament that would pit us against some of the best high school ballplayers in the country. Initially, I had not wanted to stray out from under the luxurious green and leafy canopy surrounding our New England home, where the woods near our house beckoned, shady and cool, just like those in which I'd spent my childhood in Canada. I dreaded the prospect of Florida in July; "hot, thick, and humid" constituted my least favorite climate.

Peter paused again before answering my question. "The last time we were at the ocean? Probably when we came down to visit you last fall."

"Oh, that's just the Sound." I referred to Long Island Sound, the swirling gray bathtub of fresh and saltwater that rings the north shore of Long Island and the southern shores of Westchester and Connecticut. To my surprise and delight we'd found, though, an hour's drive from our home to the corner of Rhode Island, the open Atlantic rippling outwards in an endless spread of mint jelly, and dotted along the coast, quaint seafaring villages with weathered wooden piers like wrinkled fingers pointing out to sea. The discovery of this maritime scenery helped soften my docking in America.

I'd felt ambivalent about the whole move. Torontonians typically are not a migratory species. For the most part, those who hatch in Toronto nest there, attend college somewhere close, and settle in the suburbs for the long haul. That life, I had imagined for myself, too. When we moved away, I felt guilty, selfish for leaving my parents. They'd been immigrants themselves. Surely when they landed in Canada in 1956 they assumed that their family would huddle there together forever. When Craig and I left with two of their grandchildren, we effectively took away half of their family.

I'd cried when we all sat down at my parents' kitchen table to break the news. My mother had nodded slowly and said, "Anyvay. You have to do vhatever is best for your family." My father stood up quietly and walked out, but not before I saw that his eyes were wet.

But still, the company that Craig worked for, Trans-Lux, had offered him a good job and we were flattered that they seemed willing to go to great lengths to move us to the States. The tight economy in Toronto in the mid-nineties meant that another, equally good job might not be so easy to find. I'd left my own job in public relations to stay home full-time with Jordyn, a toddler then, and Jake, a baby. In the end, Craig and I agreed: We'd be a Swiss Family Robinson of sorts. We would embark on a year-long adventure, and after that we would come home. One year, we gave ourselves.

Trans-Lux sent a team of movers, and I watched as they packed our tidy little life into boxes and onto a moving van bound for the border.

Craig had wanted to live in or as close to New York City as possible since he would be working on Wall Street for three weeks out of each month, while the fourth week would be spent in Norwalk, Connecticut, the headquarters of Trans-Lux. To Craig, New York held all the allure of Oz: a furious pace, vast business opportunity, endless entertainment, and a spinning kaleidoscope of humanity that appealed to his adrenaline-junky personality.

I had no interest in living in Manhattan. Even though metropolitan Toronto bustled just as much, I perceived New York to be dirty and dangerous. I wanted more living space, not less. I hated traffic jams and parking hassles. And I wanted a stroller-friendly front porch, fresh air, and lots of green grass for our kids. We expanded the home search progressively north of New York City, moving along the Hutch to the scenic Merritt Parkway in Connecticut. As the numbers on the exit signs increased, the property prices decreased.

Eventually, our real estate agent brought us to Trumbull. Our agent had pegged Craig as a huge sports fan. When she pulled up in front of Unity Field, the town's main baseball complex, the sun appeared from behind the clouds and shone down, brilliantly illuminating a banner at the entrance. The sign read, *"Welcome to Trumbull, home of the 1989 Little League World Champions."* Craig practically drooled. I could almost hear a chorus of angels burst into song. *Well, that's that*, I thought. *Here's home.*

In 1996, when my husband and I and our young family first arrived in Connecticut, I'd heard some new friends say to their kids, "Let's have a catch." The phrase rolled around in my head. You "have" a headache or you "have" an appointment, I thought. My dad never said to me, "Let's have a slalom" when we went skiing. But having a catch seemed to be what people in Fairfield County, Connecticut, did on their wide, manicured lawns.

We found a sprawling, if dated, house on a flat acre of land with towering oaks and spacious rooms. Bigger than anything we could afford in Toronto, Craig said. Great bones, I said. Surely, with some modern finishes, we could turn a profit in the twelve months we planned to live there before flipping the house and returning home to Canada. It felt, as we say in Yiddish, *bashert:* fated, meant to be.

And it seemed safe, this little town. A keep-the-front-door-open, leave-your-car-unlocked, let-your-kids-play-outside kind of town. Where all sorts of townsfolk, Jewish or not, drove to the local temple every Monday night to play Bingo. We signed on the dotted line.

Somehow, as we settled into a warm and welcoming community, a wide circle of friends, and a comfortable routine of school, work, and family life, that one year stretched into two, then five, then ten. In 2010, we had been in the States for fourteen years.

In that time I had morphed into an all-around Trumbullite: Suburban mom, carpooling in a minivan and hosting cookie-baking play dates and sleepovers, birthday bashes and after-sports pool parties for the kids and their friends. And publicist, earning media for an eclectic clientele throughout the Northeast. And journalist, interviewing movers and shakers around the state for a local paper. And volunteer, member of this committee and that, fundraiser for this project and that, room mother for this class and that.

I transformed from *alien* to *citizen* on April 8, 2005, my husband by my side, both of us eager to obtain dual citizenship, to vote, to give our children opportunities that came with being American. I didn't want to be an alien. I wanted to belong. I pledged allegiance to the flag of the United States of America, learned the words to the Star Spangled Banner, and celebrated Thanksgiving with all its trimmings ... a holiday that in Canada, as Jews, we'd ignored.

Gradually, and without meaning to, I dropped my Canadian identifiers, shedding *"aboot"* for "about," "Mummy" for "Mommy," "pop" for "soda." I understood what the kids meant when they asked for my "pocketbook," not purse, so they could buy "cotton candy," not candy floss, or a "candy bar," not a chocolate bar. *Runners*? Sneakers. *Duotang*? Folder. *Eaves troughs*? Gutters. *Garburator*? Garbage disposal. I took care not to ask for homo milk, and soon I became accustomed to buying it in jugs rather than bags. I lost track of Canadian exchange rates and Members of Parliament and stopped loading up on Canadian-brand groceries during visits to the place I still called home. And I gave birth to a third child, an American.

I connected more to being Jewish than I had earlier in life, an aspect of my persona that I had minimized as my parents worked hard to assimilate. Perhaps my own marriage and motherhood had provided the impetus, or perhaps my yearning for a sense of community had propelled me along. Whatever the reason, trying on Judaism for size reminded me of standing in a dressing room surrounded by dozens of rejects, zipping the one thing that – at last! – fit perfectly.

And I embraced baseball.

After years spent on the bleachers at Unity, I'd finally figured out the game. I'd come a long way from the days of yelling "SLIDE!" to a runner headed for first, or referring to the dugout as a penalty box. I could recite the rules, use the lingo, follow the plays. I shouted "Give it a ride!" to the batter or "All right, one, two, three!" to the pitcher. I felt comfortable speaking *baseball;* it was yet another language I had learned.

Craig and the kids seemed thrilled to be here in Florida, and now, standing in the mild breeze on the terrace, I felt excited, too. During school vacations, three or four times a year, we invariably returned to Toronto to visit our families – a marked contrast to this rare junket due south. Here, we'd swim in the sea and bask on the beach. In downtown Fort Myers, we'd treat the kids to ice cream cones, browse the surf shops. Jordyn would try on straw hats. Jake and Coby would ask for necklaces with a shark's tooth. Something for everyone.

It would be a great vacation.

"You should come down for a few days," I urged my brother on the phone. "A change of scenery would do you good. It's a pretty hotel."

I leaned on the railing and gazed out at the tops of swaying palm fronds. The surf rippled, crystal clear and glistening in the late day sun. Gulls circled in the sky. Sailboats and ships floated across the horizon. Pastel colored umbrellas polkadotted the coastline and little kids with plastic shovels dug for shells in the sand. I tilted my face upward to catch the sun's rays. *Ahhhh.*

Over the phone, my brother suggested I sit down. Slowly I lowered myself to the edge of a chaise lounge.

"Something's happened," Peter's voice dropped low.

The needles of anxiety returned to prick at me. "Peeps. For God's sake. What is it?"

"There's been a murder ... at the cottage."

http://wbp.bz/cratea

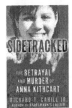